For we are sold, I and my people.
—Esther 7:4

SUNY Series in the Anthropology of Work
June Nash, *Editor*

For We Are Sold, I and My People
Women and Industry in Mexico's Frontier

María Patricia Fernández-Kelly

Center for U.S.-Mexican Studies
University of California
SAN DIEGO

Centro de Estudios Fronterizos del
Norte de México
TIJUANA

State University of New York Press
Albany

Published by
State University of New York Press, Albany

For information, address State University of New York Press, State University Plaza,
Albany, N.Y., 12246

Library of Congress Cataloging in Publication Data

Fernández-Kelly, María Patricia, 1948-
  Women and industry in Mexico's frontier.

  Bibliography: p. 195
    1. Women textile workers—Mexico—Ciudad Juárez.
  2. Women electronic industry workers—Mexico—Ciudad Juárez. 3. Textile indus-
  try—Mexico—Ciudad Juárez. 4. Electronic industries—Mexico—Ciudad Juárez.
  I. Title.
  HD6073.T42M63   1983   331.4'877'0097216   82-19249
  ISBN 0-87395-717-2
  ISBN 0-87395-718-0 (pbk.)

10   9   8   7   6

Contents

Acknowledgements

To the following persons the author wishes to express profound gratitude and appreciation. Without their wisdom, support and valuable guidance, the elaboration of this volume would not have been possible:

Helen I. Safa
June Nash
Lynn Bolles
Michael Burawoy
Wayne Cornelius
Louis W. Goodman
Marvin Harris
Laura Nader
Alejandro Portes
Donald Roy
Melanie Z. Strub
Guillermina Valdés Villalva

Funding for the original research contained in this book was generously provided by The Social Science Research Council and by The Inter American Foundation. The Centro de Orientación de la Mujer Obrera of Ciudad Juárez, Chihuahua, offered the author hospitality and the great opportunity of learning from working women during one long, memorable year of field work.

CHAPTER 1

Introduction

Points of Departure

Contemporary social science is characterized by an enthusiastic turn of interest toward political economy and world system analysis. Such a concern is at the same time a result of a generalized disenchantment with the explanatory powers of modernization theories and an intellectual counterpart of current economic, political and ideological changes operating at an international scale. Modernization and its anthropological equivalents, assimilation and acculturation, represented a theoretical view associated with a perception of the world in which independent nation-states were identified according to their degree of industrialization in a progress-oriented scale (O'Brien 1975, pp. 7-27). Comparisons arose to examine the forces which accounted for differences in development among the various components of the international mosaic. Within this framework, it was possible to entertain the notion of national autonomy and to initiate inquiries about the reasons that explained different levels of modernization in different countries.

With the appearance of the so-called *dependentista* school of thought and more recent critical structural perspectives which focus on underdevelopment, such a perception was severely shattered. The alternative provided was based on an understanding of the world as a web of historically related political and economic events, in which the underdevelopment of certain areas is viewed in inextricable relation with the development of others (Sunkel 1962; dos Santos 1970; Frank 1970; Cardoso and Faletto 1971; Furtado 1971; Amin 1974b). Modernization ceased to be the ideal to which most nations should aspire in order to be recognized as an ideological construction destined to legitimize the established international social order (Portes 1978; Cardoso 1977).

A point deserving further analysis focuses on the link between the change in perspective outlined above and modifications in the economic and political structure of the contemporary world. Both interpretations have evolved within the realm of monopoly capitalism. But the first one corresponds to a period in which productive processes largely took place within the framework of the nation state. Highly industrialized metropoles competed over the monopoly of internal and foreign markets and for control over raw materials from underdeveloped countries, while administrating the flow of technology and expertise (Palloix, 1973; Wallerstein, 1974).

By contrast, since the end of the Second World War and particularly during the last two decades there has been an increasing trend toward the internationalization of capital investments in manufacturing activities which has coincided with the transfer of part of the productive processes (particularly in certain branches of industry) to underdeveloped areas of the world (Nayar, 1977; Frobel, Heinrichs, and Kreye, 1979). Such a trend has been accompanied by a modification of the function of core states vis-à-vis private enterprise in central as well as in peripheral areas, and by the growth of export-processing zones as a symptom of a renewed adaptation of the capitalist sector to prevailing conditions of production (Buckley and Casson, 1976). Increasingly, core countries become administrative and financial headquarters for the management of refined manufacturing activities which bring together in one swift embrace various distant geographical points (Frobel, Heinrichs, and Kreye 1976; Nayar 1977). At the same time the impact of multinational investments is felt by large numbers of working people throughout the underdeveloped world.

These changes have influenced the social sciences both as a subject matter for research and as an underlying guide for interpretation: to a tightly woven net of international investment, production, exploitation and profit concentration, corresponds a social-anthropological view in which the preferred unit of analysis has become "world system" rather than "society," "ethnic group" or isolable "culture."

Although the world system perspective offers important refinements to preexisting views, one of its main limitations should not be overlooked; that is, a somewhat mechanical tendency to interpret social phenomena in underdeveloped areas as an automatic effect of the requirements of capital accumulation at a global level, without regard for local diversity particularly among working classes and class fractions (Kay 1975).

2

For example, the reduction of workers to the notion of "cheap labor" (a concept which has crucial importance for the understanding of this work) may fail to identify variations which have theoretical and practical significance. It is necessary to investigate the meaning of "cheap labor" in concrete circumstances. At the same time, the understanding of the general processes that explain international capitalism should include detailed case studies that examine and underscore the wide spectrum of effects of, and responses to, the international political and economic system at the level of the household and the community, both in central and peripheral areas (Friedman and Sullivan 1974; Schmink 1979).

Anthropological techniques can provide a valuable contribution in this respect. It does not have to be the inexorable fate of ethnography to produce esoteric or anecdotal descriptions. Rather, a collection of ethnographic data informed by the knowledge derived from political economy should illuminate broader analytical efforts and offer guidelines which are difficult, if not impossible, to appreciate when an all-encompassing approach is adopted. The purpose of this work is to illustrate such a proposition, albeit in a limited manner.

I focus upon a growing phenomenon of the contemporary world, that is, offshore production, which has resulted along the Mexican-American border in the expansion of multinational industrialization and the incorporation of large numbers of women into direct production. I adhere to a view which sees the tendency toward the transfer of production centers (mainly in the form of assembly plants) from core countries to underdeveloped areas, as an effect of the requirements of capital accumulation at an international scale (Mandel 1975, pp. 127-128).

Nevertheless, such requirements are fulfilled in many ways depending on the position of various manufacturing branches vis-à-vis the international economy. For example, when comparing the electric/electronic and textile garment industries (which dominate assembly operations along the Mexican-American border) it becomes apparent that the two are characterized by different forms and sizes of capital investment in underdeveloped areas. They also face different constraints in the international market as a result of supply/demand fluctuations and changes in technology.

To a large extent, such variations determine the nature of labor recruitment strategies and the form that control over workers take in each industry (O'Connor 1973, chap. 1). More importantly this means that the characteristics of a specific work force are closely related to the size and type of industry (whether it be electronics or garment manufacturing). Moreover, the kind of relationship (i.e., directly owned subsidiary or subcontracted firm) between a multinational corporation and its affiliate abroad also plays a significant role in affecting the traits of its labor force.

Therefore, one of the central theoretical assertions in this volume is that differences among the various subgroups that form an otherwise homogeneous labor force reflect more fundamental distinctions in the process of production itself. To understand this relationship it is necessary to give attention to the institutional arrangements governing production, that is, the "social relations of production" (Edwards 1975, p. 85).

Ciudad Juárez, located a few minutes away from El Paso, Texas, across the Mexican-American border, provides a good illustration of this point. As a result of the implementation of the Border Industrialization Program (BIP) since 1965 there are currently in that city more than one hundred assembly plants, or *maquiladoras*, which operate as direct subsidiaries or subcontracted firms of multinational corporations (Flamm and Grunwald 1979). More than half of the total number of maquiladoras in Ciudad Juárez are of the electric/electronic kind, while the rest are by and large dedicated to the assembly of apparel, with a small number involved in the manufacture of toys, asbestos yarn and other miscellaneous products (Barrera Bassols 1976; Newton and Balli 1979).

While all maquiladoras employ an overwhelming majority of women in direct production, significant differences among them surface when those employed in the electric/electronic industry are compared with those working in apparel manufacturing (Fernández Kelly 1982). The former are in general younger and have a higher average level of schooling than the latter. They are predominantly single and tend to contribute more than half of their weekly earnings to their families or orientation (i.e., parents and siblings with whom the majority live). They are an urban population whose members have grown up and been educated in Ciudad Juárez.

By contrast, women working in the apparel industry tend to be older and less educated. A large number of them have lived in Ciudad Juárez five or less years, a finding that probably indicates the presence of a greater number of recent migrants from the interior of Mexico in this group. One out of every three women in the Ciudad Juárez apparel industry provides the only means of support for their family. More often than not, these women support their own children rather than parents or siblings.

In sum, although a similarity of gender is shared by both groups or workers—all of whom are sought by international capital as sources of cheap labor—there are palpable differences among them which merit explanation. Such an explanatory effort (attempted in these pages) should take into consideration two levels of theoretical analysis. At one level we must account for the general process that governs the demand of labor in consonance with the requirements of capital accumulation at a global scale (Frank 1970; Bukharin 1972; Weeks and Dore 1979). At a more concrete level we must examine the structure of labor markets and the from that smaller reproductive units such as the family and the household take within them (Schmink 1979; Safa 1980).

Four complementary themes overlap in this work. First I will ① draw a sketch of the general and particular circumstances that enabled the implementation of the BIP, both as a profitable investment strategy for foreign business and as a government-sponsored project for development. Second, the impact of multinational investments on local labor markets will be underscored. In Ciudad ② Juárez (as well as in other Mexican border cities) this impact has entailed the fracture of the local labor force by gender (Pearson and Elson 1978) and real differences in employment alternatives for men and women and for various fractions of the working class (Doeringer and Piore 1971).

Third, the correspondence between the local labor market in ③ Ciudad Juárez and the position of the two manufacturing branches that dominate maquiladora activities (i.e., electronics and apparel manufacturing) in the international market will be examined. Finally, the function of household structure as a necessary precondition that determines labor supply vis-à-vis the requirements of international capital will be illustrated with a basis of ethnographic materials.

Methodology and Data Collection

The data which guide this study were collected during 1978 and 1979 in Ciudad Juárez, Chihuahua. Research was divided into four complementary stages.

1. The author had the opportunity to seek employment and work at an apparel manufacturing plant for almost two months. Participant observation was used as an exploratory technique. Its objective was to deepen familiarity with the nature of operations performed by maquiladoras, increase knowledge of production quotas, working

conditions and rhythms, hiring policies and time/resources invested by potential workers when trying to gain access to jobs. This technique was also used to initiate contacts with working women whose acquaintance was maintained in the later stages of research.

2. This initial facet of the investigation was followed by a survey of 510 women working as direct production operators in fourteen different assembly plants. With a basis on background information available to this author and taking into consideration the experience of work at a maquiladora, a questionnaire was designed which included more than one hundred items on migration, household composition and income distribution.

Because of the interdisciplinary nature of this research, a survey of limited scope as the one described above was used to gather aggregate data complementary to the ethnographic descriptions. All of the women in this sample were interviewed during work shifts and at the place of their employment. In part thanks to this, it was possible to exert a high level of control over the process of research and over the quality of the sample.

3. Participant observation and the interviewing of a large sample was complemented by the compilation of approximately fifty-five hours of ethnographic recordings derived from conversations between this author and working women. With a basis on the information afforded by the survey, a group of women (prototypical of the various subgroups into which the maquiladora work force is divided) was selected for in-depth interviewing.

After initial contact with these women, they were visited at their homes, and extensive conversations with them and the members of their families were recorded. These conversations are a rich reservoir of perceptions, attitudes and descriptions, many of which are incorporated into the present work.

4. Although this research was centered primarily on the characteristics of the maquiladora work force, limited ethnographic materials were also collected from government officials, private enterprise representatives, promoters of the maquiladora industry, members of upper- and middle-level management at many plants, and trade union leaders. This was necessary to form a context in which to place and contrast the narrations of workers, as well as to gain insights from those who have been involved in the development of the maquiladora program in Mexico.

Before describing the empirical information yielded by this investigation, it is useful to prepare a context on the basis of recent writings that focus on working women.

Women and Work: A Review of Literature

Although there were isolated works stressing the importance of women's social participation written in the last two centuries, only recently have social scientists given systematic attention to the way in which gender is related to political and economic life. As a consequence, a stimulating literature has emerged exploring the connection between gender and work in both highly industrialized and developing countries. Besides providing us with profuse empirical information, these works have also generated significant theoretical issues. They offer a portrayal of mothers, daughters and companions whose labor in the household is crucial to the maintenance and renewal of society. Women have also been characterized as food producers, artisans, entrepreneurs and wage earners. Contrary to a narrow interpretation of women's socioeconomic functions prevalent in the past, these works outline a rich profile marked by diversity rather than by uniformity of experience (Myrdal and Klein 1968; Tilly and Scott 1978).

In part, the emergence of scholarly interest on women's socioeconomic activities has been prompted by the rebirth of feminism as a viable political trend. This has induced recognition that the position of women within the private and public spheres is not derived from immutable biological factors but from material constraints and socialization processes (Rowbotham 1974; Sacks 1975; Hartmann 1979). In the United States and Western Europe, the attempts of women to gain access to employment have paralleled intellectual efforts to explain their economic and political disfranchisement in various cultural settings and at different points in time. Explanations of the role of gender, sexism, female subordination and the roots of a prevailing androcentric bias in cultural productions have been among the areas approached by this current (see articles in Reiter 1975; Nash and Safa 1976; Rosaldo 1976).

The close interconnection between political activism and intellectual concerns has, to a large extent, determined the nature of scholarly questions and priorities. Among these, the compound issue of women's work and class has gained increased importance (Safa 1976). As growing numbers of women claim jobs in nontraditional sectors and demand equal pay to men in similar kinds of occupations, the interest of researchers on the history of women's participation in the labor force has expanded (Tinker 1975a). Their findings have discredited some commonly held assumptions. For example, women's gainful employment—portrayed by the media and by some academic works as an unprecedented phenomenon caused by industrialization, the automation of house chores and the propagation of birth control—has been found to be a common experience rather than the exception in past generations (Scott and Tilly 1975, p. 38). Women have always had to work, although their work has often been belittled or ignored.

Many studies now indicate that for certain groups of women both in metropolitan and peripheral countries, earnings by comparison to those of men employed in similar kinds of occupations have declined rather than increased in the last years (International Labour Organisation 1976). In a similar vein other scholars have pointed to the fact that for the majority of women remunerated employment is not the result of emancipation but of economic need (Nash 1975; Beechey 1977). Thus, the most systematic approaches to this subject have stressed the importance of examining women's participation in the workforce as a fluctuating phenomenon with respect to which class membership plays a definitive role. Two corollaries of this proposition follow. First, women's gainful employment has not been the unilineal effect of technological progress and modernization (for a differing view, see Goode 1963). Second, despite disclaimers, the assumption that women's incorporation into remunerated activities indicates a furthering of individual autonomy and emancipation is not self-evident (Safa 1976).

In making the relationship between gender and labor problematic, new paths for systematic investigation have been opened. Research into the particulars of women's labor history entails the possibility of qualification of feminist generalizations based upon the experience of the middle and upper classes. It also establishes the conditions for judging concrete circumstances that prompt the incorporation or exclusion of women from certain sectors of economic activity. To reach this objective authors have alternately adopted a historical and structural perspective. They have looked at the changes in the mode of insertion of different groups of women into the local and international division of labor over time.

Ester Boserup's pioneer work, *Women and Economic Development* (1970) is generally recognized as a pathbreaking contribution in this respect. Benería and Sen (1980) have adeptly discussed some of the merits of this work by underscoring four points. First, Boserup was the first to show with a basis on empirical evidence collected in distant parts of the world that women's participation in local, regional and national economies is far from insignificant. Although not recognized by most census data and conventional economic indicators, women's labor accounts for the generation of much social wealth.

For example, in some African and Latin American Indian communities women are customarily responsible for up to 85% of food production by weight (see also Gough 1975). Thus, as gatherers, horticulturalists and farmers, women actively contribute to the maintenance of their groups' lives. However, this simple fact has been generally neglected given the emphasis of anthropologists on predominantly male economic activities such as hunting (Leacock 1972).

In the same vein, although it varies in content with culture and geography, domestic labor, a predominantly female occupation, also has economic significance. In hunting gathering societies and in many agricultural communities, the household operates as both a productive and a reproductive unit. By this it is meant that, within the home, individuals perform activities that ensure subsistence on a daily basis as well as those that guarantee the renewal and maintenance of their work force (for a discussion of the concepts of "renewal" and "maintenance" see Burawoy, 1978). Food production and consumption, alternate with the bearing, caring and raising of children as part of the flow of life. Thus, under these circumstances the modern distinction between domestic and nondomestic labor is tenuous, if even present.

Similarly, in a manner akin to Margaret Mead, Boserup underscores the widespread existence of a division of labor by gender throughout the world. Women tend to be universally responsible for the care of infants, but the degree to which individuals of both sexes participate in domestic activities has varied considerably. While it is true that in many cases women's labor tends to be undervalued, in many other cases women's economic contributions are readily recognized (Leacock 1972). Boserup and others have suggested that frequently women's status and level of socially recognized power are directly related to their food producing capacities (Leacock 1972; Gough 1975). Although it is not possible to generalize without qualification, many of these cases suggest that women's active contributions as food producers (rather than as transformers only) parallel higher degrees of female autonomy and participation in decision-making processes on a par with men.

Second, Boserup also noted, for the first time, that modernization and development policies have (more often than not) resulted in a deterioration of women's status which has paralleled their exclusion from "productive" economic activities. With this Boserup set the basis for further research (Manzoor Ahmad 1972; Nash 1975; Rubbo 1975; Aguiar 1976) whose conclusions have exposed a commonly held myth: that modernization, technification and capitalist development in general have been advantageous to women.

On the contrary, most authors now agree that "development" has generally placed women in a position of greater dependency upon men by preventing the former from gaining full access to remunerated employment and by encouraging the latter to become the sole supporters of their families. Thus, the formation of a predominantly male working class has coincided with the rise of ideological constructs that see the proper role of women as housewives. Nash (1975) notes that in areas of the world where women had been active as horticulturalists and small farmers, the penetration of capitalist developmental policies drastically reduced women's access to land, credit and other resources:

> The overall effect of the green revolution and similar development programs has been a vast increase in yields, but at the expense of the displacement of the small farmers, regional inequalities, and the accentuation of income differences. . . . The displacement of labour from a family-based context limits the ability of women to enter the productive process and thus assume a share of productivity for themselves and their children . . . commercial agriculture has often discouraged initiative for women's subsistence activities that provided a varied diet and some surplus for cash income. [pp. 31,32]

Chaney and Schmink (1976) have extended this argument to explore the relationship between technification and female employment. They point to the fact that higher levels of mechanization and technological expertise are consistently related with male employment even in those sectors of economic activity originally considered as women's domain (Baker 1964). In environments where subsistence agriculture was replaced by commercial crop production, the most profitable occupations, that is, those related to the handling of machinery, irrigation and transportation, went to men to the almost total exclusion of women. In a similar vein female employment in industry has been restricted to occupations requiring the intensive use of manual, poorly paid labor. When some of these occupations have been reshaped in order to incorporate the use of sophisticated technology, women have been replaced by men.

Thus, in the apparel manufacturing industries, cutting, now a highly mechanized operation, has become a male and comparatively well-paid job, while sewing, still requiring intensive use of manual labor, remains a low-paying female occupation (see Madden 1973; Huntington 1975; Safa 1979).

Other authors have turned their attention to the relationship between women and work under conditions of rapid industrialization and, especially, to the role that families and households play in the supply of labor differentiated .by gender (Lloyd 1975; Young 1978). Among these studies, those accomplished by Tilly and Scott deserve further attention. As a historian Tilly has looked at the particulars in the participation of European women in the industrial work force during the nineteenth century. Her contribution is equally significant for historians, economists, sociologists and anthropologists as it places emphasis upon the concept of *family strategies*, which affect not only the immediate survival of kin groups but the participation of their members in wage employment.

According to Tilly (1978) the analysis of family strategy

> tries to uncover the principles which lead to observable regularities or patterns of behavior among households. It asks who bears the costs or benefits from strategies in which individual interests or needs are often subordinated . . . . It moves away from, on the one hand, any implicit acceptance of the powerlessness of people caught up in a process of large scale structural change, or, on the other hand, the attempt to see into people's minds, to study mentality or attitude, which is often tautological. [P. 3]

The point of view that has developed around this concept has added a necessary corrective to overly deterministic conceptions (including certain Marxist and neo-Marxist trends) which view individuals and groups as the creatures of structural economic and political forces entirely beyond their control.

While Tilly does not deny the importance of structural forces at play, she also observes that there are family strategies about migration, fertility, schooling and labor force participation, about the coresidence of children and the age of marriage. Thus,

> the concept of family strategies works as a series of hypotheses about . . . implicit principles, less rigid or articulated than

decision rules, by which the household, not the individual, not the society as a whole, acts as the unit of decision making. [Ibid., p. 3]

The important point to be stressed here is the following. When observations about family strategies and broad political, economic and ideological forces are combined, the participation of women in the labor force acquires its full meaning. Such a phenomenon is not the unmitigated effect of capitalist requirements for cheap labor, nor is it the result of free choices made by individuals. Rather it is a complex phenomenon influenced by both levels of social activity and mediated by the household as the locus where conscious or unconscious strategies are enacted.

In several recent articles, Tilly suggests that just as there were variations of proletarianization in nineteenth-century France, so in turn there were differences in family strategies and patterns of behavior among working-class families. Although in the first instance these strategies may be seen as adaptations to wider structural constraints, they also affect the nature of labor supply, and the constitution of society in general—whence the dialectical relationship between family organization and labor market requirements.

The changing role of women in the wage labor market has also received attention recently. Lamphere, Hauser and Michel (1978), for example, have studied the conditions surrounding women's employment in the New England textile industry. They notice that although during the early decades of the twentieth century most women employed outside the home were young and single, those who were married worked within the home both to provide services, attend to the needs of their families and frequently to supplement family income by taking in boarders. This was the case among migrant women, especially Polish women.

Using historical data she argues that although there may be important ethnic differences in women's work experiences, many can be explained in terms of the moment when a particular ethnic group immigrated to the United States and in terms of the characteristics of the local niche into which a group was pushed.

Echoing some of the insights present in Tilly's use of family strategies. Lamphere underscores the differences among Polish and French immigrants in New England:

The high percentage of boarding and women's labor force participation among Poles could be mainly a product of the young population in 1915, the lack of housing in the neighborhoods available to them, and the low wages which Polish men earned in the textile mills. Though there may be cultural values which encouraged French women to leave paid work at marriage, it is also true that French husbands had access to a wider and better range of jobs which may have made it possible for French women to follow a strategy of having larger families whose children could provide added support after they reached adolescence. [P. 43]

Thus Lamphere underscores economic factors rather than ethnic differences affecting women's employment after migration. Simultaneously, family organization and needs are incorporated in this perspective as an important explanatory variable. As are other authors, Lamphere is cognizant of the fact that decisions regarding employment and occurring at the level of the household are determined by the costs of reproducing the daily and long-term existence of its members. Among most working-class peoples, such costs cannot be paid by the wage of only one provider. Therefore choices must be made about the number of household members that need to work outside of the home to enable family subsistence. The pooling of resources maximizes the chances for survival of both individuals and households. In these circumstances, personal autonomy is subsumed under the constraints imposed by family needs.

The interplay between individual and family needs as well as the manner in which they have affected and been affected by labor market conditions is another point recently examined by anthropologists and historians. Minge-Klevana (1978,1980), for example, has studied the changes in the concept of childhood during the transition from peasant to industrial society. Following concepts present in the work of Aries (1965) and Shorter (1975), Minge-Klevana points to the fact that the definition of childhood as a social institution varied over time in response to the fluctuations of economic and political factors. In peasant communities where the labor of youngsters was incorporated as part of family productive activity, childhood was recognized as a brief period in human development. Privacy and personal life and needs were subordinated to family requirements. Industrialization brought about the conditions for a redefinition of childhood in terms of duration and psychological content. In these circumstances children lost value as home laborers. Increasing restrictions over the use of child labor and the implementation of compulsory education, as well as the expansion of clerical work, imposed limitations upon the value of young sons and daughters as wage earners. Increasingly children became fully dependent for survival upon their parents. Women, in particular, were held responsible for the educational and psychological well-being of children, while men acted primarily (although not exclusively) as material providers.

As Minge-Klevana notices, this process had a multifaceted impact upon the life of families and households. First, it had an effect on birth rates and fertility. As children became dependents rather than young workers, the economic advantages of bearing a large number of offspring decreased. Couples had smaller families to dedicate more time, energy and resources to a few children, maximizing their chances for success at a later age in an increasingly restricted, demanding and competitive labor market.

Second, besides its demographic impact, this process was also attached to an increase in importance given to motherhood. Gradually women specialized in nonremunerated domestic chores, which in turn were redefined in order to consume more time and energy. Ehrenreich and English (1976) have noted that as women reduce their participation in productive and/or paid work, they take over many new and complex functions within the home. The increase of time, energy and resources required to adequately fulfill the role of housewife effectively diminishes the possibility of success of entry by women into the labor market. On the other hand, new household needs and a continuous reshaping of standards of living generate a growing market for material goods and services. Consequently, the family is transformed into a primarily consumptive unit.

Third, the same development has had political significance insofar as families become growingly dependent on wages earned by male workers. The permanence of men in the labor force is often insured by their familial responsibilities which make women and children entirely dependent on them for survival. At the same time women's economic and policical autonomy is significantly reduced by their impossibility to gain access to paid employment and by their characterization as supplementary earners; housewives and mothers dependent on men (see also Hartmann, 1979).

But while this description is helpful for understanding general historical developments particularly in Europe and in the United States, it must be qualified by observations of national and class background. Class in many ways determines the kinds of economic and political options available to men and women. Nationality (and

14

very often ethnic background) have considerable impact in this respect, as they indicate the particular position of individuals and groups in the social division of labor. While women belonging to the middle and upper classes may have been able in the past and in the present to fully dedicate their attention to home responsibilities (this being at the same time a luxury and the source of severe economic and political subordination), working-class women have often had to work for a wage, while at the same time attending to domestic labor. This circumstance has inevitably placed women in what may rightfully be called a "double bind."

In response to this observation many scholars have focused attention upon the situation of women in third world countries, modifying commonly held assumptions on the subject. For example, the stereotypical notion of Latin American women as conservative, apathetic and totally dependent individuals has been questioned on the basis of empirical research. Works by Saffioti (1969), Arizpe (1975), Jelin (1976), Deere (1977, 1978), Lomnitz (1978), Young (1978), Nash (1979), Safa (1980) and others have pointed to the range of methods by which women (particularly poverty-stricken women) actively contribute to the maintenance of their dependents.

Contrary to what some have assumed in the past, the majority of migrants in Latin America are women rather than men (Jelin 1976). Deere and de Leal (1980) have assessed the economic contribution of peasant women in Andean communities. Lomnitz, Nash and Safa have stressed the role that women play in Mexican, Puerto Rican and Bolivian communities as active generators of informal kin and friendship networks within which vital resources are produced, shared and exchanged. Finally, Young and others have stressed the participation of women in rural communities as artisans and merchants.

A general summary of the contributions of this literature to the study of women and work is offered by Moser (1980) through observation of poor urban women in Guayaquil, Ecuador:

> In peripheral economies such as Ecuador the abundance of available labor is sufficient to insure that wages are kept below the value of labor power. The value of labor power determines the extent to which women must work both in domestic labor . . . and also the extent to which they are forced to look for wage work. A variety of strategies are adopted. At the household level, for example, the decision of rural migrants to squat and

invade on a peripheral city swamp . . . is designed to lower the cost of living, while sending out other members of the family to work for a wage. [P. 19]

Thus,

the strategies women adopt depend on their age, marital status and skills. Nevertheless, in slum communities . . . the majority of low-income women are involved in different domestic-related activities (in all of which there are low rates of pay, no security of work and exploitative labor relations) throughout their adult lives, providing a significant input to the "family wage." [P. 21]

A review on the literature on women and work leads to five central conclusions.

1. An abundance of historical and recent empirical information demonstrates the significance of gender as a category which has powerful analytical and explanatory value in the study of social, political and economic processes. The theoretical meaning of this assertion has been clouded by two factors. On the one hand, there is reluctance on the part of certain sectors of the academic community to acknowledge studies focused on women as more than a reflection of "trendy" group interests. On the other hand, ongoing political debates (among Marxists, feminists and a combination of both) about the superiority or inferiority of gender with respect to class as sources of oppression have often confused rather than clarified issues about women and work (see Sokoloff 1979).

Nevertheless it should be clear that as with ethnicity, national background and class, gender plays a fundamental part in clarifying past and contemporary history. In the majority of cases social, economic and political developments have had a differential impact upon men and women. At the same time these have been influenced by individuals whose behavior is shaped by gender-specific socialization processes. Thus generalizations about classes, groups or nations remain partial unless qualifications by gender are effected. Here lies a fruitful path for future research not only on the part of ethnographers (whose attention generally focuses on the minute details of human existence) but also by those who wish to refine and expand the explanatory potential of social theory.

2. This literature also shows that the term "women" is an elusive abstraction. It escapes all sorts of generalizations unless questions

of class, ethnicity, culture and national background are taken into consideration. The history of women and their participation in paid and unpaid labor is the history of individuals of a particular gender, immersed in a world bounded by numerous social and economic factors. Although gender may provide the basis for commonality of experience among women of different backgrounds, often these similarities are dramatically modified by class position. The importance of this consideration has not been ignored by the authors mentioned above.

3. The available research tends to confirm the idea that a division of labor by gender has existed universally both in past and present times. However the degree to which this division inevitably causes the political and economic subordination of women is a question subjected to ongoing debate. In general authors agree that capitalist development has had as a consequence the deterioration of the status of women (especially working-class women) in many parts of the world. Moreover the issue of women's economic and political autonomy has not followed an unilinear development. It has varied according to particular historical moments and in relation to broad structural parameters.

4. In agreement with the last observation, this literature also suggests the economic importance of women's labor in the domestic and public spheres. A recent accomplishment of the social sciences in this respect is that women cannot be conceptualized only as the tenets of biological and social reproduction. At every stage of their lives most women participate in productive economic activities, either within or outside of their home even though this fact has been seldom acknowledged by official economic indicators. This opens the possibility for a rich assessment of households as the locus where domestic labor subsidizes the generation of capitalistic profits. Moreover, it indicates that women's contribution to the creation of social wealth cannot be measured only in terms of their participation in the wage labor force (see Larguía and Dumoulin 1975).

5. Finally, this literature underscores the importance of family strategies as effects of decision-making processes that take place at the level of the household. These strategies (conscious or subconscious, tacit or deliberate) mediate between the choices perceived by individuals and the constraints imposed by larger labor markets. In other words, the authors mentioned above have called our attention to the importance of household organization and needs as factors which influence the supply of labor. With this they have added an

important qualification to views that see the fate of working peoples as the fatal result of capital's requirements and demands. If the notion of *dialectics* ingrained in social and historical processes is to have any meaning at all, it should take a thoughtful account of this point.

This volume aims at providing a limited contribution to the literature on women and work by examining the birth of new groups of workers formed by women under conditions of rapid and planned industrialization along the U.S.-Mexico border. As will be seen, the five points listed above have had importance as guidelines orienting my study. Before assessing the position of women employed as assembly workers in Ciudad Juárez's offshore production plants, a description of the social and economic conditions that characterize Mexico's northern frontier and of the process that has led to its industrialization is necessary. This is the purpose of the following chapter.

CHAPTER 2

The Border Industrialization Program

Socioeconomic Features of the Mexican-American Border

Mexico shares with the United States a 1,947-kilometer borderline whose history has, in many ways, prefigured trends in the political and economic relationship between the two countries. Since its inception during the middle half of the nineteenth century, the border has experienced events of definitive consequences in shaping Mexico's history. Its own existence as an international demarcation line is linked to the loss of a large part of territory by U.S. conquest (Fernández 1977, p.48; Martínez 1978, p. 27). The shattering epic that was the Revolution of 1910 was initiated in areas close to the border. In more recent times the exacerbation of problems linked with smuggling, equitable terms of trade, transculturation (see Ortíz 1947 for a useful discussion of this concept) and undocumented (or illegal) migration, have transformed Mexico's northern frontier into a highly volatile area that may well determine the fate of Mexico in the years to come.

In many ways, the Mexican border departs from the typical features that characterize the rest of Mexico. Mexican border municipalities are the most rapidly growing in the country after Mexico City. Demographic expansion has been particularly impressive in the last five decades (Secretaría de Industria y Comercio 1974a). Luis Uniquel et al. (1974) suggest some implications of this trend by pointing to the fact that they are owed more to the proximity of the region to the United States than to the internal dynamics of Mexico. That is, rather than responding to a greater participation in national development (as would be the case of Mexico City, Guadalajara or Monterrey), the growth of border municipalities is directly related to demands and circumstances emanating from the United States.

When comparing population trends in both U.S. and Mexican border cities it is possible to see that the latter have grown at a more rapid speed than the former. An effect of this has been the increase in the concentration of workers in the services sector (tertiarization) for the majority of border cities with the exception of Reynosa (Uniquel et al. 1974, p. 33; Bustamante 1976b). Aggregate data referring to the economically active population indicate the growing predominance of the service sector in Mexican border municipalities as compared to the rest of the country. At the same time, border cities where the services sector predominates had the highest rate of population growth (5.23%) in the decade from 1960 to 1970. During the same period the average growth rate for the nation as a whole was 3.04% (Bustamante 1976b,p. 2).

The Mexican border also shows considerable demographic concentration. Seventy-five percent of the population in that area is concentrated in the cities of Tijuana, Mexicali, Ensenada, Ciudad Juárez, Matamoros, Nuevo Laredo and Reynosa (Secretaría de Industria y Comercio, 1975). In 1970 the population of Ciudad Juárez, Tijuana and Mexicali alone represented 50% of the total border population. One of the reasons for both population growth and demographic concentration lies in the very high rates of migration to border cities. Of a total population for the country of almost fifty million in 1970, 15.3% came from different places than those in which they resided in January of the year in which the census was taken (1970). The total population of migrants for the border cities was 29.3% in that year (Garibay 1977, p. 10). For the city of Tijuana the proportion of migrants was 47%, for Mexicali it was 34%, for Juárez 23%, for Ensenada 35.7%, for Matamoros 21%, for Nuevo Laredo 33.2% and for Reynosa 30.9% (Bustamante 1976b).

Some small communities like Sario, Sonora and Ojinaga in Chihuahua or Ocampo, Coahuila have upwards of a 90% native-born population. Although these towns are near the border, they are not border crossings. Cities like Ciudad Juárez, Nuevo Laredo, Reynosa, Matamoros and a large part of cities in Baja California, have numerous immigrants from other Mexican cities (Duncan 1974; García Moreno 1979).

According to the 1970 Mexican Census, the six states bordering with the United States had a total of 7,912,390 persons. This figure represents 16.4% of the country's population. Border cities are also characterized by a specific age distribution. The vast majority of border cities have at least about 42% of their populations 14 years of age or younger. In fact 46.4% of the population are less than 15 years old in all border cities (Urquidi and Méndez Villarreal 1978, p. 263). This compares closely to the national figure of 46.2% in this category (ibid., p. 265).

When comparing birth rates for Mexico and the United States, it may be seen that the former country has had birth rates at least $2\frac{1}{2}$ times those of the latter between 1965 and 1972. During this time Mexico has had approximately 44 births per 1,000 while the United States has had about 17 births per 1,000. Despite their steady demographic growth, aggregate data show that the average birth rate for the border towns in 1970 was 44.2, that is, almost the same as the national figure. Thus it is migration rather than vegetative growth that accounts for the expansion in the size of border cities (Uniquel et al. 1974, p. 37).

These figures express more than regional peculiarities. Mexico as a whole has experienced enormous growth in the last few decades. In 1940 there were 20 million inhabitants in that country. By the beginning of the 1950s, this figure had grown to 26,606,000. In 1975 it was 59,204,000. Finally, by the end of 1978, it was estimated that there were approximately 65 million people living in Mexico (García Moreno 1979; see also Alcalá Quintero 1969).

The dramatic nature of these figures is surpassed by future projections. It is estimated that by year 2000 the population in Mexico will reach 132 million if current growth trends persist. However, Mexican authorities have recently noted that the 3.5% growth rate that has characterized Mexico in the last decade and a half has been reduced to 3.3%. Although it is too soon to judge the validity and long-term durability of this change, it is true that the Mexican government has implemented massive birth control campaigns in the last five years.

Migration to the border cities combined with high birth rates have exerted much pressure upon the border communities' capacity to provide for their citizens' welfare. The burden of generating employment opportunities along the border is illustrated by employment data. For example, a 1970 survey showed that in six Mexican border cities unemployment and underemployment ranged from 11.6% in Matamoros to 42.1% in Nogales. The four other border cities in the survey (Ciudad Juárez, Mexicali, Nuevo Laredo and Tijuana) had an unemployment level that hovered around 20%. At least 80% of the unemployed and underemployed in each city were men (Engineer Agency for Resources 1970; Banco Nacional de México 1976).

The economically active population in Mexico is estimated to approximate eighteen million. However, of this contingent only ten million are currently employed. Added to the near 3.5 million undocumented workers who labor in the United States, it turns out that roughly 11.5 million persons live without permanent work (Bustamante 1976b, p. 13). This also implies that there are more Mexicans without employment than with gainful occupations. Of ten Mexicans of a working age, only six are employed, the rest are either unemployed or underemployed. In addition to this, governmental calculations indicate that every year 80,000 young adults become job seekers. Not even half of these persons are successful in their efforts (García Moreno 1979, p. 2).

Although per capita income in the country surpasses $1,000 (U.S. dollars), this is more of a fictitious indicator rather than a true expression of development. Mexico is one of the countries in the world where income distribution is very uneven. Only 5% of the total population enjoys acceptable living conditions, while the rest, peasants, indigenous groups and the urban poor, are increasingly pauperized (Conroy 1973; García Moreno 1979).

In the agricultural sector, border municipalities have 13.1 million hectares of which only 7.6%, that is, one million hectares, are arable. This represents approximately 19% of total arable lands in Mexico. Regional agriculture is characterized by its high degree of technification and its need for extensive irrigation systems (Secretaría de Industria y Comercio 1975, p. 36). Despite its potential for high levels of productivity, agricultural activity in the border area has decreased in recent years, especially during the decade of the sixties.

Agricultural activities barely incorporated 29.2% of the economically active population in contrast with 39.4% for the whole nation in 1970. Between 1950 and 1970 the economically active population dedicated to agriculture in the Mexican border states decreased from 50 to 29.2%. In contrast the population participating in the services sector grew from 15.2% in 1950 to 27.4% in 1970 (Bustamante 1976b, p. 26).

With respect to commerce, operations along the border have generally favored Mexico. For example, in 1973 and 1974 the gains derived from border transactions were of $512 and $554 million respectively (Comisión Económica para América Latina 1976). However, these benefits have been weakened by their relationship to the balance of payments between Mexico and the U.S. In 1970, $879 million represented almost 30% of total export of goods and services; by 1976—only six years afterwards—the $1,610 million received for similar exchanges represented a reduced participation of 23.2% (García Moreno 1979, p. 11). During 1977, border transactions produced gains for Mexico that amounted to $394 million. Lastly, between January and May of 1978 tourism and border transactions represented gains of $482.2 million, a figure 16.4% higher than its equivalent for the same period of the preceding year (*Panorama Económico* 1977, p. 6).

The proximity of Mexico to the United States as well as the historical relationship of interdependence between the two countries has resulted in a modicum of economic symbiosis. U.S. citizens spend more in Mexico than vice versa. However, economic exchanges are intense on both sides of the border (Urquidi and Méndez Villarreal 1978, p. 370).

The contribution of industrial activity has been central for the development of border economy. In 1965 border industries generated net production with a value of 3,482.0 million pesos (Secretaría de Industria y Comercio 1974a). Until 1965 border industry was distributed in the following way: food and drink in Baja, California, Norte, Chihuahua, Juárez, Laredo, and Anáhuac; activities related to the needle trades and the production of textiles were located in Tamaulipas (Matamoros); iron and steel industries predominated in Coahuila (Piedras Negras); and mineral exploitation with the exception of iron-related industries, focused in Sonora (Nogales) (García Moreno 1979, pp. 12, 13).

Urquidi and Méndez Villarreal note that the value of mineral production in the border area represented 11.2% of total value in the national mining industry for 1972. Manufacturing industries represented 9.2% of total production in the border area. In part this has been due to the enormous impact of maquiladora industrialization.

Antecedents of the Border Industrialization Program

The strategic geographical position of the border has also been decisive in its transformation into an area where various developmental programs have been implemented by the government in the last two decades. In 1961 during the administration of Adolfo López Mateos, the National Border Programa (Program Nacional Fronterizo) was enacted to promote the commercial improvement and beautification of the region. It was the objective of this program to transform the border region into a national windowcase *(la ventana de México)*, to attract tourism and to provide formal mechanisms aimed at encouraging consumer purchases in Mexican territory *(El Paso Economic Review* 1969; Evans 1973).

Under the auspices of Nacional Financiera, the major government bank, PRONAF attempted to (1) substitute Mexican manufactured goods for imports; (2) boost the sale of Mexican products to foreign consumers; and (3) upgrade the social environment and living conditions along the border. The objectives of PRONAF were to be achieved through a combination of public works expenditures and subsidies (Diario Oficial de la Federación 1971; James and Evans 1974). The former were directed towards the expansion of customs and entry stations, shopping areas and other services related to tourism. The latter consisted mainly of gross receipts tax rebates and reductions in freight charges linked to the sale of Mexican manufactured products along the border (Alcalá Quintero 1969).

With the aid of the Mexican government and local private enterprise large investments were made by PRONAF to develop the most important border ports of entry according to the criteria listed above. The most positive achievement of the program was to stimulate tourism. Revenues from that sector increased from 40 million dollars in 1960 to 56 million dollars in 1970 (James and Evans 1974). But with respect to its other goals, PRONAF's success was very limited specially when considering the resources invested in its implementation. For example, PRONAF failed to gain the border market for Mexican products. According to a report of the commission for the two Californias, presided by government officials in California and Baja California, the number of Mexicans making regular purchases in the U.S. side of the border increased by 6 percent between 1966 and 1967. This figure is particularly significant when considering that such an increase in previous years amounted only to 3 and 4 percent (Banco Nacional de México January 1976).

However, it is difficult to evaluate the meaning of such an increase. The recent establishment of the maquiladora program may have boosted the purchasing power of many Mexican families whose members may have started crossing the border to acquire U.S. goods (American Chamber of Commerce 1970). If this were the case, it could be argued that the effects of the new development program, based upon industrialization, initially worked against some of the major goals espoused by PRONAF (García Moreno 1979 p. 23).

Despite its limited success PRONAF resulted in an impressive assortment of modern shopping malls, public markets, museums, renovated municipal buildings and theaters. An offshoot of this effort was the so-called "artículos gancho" ('enticement products') program which since 1971 permits the importation free of duty of certain U.S. manufactured goods to be sold in Mexico at prices lower or equal to those in the neighboring country. Again, its purpose has been to strengthen the internal market. Again, its success has been limited.

More relevant to the context of the present work was the implementation of the Border Industrialization Program in 1965 that was followed at the beginning of the 1970's by the "In-Bond Plant Program or "Maquiladora Program." The two are part of a systematic effort to encourage foreign investment in export manufacturing through a combination of stimuli stemmed from tariff laws and fiscal incentives. This has caused an impressive growth of economic activity along both sides of the Mexican border.

When seen in a historical frame of reference, the Border Industrialization Program is but the last in a series of systematic efforts directed toward the industrialization of the area. As early as the 1930's the Mexican government attempted to encourage industrialization along its northern frontier through the establishment of free-trade privileges in the region (Martínez, 1978, pp. 58–70). In part, this was a response to the economic problems brought about by the onset of the 1929 Depression and the 1933 repeal of the Eighteenth Amendment to the Constitution of the United States. The former diminished the availability of money and consumption power disrupting economic activity on both sides of the border. By ending Prohibition, the latter undermined manufacturing and sales of alcoholic beverages upon which many border towns based their tenuous prosperity (De la Rosa 1965, p. 32).

Because of these reasons, means were sought to provide the basis for strengthened industrial growth. The state and territory of Baja, California and the northwestern fringe of Sonora were given a free-trade zone status in 1934, while border areas in the circumvicinity of Nogales and Agua Prieta were transformed into free perimeters. With these measures the government expected to reduce living costs in the region, attract foreign investment, and foster population growth. The free-trade status of the northwestern border has been maintained to the present although in a somewhat modified form.

This was instrumental in attracting foreign industry to the region even before the Border Industrialization Program was institutionalized.

Another series of events that had considerable impact upon the current shape of the Mexican-American border were those linked with migration policy. In 1942 the Mexican Labor Program (commonly known as Bracero Program) was constituted by official bilateral agreement to regulate the transfer of Mexican agricultural laborers to the southwest of the United States. It operated intermittently until December 31, 1964 (Bustamante 1975b). Although this program sanctioned the legal entry of Mexican workers during, roughly, two decades, during the same period, undocumented migration grew at a surprising speed (Comercio Exterior, August 1978). By the beginning of the sixties there was increasing pressure from Congress to end abuses resulted from the tax application of many of the program's statutes.

With the termination of the Mexican Labor Program by unilateral decision of the U.S. government, the economic problems along the border were accentuated. Two hundred thousand braceros were abruptly faced with unemployment at the same time that a growing number of agricultural workers continued to migrate to the border (Bradshow 1976). Unemployment rates approached 50% in part as a result of many displaced braceros' decisions to settle in border communities. Political unrest fostered by the inability of local labor markets to absorb these workers became a likely possibility. Measures aimed at assuaging discontent by providing viable channels for livelihood became an imminent necessity.

At the same time, U.S. multinational firms were steadily increasing their overseas exports of components and raw materials for assembly into finished products to be sold in the United States or in third world countries (Baerresen 1971). Growing investments of this kind in the Orient had resulted in the proliferation of assembly plants in points such as Singapore, Taiwan, Hong Kong and the Philippines. From the point of view of the Mexican government, this suggested the possibility of attracting foreign capital into the border region by developing a series of incentives while at the same time, reserving the domestic market for enterprises controlled by Mexican capital (Fernández 1977; p. 225; Martínez 1978, p. 360). Thus, a new effort under the rubric of the Border Industrialization Program was instituted in 1965. Its expressed objective was to generate the infrastructural and juridical conditions that would enable increased foreign investment in the area and, consequently, occupational opportunities for unemployed or underemployed Mexicans (Newton and Balli 1979, p. 2).

According to the U.S.-Mexican Commission for Border Development and Friendship, the border industrialization project was likely to provide major benefits for the business sectors of the world by reducing the costs of production through a combination of advanced technology and the employment of Mexican labor which would offer proven efficiency and lower relative cost. Morever, the plan was a logical solution for those foreign firms which were unable to penetrate international or domestic markets because of high manufacturing costs and their impossibility to sell at competitive prices (Flamm and Grunwald 1979, p. 3). By permitting the duty-free importation of machinery, equipment, and raw materials along the Mexican border on the condition that everything produced was exported, the Border Industrialization Program would enable these firms to compete in the international market.

To some U.S. economists the idea of the Border Industrialization Program appeared "simple in its approach" (Taylor and Bond 1968, p. 36). Based upon what was going to become a fashionable notion of economic interdependence, BIP was seen as a mechanism to

> . . . merge American capital and technical knowledge with relatively inexpensive Mexican labor. As such, attempts are made to lure American enterprise to the region by contending that labor costs are significantly lower. This program is analogous in many ways to other ongoing U.S. operations in Korea, Denmark and Hong Kong (Taylor and Bond, 1968:38).

On his part, Fulton Freeman, U.S. ambassador to Mexico during 1965 suggested broader implications for the Border Industrialization Program. He saw this effort as a potentially effective vehicle for opening jobs in Mexico that would arrest the flow of illegal migration from this country into the United States (NACLA 1975).

International Conditions and Local Incentives

Of no little importance in the development of border industrialization were the large wage differentials existing between Mexico and the United States. In 1968 the daily rate for an eight-hour day—roughly three dollars—was only a small fraction of what firms paid in their own countries while there existed (and continues to exist) a consensus that the efficiency of Mexican labor is as high or may even be higher than that of workers performing similar activities in the United States (James and Evans 1974). In the United States, for example, a similar day's work requires a wage at least six times larger. Although there have been annual increases in the Mexican minimum wages, several factors including recent peso devaluations have combined to maintain ample wage differentials.

Besides lower labor costs, the Mexican-American border offered other less quantifiable advantages to foreign business. The cities in the area possess labor and technicians of various grades and skills; industrial services; unlimited electric power; limitless supplies of fuel and lubricants; viable air and land connections; excellent roads and railways leading to major ports; telegraph, telephone and telex services; banking facilities and "a social climate that guarantees uninterrupted production and a high level of output" (U.S.-Mexico Commission for Border Development and Friendship 1968, p. 7).

The issue of the extent to which low wages determined the transfer of assembly operations from the United States to underdeveloped geographical areas deserves further clarification. Some observers have pointed out on various occasions that low wages and the availability of services required by industry are necessary but not sufficient causes of the expansion of the Border Industrialization Program. Two other features must be taken into consideration. One is the high level of productivity which can be extracted from Mexican workers at comparatively low operation costs. Another one is the panoply of benefits which accrue to U.S. business as a result of its proximity to the Mexican border (Dillman 1970.)

With regard to high levels of productivity, business representatives have noted that Mexican workers yield between 10 to 15 percent increases when compared to workers performing similar activities in the U.S., with absenteeism and turnover (both at 2 percent), comparing favorably as well (Newton and Balli 1979, p. 5). In addition, it is often remarked that labor availability, as opposed to costs or productivity is the pivotal consideration for locating in Mexico. Of special interest in this respect is the willingness of Mexicans to do shift work on a six-day week basis, a feature scarce in the United States.

On the other hand, proximity to the United States, offers the possibility of residence in U.S. border cities and work in Mexico for the members of management. This, in turn permits families of corporate executives with assembly interests in Mexico, the convenience of schooling, insurance, shopping and entertainment in their own country. In short, Border industrialization has provided an ideal situation for U.S. businessmen wishing to operate in Mexico but reluctant to forego the "American way of life." Locations in the interior of Mexico or in more distant geographical points cannot offer this privilege.

This feature has been broadly used in the publicity materials prepared by Mexican promoting agencies to encourage foreign investment. For example, in 1970 the Antonio J. Bermúdez Industrial Park promoters referred to the benefits of locating in Ciudad Juárez, only a few minutes away from El Paso, Texas, in these terms:

> The advantage of the U.S. manager, his family and his company, living in El Paso while supervising a foreign plant, are substantial. The company avoids the expense of moving the manager and his family to a distant foreign location; the family's living pattern is not markedly changed with the fully developed schools, hospitals, clubs and beautiful environment and climate offered by El Paso. In fact, the cultural experience of the family is enlarged because of the proximity of old Mexico. . . . Not the least of the advantages to the housewife are the international shopping facilities, as well as the plentiful supply of domestic services available in this area. [American Chamber of Commerce 1970, p. 75]

Undoubtedly the reference in this quote to the availability of domestic services refers to the relative ease with which U.S. households can contract the labor of undocumented Mexican maids by paying wages below the U.S. minimum.

Proximity to the United States has also meant reduction in transportation costs of goods assembled, a more fluid integration of complementary operations performed in twin plants on both sides of the border, and more expedient customs transactions. Thus, the border has been seen in recent years as an alternative location for manufacturing and assembly activities taking place in Asia.

The BIP has relied upon two crucial provisions of the U.S. tariff legislation to enhance its development. These two items (806.30 and 807) permit the basing of import duties on the value added outside the United States when the products are not substantially altered in character by manufacturing activities in foreign countries. As part of the Customs Simplification Act of 1956, item 806.30 had as a purpose to promote the manufacture of metal goods in Canada, in the event that their production in the United States should be threatened (Flamm and Grunwald 1979).

The use of this stipulation, however, has not been limited to

29

Canada. It has applied to nonprecious metal products processed overseas and returned to the United States for finishing. As such, it has had considerable interest for the electric and electronics industries. Complementary in many ways to this provision has been item 807.00, which originated in 1963 with the implementation of laws resulting from a 1954 customs court decision involving the interpretation of a provision of the tariff act of 1930. As amended in 1965 and 1966, item 807.00 applies to:

> articles assembled abroad in whole or in part or fabricated components, the product of the United States, which (a) are exported, in condition for assembly without further fabrication, (b) have not lost their physical identity in such articles by change in form, shape, or otherwise, and (c) have not been advanced in value or improved in condition abroad except by being assembled and except by operations incidental to the assembly process such as cleaning, lubricating and painting. [U.S. Tariff Commission, 1970, p. 71]

While item 806.30 has been instrumental in promoting the expansion of electric and electronics offshore production plants, item 807 has been most influential in enabling the operations of apparel, toy and other similar "light" industries. Both items rely heavily upon the definition of "added value," that is, the combination of labor costs in the area where assemblage is performed, outlays for other foreign inputs, overhead charges, a profit margin and estimates for components and supplies of U.S. origin which have either been transformed losing their identity or else used up in the process of production (U.S. Tariff Commission 1970).

The use of items 806.30 and 807 has been vehemently opposed by organized labor in the United States (see, for example, Chaikin 1976). Thus, in the words of Nathaniel Goldfinger, former Director of the AFL-CIO Department of Research:

> Item 807 is one small loophole in the tax structure for the advantage of U.S. based multinational companies. . . . It is a factor in the deterioration of both the volume and composition of the U.S. trade balance. . . . It encourages the mushrooming expansion of foreign subsidiary operations with the displacement of U.S. production and employment. [Ibid. p. 18]

U.S. industry has countered these opinions by agreeing that it is economically rational to stimulate the collaboration between countries possessing capital intensive capacities and countries specialized in labor intensive operations. From this point of view, items 806.30 and 807.00

> ... improve the competitive position of American industry by allowing a more efficient combination of the factors of production through joint utilization of American capital and advanced skills with lesser skilled labor from less developed countries ...
> They preserve jobs in the United States in those very industries that otherwise would be even harder hit by foreign competition. [Ibid. p. 27]

The debate stirred by the implementation of the BIP between U.S. organized labor and industry materialized in an investigation of the effects of the two crucial items (U.S. House of Representatives, Committee on Ways and Means, 1976). Such an investigation was requested by the executive branch in 1969 and hearings were held in May of the following year. By that time, imports from Mexico under items 806.30 and 807 had grown by 4,700% since 1966 (U.S. Tariff Commission 1970, COPY OUT).

With a basis on these hearings a conclusion was reached stating that it was not in the best interest of the United States economy to repeal the two items. It was agreed that "the labor differentials are so great that the components would continue to be made abroad and imported into the United States even if items 806.30 and 807 were repealed." [Ibid., p. 31]

While these were some of the elements that combined to insure the viability of the BIP from the point of view of foreign business, the favorable disposition of the Mexican government to aid its success should not be underestimated. During the early part of 1966, Octaviano Campos Salas, Minister of Industry and Commerce traveled through the Far East with the explicit purpose of observing assembly operations of U.S. firms. His conclusion, transcribed in the pages of the *Wall Street Journal* (May 25, 1966) was that Mexico was in a privileged position to compete in the international market as a source of highly trainable unskilled and semiskilled labor. In May and June of the same year, the Secretaría de Industria y Comercio (SIC) prepared an interministerial agreement according to which similar operations to those performed in the Orient would be permitted in Mexico (Dillman 1970; North American Congress for Latin America 1975).

President Gustavo Díaz Ordaz referred to this agreement in September during his annual State of the Nation address. With this, the program became a defacto reality, although its stipulations were only made explicit as law in March 1971 (James and Evans 1974). Prior to that date, the program developed informally through public statements by government officials and ad hoc agreements reached with particular firms.

The incentives granted by the Mexican government to foreign investment deserve special consideration in these pages. From the beginning, firms engaging in partial or complete assembly operations were exempted from restrictions on foreign ownership and management. They were permitted duty-free, in-bond imports of materials, supplies and machinery, as long as the whole of their production was exported. In general these privileges were limited to operations within twenty kilometers of the international boundary and to the entire free-trade zone (*Comercio Exterior* 1970, 1971, 1972; Bolin 1974).

Exemplary of the willingness on the part of the Mexican government to encourage the growth of the BIP is the fact that since mid-1973 a major simplification of the procedures used for BIP imports has been put into effect. Since that year, all routine import permit applications can be approved locally instead of requiring the authorization of agencies in Mexico City. Instead of the thorough inspection of total unloaded shipments that was demanded prior to 1973, authorities now perform summary spot checks (Barraesen 1971).

While every shipment of imports had to be bonded originally, it was later on possible for firms to post an annual bond, thereby saving time and up to 60% of the cost of bonding. Contrary to what occurred in the beginning (when separate storage areas were required by competent Mexican authorities), it is now possible to store imported merchandise anywhere in a plant. Stipulations over the disposal of industrial wastes have been altered to enable them to be donated to Mexican institutions (Hunt 1970).

When it appeared that the inability of foreign firms to own land along the border would hamper the expansion of the BIP, the government implemented a policy enabling them to acquire the full use of Mexican land for periods of up to thirty years through agreements in which Mexican financial institutions would act as trustees. The successive relaxations of the twenty-kilometer limit for this kind of operation are also indications of the flexible approach of the Mexican government towards the BIP (Ladman 1972).

Finally, plants operating under the BIP have been granted 100% foreign control over investment as long as their total production is exported. This is an extraordinary measure when considering that

32

under normal circumstances industries in Mexico are only allowed a maximum of 49% foreign control. The restriction of foreign investments has been aimed at preserving the national character of the Mexican economy. However, this policy—labeled "Mexicanization"—has not been applied in the case of maquiladoras.

Since 1972 all stimuli granted foreign corporations to encourage investment in export manufacturing activities were extended to the whole of Mexico with the exception of certain highly industrialized areas in the vicinity of Mexico City, Monterrey, and Guadalajara. With this, the juridical bases now exist for transforming the whole country into an Export Processing Zone (Fernández Kelly 1979b).

It was also provided that limited quantities of assembled goods could be sold domestically if import duties were paid and the products did not compare with goods of domestic manufacture. By mid-1973, BIP stipulations had been further amplified to enable twenty-one Mexican firms producing for the domestic market to use their idle capacity to perform in-bond assembly operations on a contract basis (Diario Oficial 1971).

Also since October 31, 1972, all assembly plants of the free zone and perimeters became subject to BIP regulations, enabling the Mexican government to effect tighter control over industrialization in the northwestern frontier (Secretaría de Industria y Comercio 1975). The government has taken steps designed to promote the economic development of border communities. In 1970 a trust fund was set up for the development of industrial parks, several of which were planned for border cities. In 1971 an interministerial commission including representatives of the executive branch of government was created to deal with the never-ending problems of the border region and to assist in the planning of its development. Subsidies relating to tax and freight have increased and their administration has been centralized (ibid.).

Development and Expansion

There is considerable difficulty in assessing the growth of the BIP given the ambiguity and lack of accuracy of estimates compiled by both the U.S. and Mexican governments. However, the most reliable data compiled suggest a rapid increase in the number of plants operating in Mexico and their output since 1971. Beyond question is the fact that assembly operations in Mexico have persistently

33

tended to grow more rapidly than those in other countries. The electronic/electric industry alone accounted for 77% of the value added in 1972 on goods imported from Mexico under tariff items 806.30 and 807.00 (Newton and Balli 1979).

Of the countries taking part in labor-intensive offshore manufacturing for the U.S. market, Mexico is now at the forefront, both in terms of growth and in terms of absolute value added by overseas processing. In 1978 offshore production plants provided the Mexican economy with more than 95,000 jobs and $713 million in value added, more than 70% of the total value added in this class of production in all of Latin America (ibid., p. 2).

These figures acquire full meaning when seen in the context of border industrial development since the mid-sixties. In-bond production has grown in Mexico from a negligible partaker into a major contributor to the Mexican economy. Expansion of production and revenues derived from value added have coincided with the increase in the number of maquiladoras operating in Mexico. In 1965 there existed twelve offshore production plants which employed 3,087 workers; by June of 1971, the number of plants had risen to 293 and the number of employees to 31,100. In 1974, 455 plants were in operation (429 along the border and the rest in the interior of Mexico) which employed 75,977 persons. In 1975, 454 maquiladoras (418 of which were located in the border) employed 67,214 workers. In 1976, 448 firms hired 74,496 workers. By December 1977 there were in Mexico 443 plants which employed 78,433 individuals. Finally, in 1979, the Maquiladora Program included 531 plants with 476 of these in the frontier zone and 55 in the interior. Of the 156,000 persons employed in these industries in 1982, more than 40,000 lived in Cuidad Juárez.

Value added, a definitive concept in offshore manufacturing has logically experienced a phenomenal boost during the same period. For example, in 1970 (when data on this issue were first compiled) value added by in-bond plants operating in Mexico amounted to $101.9 million. By 1974 the same figure had risen to $443.5 million and in 1978 it was $713.4 million. Therefore, in 1978, value added by in-bond industry ranked third, behind tourism and petroleum sales as a contributor to Mexican foreign exchange (Steiner 1971; Balli 1979, and Newton). Of the $713 million in value added, about one-third went to the workers employed by the plants, the rest entered the economy through rents, taxes, material costs and miscellaneous costs (Newton and Balli 1979, p. 18).

In 1978 maquiladora plants paid 12,000 billion pesos in salaries and wages along the border belt alone (García Moreno 1979). According to data collected by the Banco de México, the main financial institution in the country, the personnel employed by offshore production plants grew by 20% during the period 1977 to 1978. However the tendency appears to be in the direction of absorbing growing numbers of unskilled and semiskilled workers rather than administrative personnel. In fact, administrative employees diminished in number from 6,177 to 5,618 during 1977 and 1978; in other words a reduction of 8%.

There seems to be a clear trend towards the expansion of maquiladora production in Mexico. According to a survey carried out by the Banco de México in a sample of fifty-nine maquiladora firms, three firms employing 902 workers indicated that production volumes would not be increased given technological and market constraints. But twenty-nine firms with 20,695 workers noted that despite a weakening of external demand, they were at that time implementing new lines of production. Finally thirty-two firms with 12,781 workers expected an increase in production of 40% (*Revista Económica* 1978).

On the other hand, in accordance with the firms' perspectives, growth corresponding to the first semester of 1978 was similar to that achieved during the period included between 1971 and 1974, that is of a 45.0% annual rate. In sum, according to this survey the flow of revenue benefitting Mexico through maquiladora operations has steadily increased and will continue to increase over the years. During 1978, approximately $690 million entered Mexico through this sector, that is, $187 million (37.3%) more than the equivalent figure recorded for 1977 (García Moreno 1979, p. 22).

In sum, the impact of the Maquiladora Program in Mexico has been considerable. Goods produced during 1979 represented 24% of Mexico's total manufactured exports and 10.5% of total exports. At present it is the fastest-growing economic sector (including petroleum-related activities). Therefore, it comes as no surprise to learn that Mexican government officials see the Maquiladora Program as an integral part of Mexico's strategy for development.

Some Critical Issues

But despite its impressive expansion, the BIP (and offshore manufacturing in general) has confronted increasing criticism. In the United States the most outspoken critics have been representatives of organized labor, who see offshore production plants (runaway plants) as symptoms of a devious strategy to deflate the efforts of United States workers to obtain wage increases and better working conditions (Fernández 1977, p. 62). A source of grave preoccupation for these groups is the extent to which unemployment is accentuated in the United States as a result of the transfer of operations abroad. The line of action followed by labor leaders and representatives in the United States has been to lobby for the repeal of the two provisions in the U.S. tariff legislation (items 806.30 and 807.00) that enable the very existence and expansion of projects such as the in-bond plant program in Mexico (U.S. Congress, Committee on Ways and Means). The attacks directed against item 807.00 have been particularly virulent, constantly reminding promoters and investors of in-bond plants in Mexico of the relatively shallow ground upon which prosperity rests. However, until now such repeal efforts have not been successful.

Across the border, the Mexican government has experienced criticism from intellectuals, radical militants and labor organizers who see the maquiladora program as the most overt form of national economic servitude yet accepted by Mexico. Such critics claim that incentives granted multinational corporations undermine basic concepts of autonomy and national sovereignty. Some of these (for example, the possibility of 100% foreign control over industry, purchase of Mexican land by foreigners and the de facto transformation of the country into an export processing zone) are seen as clear violations of Mexican law or of traditional policies directed towards the Mexicanization of production. This point of view sees maquiladoras as entities which enjoy a privileged and exceptional position of dubious benefits for the country (Fernández 1977).

One of the most articulate evaluations of the Mexican Border Industrialization Program has been offered by Jorge Bustamante (1976a) in a pioneer essay on the subject. By comparing the guidelines prepared by the Secretaría de Industria y Comercio with empirical information collected after ten years of offshore production in Mexico, Bustamante reaches disturbing conclusions. Alluding, for example, to the relationship between maquiladora industrialization, rises in unemployment rates and the expansion of the services sector along the border, Bustamante points out that

> when we ask ourselves what has been the effect of the maquiladoras on the dynamics of the service sector, we have to consider the relation between the increase of migration to the Mexican

border and the changes in the occupational structure affecting the Economically Active Population (EAP). We know through data from the Department of Industry and Commerce (Secretaría de Industria y Comercio) that the proportion of the increase of the work force that finds employment in the border cities has diminished in the goods production sector, while it has increased in those sectors that generate services.

The same source makes it clear that maquiladoras have only employed 2.4 percent of the recent arrivals to the border cities. ... (It is possible) that maquiladoras operate as a magnet in the migration to border cities, but that the population attracted to the border is not absorbed by maquiladoras; it is instead employed by the services sector or not employed at all. ... In any case the important question here is whether the increase in the absorption of workers by the services sector, in the context of the border economies of Mexico and the United States, is an indication of Mexican economic development or an indication of dependency. [pp. 24, 25].

According to the explicit purposes of the government when implementing the BIP, foreign investment in the export manufacturing sector would benefit Mexico by providing and expanding employment opportunities. It would also contribute to upgrading the skills of workers, instilling in them industrial discipline while affording channels for upward socioeconomic mobility. From the point of view of production itself, the program would open ways for the transfer of expertise and technology of potential interest for Mexican industry and stimulate the elaboration of raw materials and components to be sold to in-bond plants. Moreover, in the short and long runs, in-bond plants would also help reestablish terms of trade and foster equilibrium in the balance of payments through the extraction of taxes and other similar revenues and through the sale of Mexican services (Secretaría de Industria y Comercio 1974).

However, as Bustamante suggests, none of these objectives has been achieved. The consumption of Mexican parts by in-bond plants has been negligible. In 1976 it amounted to a modest 3% of all inputs used by maquiladoras. By 1977 the same figure had decreased to 1.6% and in 1979 it was 1.5% (Christopherson 1982). Even if industries capable of absorbing sophisticated technological expertise and processing existed in Mexico, in-bond plants base their production upon the use of intensive labor rather than the development of machinery and complex productive organization. After more than ten years of existence the maquiladora program has hardly contributed to improve the balance of payments.

Perhaps more significant than these limitations have been the questions raised by observers with respect to the employment-generating capacity of maquiladoras. Bustamante points out, for example, that unemployment increased along the border by 83% during the same period that the BIP had been in existence. While this increase is in part due to rising rates of internal migration, it is also probably related to the inability of maquiladoras to expand occupational opportunities for men and to maintain a long-standing labor force. The high rate of mortality of maquiladoras (many of which have closed operations after relatively short periods of time), their reluctance to provide jobs for larger numbers of men, and the tendency of some to discourage a long-standing work force have combined to cast a negative image of the program (Teutli Otero 1976; Fernández Kelly 1982).

Policy Guidelines

Mexican government officials have responded to some of these criticisms by outlining a policy aimed at resolving the most obvious limitations of the BIP. Some basic points guide this endeavor:

1. First, the Mexican government favors decentralization of the maquiladora industry. Until now 90% of offshore production in Mexico has been concentrated in the border (especially in three cities: Tijuana, Mexicali and Ciudad Juárez) where it employs 10% of the work force in that area. During 1977 the ratio between the border and the interior of Mexico with respect to the total number of plants was 8:1. However, the same ratio with respect to the seventy-four new industries (and enlargements of existing ones) generated between January and April of 1978 was 4:1. This represents 11% of the total number of plants in 1978 as compared to 6% in 1973 and zero in 1966.

Thus, government representatives have expressed confidence that the current tendency of maquiladora production is towards the interior of Mexico and towards a more balanced integration with the Mexican economy. Statements made by directives of the Mexican Bankers' Association expressing the interest of Mexican financial institutions to sponsor maquiladora investments in various Mexican areas is another indication of this trend.

However, extensive interviews with in-bond plant managers and promoters suggest a measure of unwillingness on their part to consider operations in the interior. Costs of transportation, the scarcity of necessary services and especially the envisioned difficulties in dealing with a less tractable or trainable work force militate against the expansion of the maquiladora industry in central and southern Mexico, in spite of the fact that lower wages can be paid in those areas. When seen in counterpoint with advantages of the border listed earlier (in particular those which result from the proximity to the United States) it seems clear that the number of plants will continue to grow more rapidly in that area than in the rest of the country. The differences in opinion between maquiladora and government representatives with respect to the issue of decentralization suggest areas of potential conflict. At the same time, the excessive concentration of plants in certain points of the border may, in time, exacerbate urban problems of housing, transportation and other services.

2. It is also the intent of the Mexican government to encourage the diversification of production in offshore manufacturing and to stimulate investments in the area of capital goods. As noted earlier two manufacturing activities dominate offshore production in Mexico: electric/electronics and apparel. Thirty-two percent of the 540 firms approved in 1978 as maquiladoras and 50% of the total added value generated by them were related to electric/electronics production. Following in order of numerical importance (i.e., number of plants) were clothing and textiles (26%), nonelectrical manufacturing (21%) and transportation (3%) (Newton and Balli 1979).

While there are differences in the level of capital investment and stability between the two predominant kinds of maquiladoras, their general lightness and high vulnerability to fluctuations in the international market, rapid changes in design and technology and (in the case of apparel) seasonality, make them a feeble channel to achieve solid long-term industrialization. Furthermore, short-term contingencies throw these industries out of balance often forcing their disappearance, the dismissal of large numbers of workers and the ensuing disruption of the economy.

This was made painfully clear during the 1974–1975 recession which took over the United States with no little consequence for the Mexican-American border. In Ciudad Juárez alone, more than half of existing maquiladoras either experienced shutdowns or closed operations during that time. The majority of the plants that closed never reinitiated activities and thousands of workers lost their jobs. As one personnel director employed at an electric maquiladora put it to this author:

> I was personally responsible for the dismissal of over a hundred workers. There was no choice. As each one received, teary-eyed, her final weekly payment she had to return her uniform bearing the firm's emblem. By the end of the day I was surrounded by mountains of smocks, a sad reflection of the crisis we were undergoing. [Fernández 1978]

Although the maquiladoras recuperated and gained strength after 1975, the effects of the recession are a sharp reminder of the high degree of dependency that ties them to the U.S. economy. When asked how long maquiladoras will continue activities in Mexico, the almost unanimous response of managers is "as long as the United States market holds up." This gives credence to the belief that rather than tending to integrate with Mexican economic needs, maquiladoras observe a great degree of integration with the U.S. economy.

Thus, the interest of the Mexican government to stimulate investments in capital goods appears as a sound and necessary demand. For this, some recent, if minor, investments in heavy industry, particularly in the assembly of automotive components, have been received with optimism. However, this is far from signaling a trend. On the one hand, the response of organized labor in the United States would be disfavorable, especially in view of the fact that maquiladoras would then be competing directly against long-established industries in that country. On the other hand, investments in capital goods seem contradictory to the motivations that originally brought about the expansion of offshore production in Mexico, that is *the maximimzation of productivity and profits through the intensive use of cheap unskilled and semiskilled labor.* Because of this it is not surprising that the proportion of textile assembly plants among maquiladoras rose from 19 to 26% between 1973 and 1978, while the share of electronics assembly in value added increased from 36 to 50% during the one year between December 1977 and December 1978 (König 1979; Newton and Balli 1979). Companies involved in the production of capital goods were conspicuously absent from the Maquiladora Program.

3. It is also the intent of the Mexican government to provide mechanisms for the added consumption of Mexican components and raw materials. As stated earlier, such a consumption has been

extremely modest up to the present. However, the ratio of value added to the value of imported materials has increased from 58:1 in 1970 to 85:1 in 1978 (Flamm and Grunwald 1979). This may indicate the growing competitiveness of Mexican inputs, but the slightness of the increase also augurs only minor advances in this area.

Linked with added consumption of Mexican raw materials and components has been government's intent to provide formal mechanisms to enable maquiladoras to trade among themselves. This would prevent the now existing "triangulation," that is, maquiladora sales of semifinished products to parent firms in the United States and their subsequent sale to other maquiladoras in Mexico. This has increased operation costs from the point of view of the plants themselves and caused losses for potential producers in Mexico.

While both the additional consumption of raw materials and components and the possibility of more viable internal-trade mechanisms are worthwhile pursuits, they seem to be opposed to the original motivations of offshore production. Low quality, reduced stocks, extreme delays, comparatively high prices and general unreliability are some of the reasons given by plant managers for the tepid (at best) response to the incorporation of Mexican parts into their manufacturing processes.

It is difficult not to agree that these are important deterrents in the course of daily business activities. Nevertheless, more significant than these may be the structural foundations upon which the maquiladora program is based. In part its success as an economic strategy flows from its nature as an enclave which benefits from privileges obtained on both sides of the border. The flexibility of maquiladoras, their ability to move to distant points of the globe and their capacity to adjust to fluctuations in supply and demand are derived from their privileged position in host countries. The original incentives granted by the Mexican government and its compliance to the demands of multinational corporations have created a convenient boundary which is continuously used by maquiladoras to enhance their bargaining power vis-à-vis labor and bureaucratic requirements.

From this point of view the items of policy outlined above entail the possibility of undermining the boundaries within which maquiladoras now operate by transforming them into real instruments for national development. While in theory this is a noble objective, in practice, it is an unlikely possibility, especially given the government's commitment to allow as much freedom as possible to maquiladora production.

4. Finally, although the Mexican government has been more interested in the number of jobs than in the gender of those employed by maquiladoras, it has recently articulated a recommendation that more men be employed in offshore production plants. From this follows an interest in capital goods investment. Unfortunately, this seems an unlikely possibility in view of the political and ideological foundations which underlie the employment of women in assembly operations.

Plant managers base their preference of women (particularly young women) over men for this kind of work upon presumed anatomical and animical features that distinguish both sexes. It is consistently stated that women are more dexterous, patient and reliable than men. Their fine muscles, acute eyesight and nimble fingers make them particularly suitable for repetitive assembly work. It is also the consensus that women are more tractable in general than men. The latter are often reluctant to accept rigid work patterns, and they tend to be prompt in their exigencies and in their willingness to organize.

Because maquiladoras must rely upon the use of cheap unskilled and semiskilled labor to maximize productivity and profits, they are led to employ the most vulnerable sectors of the working class. These sectors are increasingly being formed by women. In other words, given the constraints that guide offshire production, women constitute a close to ideal working contingent. In this light, the incorporation of larger numbers of men into maquiladora production is unlikely.

Maquiladoras, Unemployment and the Mexican State

At this point a question must be asked: If the empirical evidence accumulated during more than ten years of maquiladora industrialization suggests its limitations as a viable means to achieve development, why does the Mexican government continue to encourage its expansion?

Aside for the significant structural determinants operating at a world scale which have made programs such as the BIP feasible, two other interrelated factors ought to be considered. These are, first, the role of maquiladoras vis-à-vis unemployment variously defined, and second, the part played by relatively independent state interests in promoting border industrialization. The analysis of both issues shows the limitations of rhetoric.

There is disonance between the explicit criteria that ostensibly led the state to sponsor social developmental projects and the political and economic constraints that may better explain their existence. It was said earlier that when stated in absolute figures, the number of jobs offered by in-bond plants in the last ten years is impressive. In Ciudad Juárez alone they have increased from barely 2,000 in 1969 to over 40,000 by the middle of 1982. Moreover, business representatives underscore the "multiplier" effects of ma-quiladora employment. Some promoters of the industry go so far as to suggest that ten jobs in various sectors of economic activity are generated for every job opened by a maquiladora (Mitchell n.d.).

Two factors must be considered to place these affirmations in proper perspective. One is the incontestable fact of the growth of unemployment along the border during the same period that the maquiladora program has been in existence. Another one is the meaning of predominantly female employment in offshore production.

There are no precise unemployment and underemployment statistics available in Mexico. Population censuses do not permit accurate quantification of open unemployment, and other similarly obtained surveys generally tend to underestimate unemployment figures. However, it may be noted that the 1970 census records show 28,600 unemployed workers in border municipalities. This represents an increase from 2.4% in 1960 to 4.1% in 1970. The higher proportion of unemployment along the border is found in the larger municipalities such as Juárez, Mexicali and Tijuana. These account for 53.6% of the unemployed. According to Urquidi and Méndez Villarreal (1978), these estimates are optimistic since to them should be added the number of those seeking work for the first time. Thus, unemployment in the border municipalities in 1970 was probably no less than 7% of the economically active population.

More important than unemployment is underemployment. This entails lack of work continuity throughout the year and extremely low levels of compensation given to workers. According to the most reliable information on this subject, 16.1% of the economically active population is underemployed (ibid.). Additional data provided by the Secretaría de Industria y Comercio indicate that if all workers receiving wages lower than the legal minimum are considered underemployed, then underemployment in the border region in 1970 amounted to 34.3% of the regional industrial economically active population, while construction underemployment reached 38.5% (ibid.).

The situation described by Urquidi and Méndez Villarreal has not improved after 1970 despite claims to the contrary. For example, a report prepared in 1978 by the Regional Commission on Minimum Wages for Zone no. 09, to which Ciudad Juárez belongs, indicates that of the total 194,136 economically active individuals in that area, 24,268 were unemployed. That figure is equivalent to 12.5% of the economically active population (Regional Commission for Minimum Wages 1978).

The same report notes that according to the 1970 census, 6,395 persons, that is, 5.7% of the economically active population for that year, were unemployed. Thus, unemployment rates have more than doubled during the same decade that the maquiladora program has been in existence. These figures are especially revealing when considering that the report in question was prepared by the employing sector in Ciudad Juárez. Therefore, there is little substance in the statement that in-bond plants effectively resolve occupational problems for the majority of working-class people.

However, as noted earlier, rises in unemployment and underemployment along the border are in part attributable to the increase of migration. For instance, census data covering the period from 1930 to 1970 show an exorbitant population growth in Ciudad Juárez. Current population for that city is estimated to be about 606,674 inhabitants (Regional Commission for Minimum Wages 1978) with an increased annual rate of 5.74% during the 1960–1970 decade. This growth appears to be the result of immigration and not natural demographic increases of the local population. A survey carried out in August 1977 in a casual sampling among 476 families in Ciudad Juárez showed that 1.7% of those families had been residing in Ciudad Juárez less than a year and that 11.1% had resided there for five years or less (ibid.).

While migration has undoubtedly contributed to exacerbate the problem of unemployment along the border, in-bond plants have not succeeded in meeting the challenge of an increased number of potential workers arriving in the border cities in search of jobs (only 8% of the maquiladora work force is formed by rural migrants). As noted in other sections of this work, many maquiladoras, especially those which are larger and more stable, prefer to employ local residents rather than recently arrived immigrants. The acute levels of unemployment that exist in cities like Ciudad Juárez would probably increase if maquiladoras ceased to exist.

Then again the question originally raised by Bustamante, of the extent to which industrialization along the border has precipitated increases in migration must be asked. That is, to what extent do individuals and families from the interior of Mexico move to the border contemplating the possibility of employment in the maquiladora sector?

While it seems clear that offshore production plants are short in their ability to effectively control unemployment, they do not immediately cause unemployment. Quite clearly, jobs have been generated and economic activity stimulated through border industrialization. Nevertheless, the character of employment in these plants must be assessed.

Maquiladoras have not reduced unemployment rates because they do not tend to employ the members of the traditional work force, that is, males of working age. Rather, they employ members of the so-called inactive population, that is, daughters and wives whose principal activities took place in the school or in the home prior to the existence of the in-bond plant program. In other words, these were the components of a formerly unemployable sector.

Maquiladoras have thus created a new working contingent, expanding, in fact, the size of the potential labor force while at the same time disfranchising from its rank and file the majority of male workers. The implications of this policy will be elaborated in other sections of this work. At this stage what is important to note is that given the situation outlined above, the interruption of maquiladora operations would undoubtedly *create* unemployment among the members of a recently formed working contingent. It seems evident, for these reasons, that in spite of the limitations of maquiladora industrialization, it is not feasible to arrest its growth (*Revista Económica* 1978). The program has acquired a life of its own and the political and economic perils which would follow its disruption would be considerable.

At the same time the relatively autonomous interests that the Mexican government has at stake in the continuation of the BIP should not be underestimated. The BIP has proven to be a steady source of revenues in the form of taxes and payments to municipal, state and federal authorities (Newton and Balli 1979).

The centralized nature of the political system in Mexico implies that policy-oriented decisions made in the capital for other regions are not always aimed at solving local or regional problems. Rather, in some instances, they tend to benefit Mexico City itself and particularly certain privileged groups with economic and political

45

power. Where border states are concerned and given the interests of the United States in that area and in Mexico in general, decisions made by the state are also motivated by international considerations (Barkin 1975).

Certain basic criteria have guided decision-making processes undertaken by the Mexican state in the last fifty years. One of the most important has been the maintenance of political stability. In exchange for stability certain concessions must systematically be granted the members of a growing bureaucracy. According to Ugalde (1978) the Mexican government has been inclined to take advantage of the proximity and wealth of the United States in order to solve part of its own national unemployment problem and, at the same time, find the income necessary to maintain political stability.

From this it follows that the privileges enjoyed by the border states have been granted not so much to promote development and help solve local problems but, rather, to fulfill the political and economic interests of the country's power structure, which centers in Mexico City. In light of this, whether maquiladoras are effective instruments to combat unemployment or not is a secondary consideration. What matters is that developmental efforts yield the necessary revenue to maintain an orderly social system. In this sense, the maquiladora program has undoubtedly been a success.

CHAPTER 3

The Maquila Women:
Characteristics of the Work Force
in Ciudad Juárez's Assembly Plants

If you walk along the streets of Colonia Zacatecas in Juárez, Mexico, you will see, without difficulty, the transparent image of downtown El Paso, Texas. Its modern buildings cut sharp against the background of the Franklin Mountains form a striking contrast with the drab surroundings in which thousands of Mexican workers live. Cities are the living expression of society's political and economic constitution. History shapes them and imprints in their countenance the legacy of secular inequalities. Barely separated by an international demarcation line, El Paso and Ciudad Juárez epitomize the aymmetrical relationship that has existed for more than one hundred years between the United States and Mexico.

For Mexicans trying to cross the border illegally, El Paso offers the promise of higher wages, improved occupational opportunities, and access to a myriad of symbols of prosperity: a consumer's dream of upward mobility. At all hours men and women sit along the edge of the narrow canal that divides the two cities; their bodies still suspended in Mexican territory, their feet already dangling in the United States. Calmly they challenge the omnipresent *migra** and wait their chance to pass unobserved. Many are detained and promptly deported. Many try again.

Reality is different for the U.S. executives who commute to Juárez from the plush suburban areas of El Paso. For them, the

---

*The term used in vernacular Spanish to denote the U.S. Immigration and Naturalization Service.

Mexican city is a growing industrial complex which embodies the "new international economy." A primary feature of this new order is the "alliance" of monopoly capital with labor found in underdeveloped countries. Many of these executives manage the more than one hundred maquiladoras which now exist in Ciudad Juárez. These are assembly plants which depend either as directly owned subsidiaries or subcontracted firms from U.S.-based multinational corporations. More than half (60%) of these plants manufacture electric and electronic products while approximately 30% assemble apparel. The rest are dedicated to miscellaneous activities, which include the sorting of coupons, the production of asbestos yarn and the assemblage of plastic sprays and ornamental products. The majority of those who work at these plants are Mexican women whose predominant ages fluctuate between 17 and 25 years. Eighteen-year-old Rosario Rivera is one of such women.

After she was deserted by her husband of only two years, Rosario went to live with her mother, Mariana, her young brother, Gerardo, and her two aunts, Kica and Julia, who also work as direct production workers at clothing maquiladoras. Kica and Julia work to support themselves and their two children. Rosario does so in the hope of moving to a better home and to afford her brother an education. She lives in a two-room adobe house with permanent leaks in Colonia Zacatecas. The monthly rent is almost sixty dollars. Despite her youth, Rosario must always consider her family's situation:

> When I see my mother and aunts laugh and chat, I wish we were always happy. But the truth is that we have many problems. My mother wants to move to a different *colonia* because the *barrio* is full of idle bums. They stand at the street corners smoking pot, drinking, playing, and occasionally harassing pedestrians. What a curse: It's because they have no jobs. There are a lot of unemployed men in this city.
>
> Mother does what she can to take care of the house and the children because neither Kica nor Julia can afford a place of their own. On the one hand I can understand them: Who would take care of their sons if they were living alone? On the other hand we have to contend with their demands. They feel that they have special rights because they contribute to the expenses of the household.
>
> Both Kica and Julia were living here when I ran away with Carlos. He was my last hope! I wanted to marry him because I

thought my situation could only improve. Carlos was a student of architecture then. The first time we went out he took me to Café d'Europa and ordered strawberries with cream. I had two servings, just like an elegant lady in a romantic novel. At sixteen I became pregnant and Carlos married me shortly afterwards. Then things changed. Even before the death of my baby, Carlos had started to drink. He dropped out of school and could not support me. When he finally left me there was nothing to do but to look for work at a plant. I was fortunate to land a job at RCA. They were expanding production and hiring people; all women.

Many could not get placed because they didn't have enough education. But I went to school for nine years and have some knowledge of typing and shorthand. For a time I thought management would find me a position as a receptionist or a secretary, but you need to speak English to even be considered for that, so I guess I'll just have to keep on doing assembly work.

My shift runs from 6:30 in the morning to 3:30 in the afternoon from Monday to Friday. On Saturdays I work from 6:30 to 11:30 A.M.—forty-eight hours in total every week. On Fridays I get paid 1,001 pesos (slightly less than 43 dollars). I give mother half of my weekly wage. *Ruteras* [small vans], meals at the factory and personal expenses take care of the rest. I am buying a stereo system. At least I can purchase that for myself. As long as I can work, I don't think I will get married again.

Personal experience shows infinite variation. Paradoxically, however, Rosario's story does not differ significantly from that of thousands of Mexican women employed by maquiladoras. As many others Rosario is young, single and childless. She lacks support from either father or spouse and she has considerable economic need. Not unlike many other women doing assembly work in Ciudad Juárez—especially those in the apparel manufacturing sector—Rosario belongs to a female-headed household with children. More frequent, however, is the case of the young daughter who contributes to the support of both parents and siblings. Although fathers, husbands, brothers and other male relatives may live under the same roof with these young women, evidence indicates that the majority of the men are either unemployed or underemployed.

What leads women like Rosario to seek employment in the Ciudad Juárez maquiladora industry? An outline of personal and household characteristics in this context may contribute to answer this question.

Age

The predominant ages of female maquiladora workers in Ciudad Juárez varies between 17 and 25. This confirms the findings of restricted studies done in the past (Garibay 1977; Murayama 1979). Therefore, this is a work force characterized not only by its gender specificity but also by its youth, especially when compared to workers in highly industrialized countries who perform similar kinds of jobs (see Safa 1978). At first this finding may not appear surprising considering that working peoples throughout the third world are characterized by their youth. As pointed out in chapter 2, almost half of the border population is 14 years or younger (Urquidi and Méndez Villarreal 1978). In Ciudad Juárez 49% of the people are in this age group. In part this indicates the existence of households with a relatively high number of dependent youngsters. On the other hand, because the legal working age in Mexico is 16 years, many persons of both sexes seek employment in early adolescence. Fully 21% of the female workers in Ciudad Juárez's maquiladoras are between the ages of 16 and 18 (see table 1).

TABLE 1

Age Distribution of Maquiladora Workers in Ciudad Juárez by Manufacturing Branch

Ages	All Industries (%)	Electronics (%)	Apparel (%)
16–18	21	32	4
19–21	25	38	14
22–24	18	15	18
25–27	20	12	27
28–30	7	3	14
over 31	9	—	23
	100	100	100

However, it is also true that there are significant differences in age when comparing workers by manufacturing branch. The median age of laborers in the electric/electronics industry is 20 years, while that of workers in the apparel manufacturing sector is 26.

Managers explain this difference in age by reference to the varying skill requirements of both industries. Thus, it is often assumed that workers in the apparel manufacturing industry must possess a higher level of skill than most of those employed in the electronics industry. Higher levels of skill, in turn, are predicated on years of experience as seamstresses; a reason which by itself presumably explains the older average age of workers in the clothing industry.

While there may be an element of truth in this explanation, it may also be argued that there are other equally, if not more, important reasons for the age differentials of workers in both industries. "Older" women are at a disadvantage when competing for jobs against younger women, who are generally preferred for assembly work in the electronics industry.

From the point of view of workers, employment in electronics manufacturing offers advantages which do not exist in the apparel industry. Due to the higher instability and temporality of employment, as well as the extremely inadequate working conditions that prevail in the latter'sector, it cannot attract workers who are seen as ideal (i.e., young, single, childless women). The enfeebled position of "older" women in the labor market combines with the structural limitations of the industry to bring them together. "Older" women whose entrance into more desirable employment slots is barred by their age, marital status and number of children have few job alternatives. Sewing in factories is for them the most viable.

Younger women who fall short of the stringent demands imposed by the larger and more stable maquiladoras (particularly with respect to schooling levels) and whose economic needs are acute are also found among the workers of the apparel manufacturing industry. Thus, 18% of the labor force in this sector is formed by women who are between the ages of 16 and 21. Among these, the average length of schooling is of 6 years as compared to 8 for workers in the same age group in the electronics industry.

In sum, age is an important variable when considering the employment alternatives of women seeking jobs in the Ciudad Juárez industrial sector. However, age cannot be considered in isolation from factors such as marital status, number of children, years of schooling and family composition.

Marital Status

Fifty-seven percent of the sample interviewed for this study was formed by single women. Of these the majority (69%) were daughters living with parents and siblings. The rest were divorced, separated or widowed women. When taking into consideration a comparison by type of industry, some differences were observed. Sixty-one percent of those employed in electronics were single while the equivalent figure for those in apparel manufacturing was 54%. Thus, there is a comparatively large number of married women working in apparel manufacturing (see table 2).

TABLE 2

MARITAL STATUS OF MAQUILADORA WORKERS IN CIUDAD JUÁREZ BY
MANUFACTURING BRANCH

Marital Status	All Workers (%)	Electronics (%)	Apparel (%)
Single	57	61	54
Married	43	39	46
	100	100	100

Schooling Levels

The vast majority of maquiladora workers (95%), both migrants and nonmigrants, have attended school in Ciudad Juárez. While the average education level for Mexican workers in general is 3.8 years (United Nations 1977), most maquiladora operators (55%) have completed at least 6 years of schooling. Many (20% of my sample) have taken courses in commercial academies where they have acquired typing and accounting skills seldom put to practice. Some (11%) have studied to become nurses, nurse's aides, secretaries, computer technicians, beauticians or seamstresses (see table 3).

Because of their comparatively high levels of formal education and familiarity with an urban environment, these workers can be trained easily and in short periods of time. According to managers, these are valuable traits, much different from those of rural migrants who tend to find it difficult to accept rigid work paces and inflexible production quotas.

TABLE 3

SCHOOLING LEVELS OF MAQUILADORA WORKERS IN CIUDAD JUÁREZ BY
MANUFACTURING BRANCH

Number of Years	All Industries (%)	Electronics (%)	Apparel (%)
Less than 6	5	3	8
6	55	38	59
7–11	40	59	33
	100	100	100

As noted earlier, there are also differences among workers in electronics and apparel manufacturing with respect to schooling level. In the first sector, the average level of schooling was 8 years, while in the clothing industry it was 6 years.

Labor History

In part because of their youth, most assembly operators have limited work experience prior to their employment in the maquiladora sector. Particularly in the electric/electronic branch, where the median age of workers is 20 years, the majority (60%) have not held jobs prior to the one they now have. By contrast, in the apparel manufacturing branch, where the median age of workers is 26 years, less than 30% of those interviewed by this author had not held other types of jobs.

In general, among those who had worked for a wage before their employment in maquiladoras, two distinct experiences were identified. The first group (36%) was formed by women who had worked in the services sector as clerks, cashiers, salespersons, beauticians, office auxiliaries or secretaries. The next was composed of those whose only prior experience was as maids either in Ciudad Juárez or in El Paso, Texas. Among the members of the second subgroup almost all had done so as illegal aliens. Because of familial needs many maquiladora workers have had to work in the informal economy since an early age. Fifty-six percent of those with a labor history started to work between the ages of 13 and 15 as maids.

The relationship between international undocumented migration and maquiladora employment will be explored later. At this point it will suffice to say that from the information now available, maquiladora work has become a much sought after alternative for women who have had working experience as illegal aliens across the border. Although this may result in a relative decrease of their net income when compared to earnings derived from domestic work in U.S. border towns, such a loss is counterbalanced by the access to medical care for themselves and their dependents in the clinics of the Instituto Mexicano del Seguro Social—one of the "fringe benefits" of employment in a maquiladora. For these women factory employment certainly represents an upward step in social mobility.

But for the women who were clerical workers before becoming maquila operators circumstances are dissimilar. Seen from a broad perspective, their experience represents a curious transfer of labor from the so-called white collar sector to blue collar employment. This contradicts what has been regarded as the "normal" trend in occupational mobility according to modernization perspectives.

Again, the explanation to this phenomenon may be found in the particular structure of the Ciudad Juárez labor market. Although the services sector predominates along the Mexican border, the majority of jobs found in it are lacking in stability, adequate earnings and benefits, even in those echelons endowed with more prestige than factory work. Most receptionists, salespersons and secretaries in Ciudad Juárez earn less than maquila workers.

It is also true (as the description rendered by Rosario at the beginning of this chapter shows) that the more prestigious and better-paid occupations are only accessible to those who are highly trained and/or speak English. Thus, to a certain extent, services and clerical jobs available to most women are interchangeable with wage domestic work. At the local level, the consensus is that maquiladora work offers the best employment alternative in Ciudad Juárez. This is an alarming revelation when observing that assembly operators earn an hourly wage of less than $1.00 and work 48 hours a week.

There is an important corollary of the information presented above. If the majority of the women who work at Ciudad Juárez's maquiladoras were doing so primarily as "individuals," that is, to fulfill personal needs or to supplement family income, it is probable that they would not opt for proletarian employment. Although less remunerative, there are jobs of a higher status in Ciudad Juárez which do not entail the rigorous work paces and schedules of maquiladoras. The reality, however, is that these women have joined the work force as members of households for whose subsistence their wages are vital.

Household Composition and Income Distribution

Although several forms of household organization exist among maquiladora workers, one was found to be dominant; that is, the one formed by single daughters living with their parents and siblings. Seventy-nine percent of all single women interviewed lived in households with these characteristics; 3% shared living arrangements with peers, friends or acquaintances; the rest were heads of households living with their own children (see table 4). With very few exceptions all married women live in independent households

TABLE 4

HOUSEHOLD COMPOSITION OF MAQUILADORA WORKERS IN CIUDAD JUÁREZ

Type of Household	All Industries (%)	Electronics (%)	Apparel (%)
Nuclear household (both parents present)	71	76	59
Nuclear household (one parent present)	8	15	9
Female-headed households	18	6	31
Other	3	3	1
	100	100	100

with their husbands and offspring although very often they reside in neighborhoods where other close relatives also live.

In agreement with other data mentioned earlier, daughters living with their families of orientation are particularly prevalent among workers in the electric/electronics industry (76% of all single women working in that sector). However, in the apparel manufacturing industry almost one out of every three women is a head of household. Employment in the mquiladora industry seems to be related to the proliferation of female-headed households in Ciudad Juárez; however, the specific relationship existing between the two phenomena is far from clear at this point. Some see factory work as the cause for the rise in the number of female-headed households. They believe that when women work outside the home, tensions having to do with the distribution of power and resource allocation result between men and women living together.

Women, having greater access to resources on account of their newly acquired wage-earning capacity, press to obtain greater participation in familial matters, thereby threatening the authority of fathers and husbands. At the same time, they may be accused of neglecting their proper role. Presumably both factors may cause the fragmentation of "intact" families and the formation of households headed by working women.

However, it must be noted that most of the female-headed households in this study (90% of the total number) were in existence before women began to work in the maquiladora industry. In fact, according to the unanimous report of those interviewed, it was precisely the unexpected absence of male support in their families either through death or desertion that prompted women to look for jobs.

It was found that while the average number of members per household for Ciudad Juárez in general is 5.3, the equivalent figure for maquiladora workers in general is 7. Thus, workers' households are large even by the standards of a city where sizable families are the norm.

In the first instance, it may be suggested that the size of households alone is an important variable precipitating the entrance of women into the labor force. However, this tentative proposition must be qualified. The age composition of the family unit has to be considered. Fifty-three percent of the workers interviewed reported living in houses with one to three children 14 years old or younger. Twenty percent shared households with four to seven youngsters in the same age group (see table 5).

TABLE 5

Number of Children Per Household by Age

With Children 14 Years or Younger	All Households (%)	Electronics (%)	Apparel (%)
1–3	53	59	50
4–7	20	15	23
8 or more	2	—	4
None	25	26	23
	100	100	100

To the relatively high number of children who live in maquiladora workers' households must be added the employment status of their adult members. In this respect the situation of men is particularly relevant. High levels of male unemployment and underemployment were detected in Ciudad Juárez. Eleven percent of all males in working ages coresiding with maquiladora workers were without employment at the time when the latter were interviewed. Among those who were employed, certain occupations were found to be prevalent. In order of importance these were unskilled construction worker (30%), petty clerk (27%), general unskilled worker (15%) and street vendor (7%).

The typical household to which a maquiladora worker belongs is formed by her parents (whose age fluctuate between 45 and 65 years of age) and siblings. In the vast majority of cases, mothers are fully dedicated to household chores and child care. They administer family income and are, thus, the receivers of their working daughters' contributions. Fathers are often irregularly employed or employed in low-paying occupations. In 20% of these households one single working daughter acted as a primary provider.

56

However, in most cases, young women combine their income with that earned by other members of the household. Generally (68% of the sample) these households have two or more members whose income is pooled to cover family expenses. In 12% of the cases two to three maquiladora workers support their households (see table 6).

TABLE 6

MAQUILADORA WORKERS' PARTICIPATION IN HOUSEHOLD SUPPORT

Number of Providers	All Households (%)	Electronics (%)	Apparel (%)
Interviewee only provider	20	15	27
2–3 Maquiladora workers as only providers	12	15	9
2 or more providers (maquiladora workers and others)	68	70	64
	100	100	100

The case of married women differs to some extent. The majority of these live in independent households and have an average of two children living with them. However, the number of children naturally varies with the age of the woman. It was found that 4% of all married women living regularly with their husbands are the sole supporters of their household, while only 1% reported using her income exclusively for personal expenses.

In general, workers reported using 55% of their weekly wage to cover household needs. An average of 14% was used up by transportation and meal expenses during working hours. However, the allocation of income varies significantly depending on family needs. Twenty percent of all daughters interviewed reported giving all of their weekly wages to their mothers, while 73% of all married women used all of their income for family and work-related expenses.

In sum, most maquiladora workers can hardly be considered as supplementary wage earners. The size and age distribution of their households, as well as the weak employment status of the men in their families, are precipitant factors which explain the entrance of women into the industrial labor force.

There is, therefore, a convergence between labor market conditions and familial needs which facilitates the flow of women as suppliers of labor for maquiladoras. The result of this has been the swift transformation of women into the main providers of stable and regular income (however small this may be) for their families. Benefits derived from this strategy are increased when several women in the same household are able to get jobs in maquiladoras.

The abundance of women in search of jobs thereby presupposes, and is made possible in part by men's inability to gain access to gainful employment. Thus, in a country where, for better or for worse, women aspire and are encouraged to become mothers and/or housewives, female factory work does not necessarily indicate an expansion of alternatives for women or their families.

Migratory Background

It is commonly assumed in Ciudad Juárez that maquiladoras employ mostly migrants. In partial accordance with this general impression, 64% of women engaged in assembly work in that city were born outside of Ciudad Juárez. Three northern states are the main sources of out-migration for this group: the interior of Chihuahua (the state in which Ciudad Juárez is located) accounted for 44% of the total migrating group; Durango for 28%, Coahuila for 14%, with only a small number of workers having been born in a state farther to the south (see tables 7 and 8).

As may be seen this is a case of highly focalized outward migration. From the total number of factory workers who came from the

TABLE 7

MAQUILADORA WORKERS: MIGRATORY BACKGROUND

Place of Birth	All Workers (%)	Electronics (%)	Apparel (%)
Ciudad Juárez	36	41	27
Other	64	59	73
	100	100	100

TABLE 8

MIGRATORY STATUS BY STATE OF BIRTH

State	All Industries (%)	Electronics (%)	Apparel (%)
Chihuahua (except Ciudad Juárez)	44	50	38
Durango	28	25	31
Coahuila	14	15	12
Other	14	10	19
	100	100	100

interior of the state of Chihuahua, fully 42% were born in the circumvicinity of Hidalgo del Parral, including the cities of Santa Barbara and San Francisco del Oro.

However, although the majority of workers employed in the maquiladora industry are migrants, it was also found that they have lived in Ciudad Juárez for an extended period of time. Migrant factory workers have lived in the city an average of 14 years. Both by place of birth and by length of residence, this work force is urban in nature. In addition, differences with respect to migratory background and length of residence in Ciudad Juárez were found when comparing the electronics and apparel manufacturing sectors. Thus, in the clothing industry, the average length of residence is 11 years, while workers in the electronics industry have lived in Ciudad Juárez for an average length of 16 years. While 7% of all migrant workers in the first sector had arrived in the city within the last 5 years, only 2% of those in the second were in similar circumstances. Thus, larger numbers of relatively recent migrants are found working in the clothing industry.

The extended period of residence of migrating factory workers in Ciudad Juárez has special significance when considering their relative youth. This indicates that the majority arrived in Ciudad Juárez as children, in many cases long before the BIP was in effect. Therefore, at least for the sample interviewed in this study, it may not be said that maquiladoras acted as "pull factors" for migration.

It is also important to note that most of these migrants came to Ciudad Juárez accompanied by members of their families, generally parents and siblings. An average of five persons (mostly relatives) were with the migrant at the time of her arrival in the city. Seven percent had traveled with distant relatives of friends of their families and 3% had migrated alone, as young women in search of a job. But even among those who had migrated alone, all but a few had promptly reestablished coresidence with members of their families who had migrated previously. For women who migrated alone, some scattered evidence suggests that they were in unusual circumstances. For example, one young woman gave as a reason for migration, attempted rape by her father. Another one, an orphan since early childhood, had escaped from the institution where she had lived for eight years.

But while a large number of assembly workers are migrants, only 8% of them came from a rural environment. The rest were born in cities. This suggests the existence of an urban-urban (rather than rural-urban) migration where maquiladora workers are concerned.

This observation is interesting because it contradicts to some extent the statements made by local and federal public officials that maquiladoras have opened employment opportunities for migrants from the countryside. While maquiladoras may have acted as a factor of attraction for rural migrants, these have not been incorporated into the industrial labor force. The employment of a predominantly urban population is owed to the recruiting policies of plants themselves. Managers state that workers who have lived in the city for long periods of time tend to be more "stable," "disciplined" and "reliable" than rural workers.

On the other hand, the fact that the migration described above anteceded the implementation of maquiladora industrialization makes it difficult to establish a direct causal relationship between this program (as a factor of attraction) and the movement of workers now employed in industry and their families.

Other Migration-Related Issues

The present study is in agreement with critical sociological perspectives which see migration as a particular strategy for labor allocation rather than as a random occurrence due to individual choices and preferences (Castells 1975; Portes 1978; Sassen Koob 1982). The mode of insertion of migrants into labor markets is directly determined by the structural needs of capital movements in general and by the requirements of specific industries or economic activities. The findings listed above suggest that even when there is commonality of gender, migrants with different personal attributes and length of residence in the city enter the labor market in a distinct and nonfortuitous manner. Thus, there is a propensity on the part of the clothing industry to incorporate a larger number of "older" women and women recently arrived in the city.

In the same vein, other issues related to migration and the BIP deserve consideration in these pages. This is necessary for two reasons. First, there is a historical connection between the termination of the Mexican Labor (Bracero) Program and the emergence of maquiladoras. While the first enabled the transfer of Mexican agricultural workers, the majority of whom were male, into the United States, the latter have fostered the movement of productive industrial stages from the U.S. to the Mexican-American border.

Second, there has been considerable speculation about the way in which the BIP relates to both internal and international migration

(Bustamante 1976a). Some believe that by providing employment alternatives, maquiladoras reduce the need for illegal migration to the United States. Others argue that by attracting a larger number of internal migrants to border cities, and failing to employ most of them, maquiladoras exacerbate the conditions that lead workers to cross into the neighboring country illegally.

Therefore, two convergent although analytically distinct aspects of migration must be mentioned at this point: (1) migration from the interior of Mexico to the border area, and (2) migration from Mexico to the United States.

Until fairly recently, massive migration did not constitute a distinctive feature of the Mexican-American borderland. Only during the second decade of the twentieth century did migration, both legal and undocumented, become a quotidian aspect of Mexico-U.S. relations (Fernandez 1977). In the past, this phenomenon was attributed to the pernicious effects of the Mexican Revolution, which presumably led exiles to abandon the country and at the same time forced dispossessed peasants to search for occupational alternatives by crossing the border (Martínez 1978).

In more recent times, however, it has also been noted that the increase of Mexican migration to its northern neighbor coincided with the consolidation of the United States as an economic and political power on a world scale, and with a need—particularly in the Southwest—for cheap labor to be employed in booming agricultural activities. It may be said that there has existed complementarity between the failure of the Mexican state to implement viable agrarian reform (a failure which in turn has generated increasing numbers of displaced agricultural workers) and the need of U.S. capital for abundant supplies of unskilled labor (Bustamante 1975a).

Put in a somewhat different way: There is little doubt that Mexican migrants attempt to cross the border—either legally or illegally—responding to expectations, motives and calculations induced by personal experience and communications; but seen in an international context, their behavior can be said to be determined by the unequal relationship between Mexico and the United States.

During the last fifteen years, international (mostly undocumented) migration from Mexico to the United States has coexisted with booming industrialization along the border. However, the connections between these two facets of labor incorporation in the international context have not been systematically explored. While international migration continues to provide labor for certain sectors of economic activity in the United States (for example agriculture in the Southwest), other economic interests rely upon the possibility of transporting the centers of production themselves to locations where costs can be reduced, productivity can be enhanced and labor conflict can be brought to a minimum (as in the case of border maquiladoras). The most striking, although vastly neglected, feature of this development is its gender-specific nature. While the majority of undocumented aliens working the fields of the U.S. Southwest continue to be male, most of those working in the export manufacturing plants along the Mexican border are female.

Thus, the BIP has effected a transfer of capital from the United States to Mexico by sanctioning the operation of maquiladoras which function as subsidiaries of multinational corporations. In a complementary fashion, the same process has accelerated the transfer of labor from the interior of Mexico to its northern frontier (Barrera Bassols 1976).

As mentioned previously, Mexican border municipalities constitute the most rapidly growing region in the country after Mexico City (Bustamante 1976b; Urquidi and Méndez Villarreal 1978). Migration to the border zone is closely tied to the expansion of the services sector and to rising unemployment and marginality. At the same time, indications are that migration, population growth, unemployment and underemployment have intensified in these cities during the last decade, that is, during the same period that the maquiladora program has expanded (Bustamante 1976b).

What matters for the purposes of the present discussion is to underscore the special dimension that the maquiladora industry has added to the complex picture of migration from the interior of Mexico to its northern border. Contrary to their alleged intent, export-processing plants have failed to generate employment for those left idle by the termination of the Bracero Program, that is, male agricultural workers. Nor have they provided opportunities for rural women.

What is, then, the specific relationship between the industrialization of the Mexican-American border and migratory patterns both within Mexico and from Mexico to the United States? Three interrelated but different cases must be distinguished in this respect. First, there is the case of Mexicans who migrate to the border with the expectation (realistic or not) of, once there, being able to cross into the U.S. The second is the case of those who migrate to seek border jobs and/or follow relatives and/or spouses. Finally, there is the case of those who migrate to the border to acquire skills that may later enable them to migrate to the United States. Studies to clarify these phenomena are, unfortunately, still few and tentative. However, on the basis of information collected in Ciudad Juárez, Chihuahua, it is possible to identify some general trends.

For instance, the migration of young unaccompanied males (and that of males who may later on be joined by their families) may be partly explained by the expectation (linked to objective socio-economic conditions) that the border region might provide access into the U.S. It has now been established that, contrary to previously held interpretations, people frequently do not migrate believing that cities will provide them with a chance to progress and move up in the social ladder, but simply because survival in their hometowns has been severely impaired (Cornelius 1979).

There may also be attractive features in the areas where migrants choose to live. For example, Mexican border municipalities offer the highest minimum wages earned in the country. While this could be considered a powerful incentive for migrants, it should be remembered that the cost of living is also high in the borderland. Moreover, higher minimum wages may be earned in the United States. Although the relative appeal of minimum wages cannot be denied, the labor requirements of U.S. agribusiness and the overall lack of employment alternatives for young productive Mexican males along the border predominate as causal agents in male migration.

Gender intervenes in this complex panorama by defining overlapping areas of movement accessible to either men or women. Because of their relative autonomy from the household and particularly from domestic and reproductive functions, it is less difficult for men to risk the hazards involved in becoming "undocumented" or "illegal" aliens.

As Cornelius (1979) has observed, male undocumented aliens very often migrate alone and tend to remain for extended periods of time in the U.S. (unless the Immigration and Naturalization Service [INS] prevents this). Female undocumened aliens, by contrast, cross the border daily in both directions more frequently. The majority of these women find employment as domestics in nearby U.S. border towns and return to Mexico every night or, at the most, every weekend in order to care for their children and visit with their families.

Extensive interviews with women and men formerly or presently engaged in undocumented migration suggest that the appeal of higher minimum wages in the United States is sharply attenuated by the anxiety produced by possible harassment or detainment by migra officials. As one women, now working at one of the local

63

maquiladoras in Ciudad Juárez, put it to me: "All I wanted was a job. But they made me feel like a criminal. Crossing the border was simply not worth the price; it is better to stay here and struggle."

Although the nervousness induced by INS policies is shared by both males and females, their experience with respect to migration is somewhat different. Men, socialized to act as providers, are expected to send money and/or presents to their families in Mexico and to visit occasionally. Women, on the other hand, are expected to take full responsibility for the daily care of their children and their homes. If they must migrate they must also return to the homestead more frequently. Thus, the widespread ideological notion that "man was made to work, and woman to care for the house" (el hombre para el trabajo y la mujer para la casa) impinges upon the likelihood of female movement. It also reflects and reinforces a reality in which crossing the border illegally is more feasible for men than for women. Such is the nature of precarious alternatives.

Therefore, it is not surprising that the majority of female undocumented aliens who migrate alone and stay for longer periods of time in the United States are single and have either one or no children. These women can travel to more distant regions searching for better jobs, and once in the United States they tend to live with relatives or friends. Their marital status and diminished responsibility with respect to offspring bring their experience and scope of alternatives closer to that of their male counterparts.

By contrast, the experience of those women with more than one child who migrate to the United States may be graphically illustrated by the story of Manuela. In late September 1978 Manuela was desperately trying to find a job as a production operator at the largest electronic maquiladora in Ciudad Juárez, RCA Componentes de Televisión. She was 24 years old, single, with six years of schooling and two children (ages 6 and 4) to support. A year before, when her common-law husand had deserted her, Manuela looked for a job in Juárez with little success. During most of the six months that preceded our encounter, she had been crossing the border every few weeks to work as a maid in El Paso, Texas.

Although many Mexicans cross the border without legal documents, Manuela had at that time an international crossing card which had been issued in her name by migration authorities. According to INS policy, such a card allows entry of Mexican citizens into the United States for a period of seventy-two hours in an area restricted to 12.5 miles. Holders of international crossing cards are explicitly forbidden from seeking or keeping jobs. The purpose of the cards is solely to stimulate tourism and purchases in U.S. border towns.

Nevertheless, thousands of Mexicans, especially women, use them to gain access into the secondary sector of the U.S. labor market. Although she was able to earn up to twenty dollars a day, Manuela's problems grew over time. Her mother, a widow of forty-four, also an undocumented maid, was not available to care for the children while Manuela was at work. This forced the latter's return to Juárez more frequently than safety advised. After a few months Manuela's illegal activities were reported to the INS by an anonymous caller. She was promptly sent back to Mexico and her international crossing card was confiscated.

In the weeks prior to our conversation, Manuela had been supporting herself and her children by taking in laundry, up to three dozen garments a day for less than three dollars. She was understandably eager to start work at an assembly plant. I asked what she would have to do in order to surmount the problem of day-care for her youngsters. Her answer was revealing. An unmarried cousin from her hometown had already agreed to come to live in Ciudad Juárez and help out with the children in exchange for a weekly allowance. But this arrangement depended upon the uncertain possibility of Manuela getting a job at a maquiladora.

As may be seen, there is an important relationship between women's decision to migrate and local job alternatives. A complementary connection exists for males sharing households with maquila workers. Assembly plants offer few options to those who cross the border illegally most frequently; that is, working Mexican men. Thus, it comes as no surprise to find that more than half of the women interviewed in my sample reported having one or more male illegal aliens among their immediate relatives, the majority of these brothers and fathers.

Among married women and former common-law wives there are many who have been deserted (either temporarily or permanently) by husbands eager to begin a new life in the United States. In Ciudad Juárez there is a widespread tendency to pass judgments on the irresponsible behavior of these men. Nevertheless, when the objective realities of their lives are taken into account, it becomes apparent that those who leave their families are often prompted by their failure to meet the economic demands of wife and children. Luisa's plight is a case in point.

65

Luisa married Martín when she was nineteen and he twenty-two. At that time Martín was working as a mechanic in a car repair workshop. By twenty-three Luisa was expecting her second child:

> Things went well for us at first, but then the workshop was shut down and Martín lost his job. He looked around for work but couldn't find anything. Then he started hanging out in bad company and drinking heavily. Finally he left us. He crossed the border as a wetback more than a year ago and we haven't heard from him since. I believe he is in California. Maybe he's married to another woman. Men can't be trusted; that's the reason I'm working at the maquiladora.

Luisa is now, at age twenty-four, working as an operator in an apparel plant and her chances to achieve a more prosperous future are slim.

As Luisa's case suggests, single women who support their children through maquila work do so either because their male companions are unable to meet the economic needs of the family or because they have been deserted. The absence of a male provider is a crucial factor that forces the entrance of women with children into the work force.

These statements are central for an understanding of the effects of the BIP upon the living and working conditions of workers. They clarify the relationship between women as a particular kind of labor reserve and the occupational opportunities available to males. According to maquiladora managers and promoters women are hired because of their putative higher levels of skill and performance, because of the quality of their hand work, because of their willingness to comply to monotonous, repetitive and highly exhausting assignments and because of their docility, which discourages organization efforts on the part of union leaders. Men, on the other hand, are invariably described as being more restless and rebellious than women, less patient, more willing to unionize and, perhaps most importantly, less resigned to tolerate rigorous work paces and inadequate working conditions for a low wage.

Rather than being the result of inherent feminine or msculine psychological and physical attributes these traits are explained by the economic and political position of men and women vis-à-vis international capitalism. The employment of women with acute economic needs by the maquiladora industry represents, in objective terms, the use of the most vulnerable sector of the population to achieve greater productivity and larger profits. The employment of men to perform similar operations would require higher wages, better working conditions and more flexible work schedules, all of which would increase labor costs and reduce capitalist gains. Furthermore, the use of female labor under the conditions described earlier diminishes the bargaining capacity of the working class as a whole. In the same vein, the employment of young women who were not part of the work force before the appearance of the BIP does not support the allegation that maquiladoras genuinely expand occupational alternatives along the Mexican border. It is in part because of this that unemployment rates continue to rise at the same time that the number of jobs opened by maquiladoras increases.

Another paradoxical feature of the maquiladora program should be mentioned. During the period that this type of industry has expanded, the age and composition of its work force has varied only slightly. This reflects the puzzling discovery that the majority of female workers tend to leave their jobs after a relatively short time. Permanence in a maquila job averages only three years (James and Evans 1974). There exists a tendency on the part of employers not to encourage the permanence of women in assembly operations over a long period of time. Women are often either laid off or persuaded to leave work voluntarily. In many cases, they are not hired permanently but on a temporary basis. At the outset, it may be said that a rotating labor force spares industry the need to comply with legal regulations emanating from Mexican labor law regarding seniority, indemnity and vacation periods. According to these regulations, employees laid off or released by a firm without special cause are entitled to three months wage indemnity plus twenty days of wage for every year spent under the firm's employment. Additional compensation is also allowed for vacation and yearly bonuses.

By contrast voluntary resignation is not accompanied by compensation payments other than a proportion of the vacation period calculated in relation to the days worked up to the moment of severance. When originally formulated, Mexican labor law intended to protect the interests of workers considered as the weakest part in a contractual agreement. In practice, nevertheless, it has resulted in policies that discourage permanent employment because of the potentially higher expenditures that it requires.

Moreover, from the point of view of industry there are other variables to be considered. Managers agree that the productivity of workers tends to decrease after the second year of work while absenteeism tends to increase. Discontent over low wages, the tediousness of assembly work and frequent complaints over eyesight deterioration, and nervous and respiratory ailments appear to coincide with this decline. Thus, it may be counterproductive to maintain, for extended periods of time, a less productive and potentially restless work force. On the other hand, it is pointed out by managers and researchers alike that workers tend to leave their jobs voluntarily. Why?

The nature of the work performed at the plants is a contributing factor for high turnover rates. Highly monotonous, repetitive operations, accelerated work rhythms, lack of promotions and inadequate working conditions combine to prevent long-term employment. It is not in the interest of the maquiladora industry to maintain a stable and permanently employed work force, especially in an environment where assembly operators may be easily replaced. A recent study (University of Texas, El Paso 1974) calculates that there are at least three women with similar needs and skills for every maquila operator in Ciudad Juáez.

Women interviewed by this author offer three motives for leaving their jobs. First, they tend to leave their jobs to get married or to provide better care of their homes and children. Second, they tend to leave jobs in order to "rest" after periods of monotonous work. In these cases they admittedly make plans to rejoin the labor force in a different capacity. However, every time they resign, they forfeit the cumulative benefits that continued work in the same firm potentially carries. Finally, workers leave work voluntarily for problems of health even in those instances when the ailments seem to be work-related. In cases of discontent or grievance women seem to prefer passive response (such as withdrawal) rather than direct confrontation with their employers. Also, women are likely to avoid arguments with their employers for fear that they will be blacklisted and unable to find a job later on.

Overriding these three motives are a generalized ignorance of workers' legal rights and women's tendency not to see themselves as permanent wage workers. These factors combine to make women a particularly cheap and manipulatable work force.

An important reason given by women themselves for deserting their jobs is marriage, coupled with the intention to have a child or the desire to give better attention to children and home. In both cases women, almost without exception, opt for this course of action responding to the pressures of their male counterparts who urge them to leave their jobs in order to give full time to their homes, that is, to fulfill what is considered their "normal" or "proper" role. Such women never stay on a job long enough to acquire seniority. It is in this sense that one of the functions of the domestic unit vis-à-vis industry may be better appreciated. At certain stages of its development, households tend to produce and put into circulation young factory workers (that is, daughters), who after a few years of work in one or several factories tend to be reabsorbed by newly formed homes as wives, while a new wave of younger women take their places along the assembly lines. But because of the inability of males to meet the economic needs of their households many of these women have to reenter the labor force after becoming mothers. Their age and offspring at this point in their lives are handicaps in a highly discriminating labor market in which single, childless women are preferred for maquiladora work. It is among these women who have previous factory work experience but who are unable to get new jobs in that sector that a large number of undocumented workers are found. Beatriz, a thirty-year-old single mother who has worked in the maquiladora industry for seven years told me: "If you are alone and have children to support there is no future for you in Ciudad Juárez. That is why I am trying to go to the United States. It is not me I am thinking of, it is my children's future that worries me."

To sum up, the impact of the maquiladora industry in deterring illegal migration to the United States is far from obvious. Because they do not provide jobs for the majority of males who need them, and because of their temporary nature, maquiladoras are probably insufficient as a tool for retaining laborers in Mexico.

It has been the objective of this chapter to describe the general characteristics of the maquiladora work force and the connections among gender, family structure and occupational alternatives for both men and women along the Mexican border in the context of its recent industrialization. Only by taking into account these issues does the study of migration acquire its full significance. Migration is not a random phenomenon. Rather, migratory flows are the consequence of specific structural, economic, political and ideological conditions which affect social actors in a differential manner.

CHAPTER 4

Maquiladoras and the International Division of Labor

Gender and Labor in a Historical Context

Seen in the context of Latin America, where one out of three women who work for a wage do so as domestics, maquiladora workers represent a relatively recent and unusual occurrence. Of the 19.4% women who are employed by industries in Mexico, only 0.7% do so as direct production operators (González Salazar 1976). By contrast, in Ciudad Juárez almost half of the work force is composed of women as a result of maquiladora operations. This development is not fortuitous. Rather, it is a symptom of current tendencies that appear at a world scale and which affect the international division of labor. Indeed, women working at maquiladoras are the bearers of labor sought for "alliance" by monopoly capital in a new international division of labor (Nash 1979).

To fully understand the implications of this phenomenon an investigation of the economic and political factors that have effected the massive employment of women in maquiladoras must be undertaken. As stated earlier, the immediate roots of this development are found in the implementation of the Border Industrialization Program since 1965. Offshore industrialization has made possible the collaboration of multinational firms, the Mexican state and private enterprise. Maquiladoras have enabled the penetration of international capital into local economies. This penetration has been motivated by the search for wide wage differentials, the availability of what appears to be an inexhaustible supply of unskilled and semiskilled labor, high levels of productivity and a tractable work force, a process which is consistent with capitalist business rationality (Sunkel 1973; Blanpáin 1977; Sciberas 1977).

Thus, the expansion of the BIP suggests the existence of profound structural determinants which operate independently from the policy guidelines advanced by the Mexican government. But there are also conjunctural factors to be considered. Historically the most important of these was the bracero program. The dramatic rises in unemployment that followed its termination made it convenient to contemplate efforts aimed at neutralizing the political risks posed by large contingents of idle agricultural workers (the majority of whom were male (Bustamante 1976a).

However, the unintended result of industrialization along the border was that far from providing occupational opportunities for those who had been most affected by the elimination of the bracero program—that is, male agricultural workers—it instead precipitated the entrance of formerly unemployable women (particularly young and single women) into the work force. In this manner a new contingent of industrial laborers emerged. Evidence of this is the fact that 85% of the maquiladora work force in Ciudad Juárez is female. The equivalent figure for similar plants in all of Mexico is 75% (Flamm and Grunwald 1979).

The rapid incorporation of women into direct industrial activities is a feature shared by the Mexican-American border and other geographical areas of the world—particularly the Orient—where a similar penetration of multinational investments into the export manufacturing sector has occurred (see Grossman 1978; Lim 1978; Barthomieu and Hanaut 1979). This is an important point for two reasons: on the one hand, it reveals the function that women fulfill in the industrial wage labor force at the present stage of capitalist development, and on the other hand, it enables the understanding of the particular impact of multinational investments upon local labor markets.

With respect to the employment of women in multinational assembly operations, the conventional wisdom among government officials and personnel managers is that because of their patience and high levels of manual dexterity, women are well fitted for minute, monotonous operations (Barraessen 1971). While it is true that women have historically been employed in poorly paid, repetitive, unskilled or semiskilled work, this argument is mostly ideological; it constitutes a superimposed definition—of what men and women are able or unable to do—upon given material realities.

When the productive system is examined as a whole, this definition reveals the importance of a gender-differentiated labor force whose members occupy different positions within the social division of labor. Women are hired to perform the tedious and unrewarding operations that accompany assembly work for reasons that are political and economic in nature (Madden 1973, pp. 45–50). Because of their behavior, expectations and attitudes (linked to gender-specific socialization processes), because of their relative youth and because of their subordinate position within their own households, these women constitute a highly vulnerable, docile and manipulatable work force. Their employment in low-paying, unskilled and semiskilled jobs offers distinct advantages from industry's point of view (Lloyd 1975).

In areas such as the Mexican-American border where racial, ethnic, national and religious differences are generally inexistent, gender takes their place. As with race, ethnicity, nationality and religious affiliation, gender differences are used to identify and preferentially hire a particular group of people to perform some of the worst-paid and least-rewarding jobs. This preference is, ironically, often based on stereotypes of, and prejudice directed against, the group in question. In this case perceptions of age and gender combine to form an image of women as supplementary income-earners and temporary workers, while patriarchal traditions sanction their submission on the job and in the household. Both features tend to prevent women from acquiring a legitimate status as income-earners and from retaining their jobs over extended periods of time (Safa 1976, 1980).

From the point of view of business these same factors may translate into the necessary flexibility that adaptation in a fiercely competitive international market demands (see O'Connor 1973, chap. 2). The possibility of maintaining an elastic labor force which can be expanded or reduced in response to rapid fluctuations of supply and demand is closely related to the striking concentration of women in certain branches of manufacturing activity, for example electronics and apparel (which predominate along the Mexican-American border). But, as has been pointed out, such a concentration cannot be explained by invoking tradition and the animical or anatomical pecularities of the sexes. Rather, we must observe the objective structural conditions that determine the predilection of one group of workers over another for certain jobs (Pearson and Elson 1981). How have such predilections developed historically? The purpose of the next section is to explore this topic.

72

Historical Antecedents

Multinational corporations operating under the Mexican Border Industrialization Program are but the last in a fluid sequence of events affecting working people in the last two hundred years. Rather than being the harbingers of "post-industrial" society, as some would claim, multinational corporations are a symptom of industrialization revisited under the conditions of late capitalism (Mandel 1975; Frobel, Heinrichs, and Kreye 1979).

In England, the period characterized by the onset of industrialization also coincided with the transformation of household organization. Households ceased to represent a unity between productive and reproductive labor in order to gradually become the arena where consumption and the regeneration of human energy took place (Rowbotham 1974; Tilly 1980). The enclosure system as well as increased taxation over the ownership of land and property induced a continuous flow of rural-urban migration with the accompanying immiseration of an uprooted peasant class.

Industrialization in general entailed the movement of labor and resources away from agriculture, fishing and forestry toward manufacturing, commercial and service activities. With the shift in the emphasis and scale of production the factory eventually replaced the household as the center of productive activity. The decline of family production also meant a decline in the number of propertied peasants and craftsmen and an increase in proletarians—propertyless people working for wages (Thorner, Kerblay, and Smith 1966; Bairock 1973).

These gradual changes prefigured the restructuring of the social organization of work and of the division of labor by gender. In particular the separation of place of work (the factory, commercial establishment, office) from home had a profound impact on the position of men and women in the structure of production (Rowbotham 1974).

The beginning of industrialization centered on the manufacture of cotton textiles, which in earlier times had been predominantly female occupations. Weaving and spinning had originally engaged the labor of household members, including children of a very young age. Capital investments during the late seventeenth and eighteenth centuries fostered the emergence of cottage industries, an immediate antecedent of the factory system (Pinchbeck 1969). From the point of view of women, cottage production afforded two advantages. First, it enabled them to maintain control over familial income. For example, Rowbotham (1974) points out that women were often the recipients of payments from investors and merchants and the administrators of family income. Second, it also allowed them to fulfill household chores and child-care responsibilities under the same roof where work for a wage was performed (Anderson 1972; Rowbotham 1976).

The rationalization of production which involved technological advances as well as the separation of home and factory placed women at a disadvantage with respect to men. Women retained the responsibility for household chores and child care, but in many instances they also had to find jobs outside of the home. The difficulties in coordinating time and energy to fulfill both roles in different physical localities generated a lasting conflict between women's activities as family members and as wage earners (Anderson 1972. p. 71).

When women have had to work for a wage they have often found themselves in a twofold bind. On the one hand, remunerated labor appears to be performed at the expense of the roles that women play in the home. On the other hand, because women have frequently had to work for wages while at the same time continuing their functions as pivots of regenerative labor, they have found themselves working a "double day" (Safa 1976).

The exclusion of women from certain sectors of manufacturing activity and their segregation into others has paralleled the development of ideas and assumptions about the "normal" function of women in society. For example, the notion that women are in general supplementary wage-earners whose income complements that of a male head of household has weighed heavily as a justification of women's employment in low -paid menial jobs (Sacks 1975; Hartmann 1976).

However, this represents only one facet of the total mosaic. Historical evidence confirms that more often than not women have had to coordinate labor within the home with wage labor (Charles-Roux et al. 1975). Therefore, a clear distinction must be made between ideological definitions of what women's place should be and the realities that women as well as men have had to confront in the course of their daily existence. Although it is true that women have participated in manufacturing activities both in core countries and in peripheral nations to a lesser extent than men, they have done so continuously since the inception of industrialization (Scott and Tilly 1975; Tilly and Scott 1978).

For example, in England in 1851, 45% of all women workers were in manufacturing, while in France they amounted to 27.3%. At the same time, working women constituted 31% and 33% of the total ← labor force in the two countries. Although the participation of women in the labor force has remained low and stable in France during the period between the mid-nineteenth century and 1960, in England in 1920 they surpassed 40% of the labor force (Tilly and Scott 1978, pp. 70–73). What then have been the conditions under which women have been incorporated into manufacturing activities?

This question cannot be answered without looking at the historical record (Kessler Harris 1975; Safa 1978). During the first stages of industrialization, women, mostly daughters from farm families, were hired to perform operations in textile mills both in England and later on in New England. Several authors note that women's work during the transition from peasant to industrial production cannot be separated from considerations about children's work within the family (Minge-Klevana 1978; Thompson 1978). A daughter began working at home at a very early age. Girls, as well as boys, were given tasks to perform as early as four or five years of age (Tilly and Scott 1978, p. 129). As members of rural households, they aided their parents in the care of animals and in harvesting and gleaning. In cottage industries characterized by the utilization of family labor, children helped in washing, sorting wool and spinning (Thompson 1978, p. 10).

With the spread of cottage industries and their ensuing competition with factory production, the need for family labor increased. Landless families were forced to rely intensely on their own children's work. The transition from farm to the putting-out system meant that children had to work longer hours. This was forced by the need to increase productivity in an environment where growing mechanization in the factories resulted in more abundant and cheaper output to the disadvantage of cottage industries. Under these circumstances children often had to begin winding thread or turning a reeling machine as young as age four (Tilly and Scott 1978, p. 135).

At times when mothers had to take on industrial work, daughters became their main aides. In general the labor needs of a family determined the type of work expected from a daughter. If a family had no need for a daughter's labor she would be sent to find a job elsewhere in towns and growing cities. In this way families adjusted their labor supply and resolved the survival needs of their members. Thus, in England girls were often apprenticed to crafts or tradeswomen or they would work for wages in textile or garment manufacture. In Caen, France, for example, the lace industry hired girls between ages five and fifteen during its burgeoning period in the eighteenth and nineteenth centuries (ibid. p. 142).

The competition between factory and cottage continued until power looms in the mills started to outproduce family labor to the extent that even by increasing the number of hours worked and the input of its members, a family could no longer work in its own shop. The importance of this change may be gathered from the following figures cited by Minge-Klevana (1980, p. 11): In 1760 most cotton was manufactured by hand in small shops throughout the countryside. At that time Britain imported 21.5 million pounds of raw cotton. A generation later the industry absorbed 22 million pounds, and a half-century later 366 million pounds.

The gradual displacement of cottage production and the rearticulation of peasant and crafts labor within an industrialized capitalist environment resulted in the incorporation of young, single daughters of farm families into factory work. Not uncommonly these were women who stopped working as soon as they were able to marry. As Safa (1979, p. 4) notes, in these conditions women's lives were divided into a paid productive phase and an unpaid reproductive phase in which their activities were for the most part directed towards the maintenance and renewal of the labor force.

In the United States the employment of women in textile manufacturing was significantly linked to the emergence of the factory town and the installment of facilities destined to upgrade to some extent working and living conditions (see, for example, Wallace 1978). In places like Lowell, Massachusetts, firms provided resident boarding houses to insure the safety and moral rectitude of their workers, who often were entrusted to them by rural families. As the industry grew, however, such services became too expensive and manufacturing firms sought other labor supplies. These were found predominantly among migrants coming to the United States from various European countries (Safa 1975). But in many parts of the country the employment of women for textile production in conditions characterized by extreme hardship and low wages continued well into the twentieth century. In her autobiography, Mary Hillis Jones documents the practice of hiring women and their young children for operations in the textile mills of West Virginia and Kentucky. These industries paid a wage to the mothers but utilized in addition the labor of the children. Thus, the type of women's employment described above must be seen more as an effect of certain conditions in the process of capital accumulation than as a sharply cut stage (Mandel 1975).

The use of predominately white, rural female labor in the East Coast of the United States was followed during the middle half of the nineteenth century by the onset of immigration as a means to supply abundant cheap labor (Lamphere Hauser and Michel 1978; Safa 1979). The employment of poverty-stricken international migrants from various points in Europe also coincided with a new intervening factor in the relationship between capital and labor: institutionalized discrimination on the basis of national origin.

In general immigrants have been seen with apparently opposed but in effect complementary attitudes. On the one hand, massive flows of migrant workers diminish the cost of labor in relative terms in a market ruled by the laws of supply and demand (Portes 1978). In principle this rebounds to the benefit of investors. Thus, they are welcome to replace native workers, and not seldom they are used as strikebreakers and to deflate the claims of an already established work force. On the other hand, a generalized attitude of contempt towards foreign workers regarded as inferior vis-à-vis the native-born population contributes to maintain them in a marginalized position while sanctioning extremely low wages and unfavorable working conditions. The influx of migrant labor during the nineteenth century and in more recent times has also exacerbated the competition among workers of various national origins (Castells 1975; Bustamante 1976a.)

In the case of women, discrimination on the basis of national origin has been compounded by discrimination on the basis of gender. The acquisition of benefits in wage levels and working conditions by native working groups was paralleled during the nineteenth and early twentieth centuries by extreme hardships imposed on foreign-born workers. This occurred because "immigrant labor was free from many of the restrictions governing native labor" (Safa 1979, p. 5). Immigrant women experienced a particularly acute need to work and therefore were pressed into accepting penurious working conditions and very low wages. Not seldom women in these circumstances had to work after marriage, sewing at home at piecework rates while trying to combine family duties with wage labor.

As will be seen later, this situation parallels contemporary cases in areas such as the Mexican-American border where, due to the peculiarities of local labor markets, women have to combine wage labor with supplementary economic activity in the home.

The number of female wage earners with a migratory background in the United States increased steadily until 1910, when a combination of factors reduced their participation in the labor force. Among

these factors must be counted the enactment of protective legislation as well as a general attitude aimed at assimilating workers
under a "melting-pot" ideology. In a contradictory but ultimately
explainable mode, these reform movements eventually hurt wom-
en's possibilities for equal participation in the labor force. Protective
legislation, for example, made women more expensive to employ by
restricting the hours when they could work and the type of work
they were permitted to perform.

At the same time, wages earned by men increased, enabling many
women to remain at home and be dependent on the earnings of their
husbands. It is one of the paradoxes of modern history that the
confinement of working-class women to the role of housewives in
replication of upper- and middle-class models was linked to the
obtention of a "family wage" by workers of both genders. While this
was a step forward in the dealings of laborers, vis-à-vis capitalists,
its benefits for women were far from obvious (Baker 1974).

On the one hand, by being removed from the wage labor force,
some women or their daughters were spared the difficulties that
accompany competition for paid work. Women were in a better
position to dedicate more time and energy to the care of home and
children without having to compete in an open job market. On the
other hand, dependence on their husbands' wages frequently increased women's vulnerability, reduced their autonomy and accentuated their economic strife.

Despite this general trend women have recurrently been incorporated in large numbers into wage labor. This has occurred in
particular during times of economic and political crisis. For instance, during the Second World War women were employed to
replace men in heavy industry. It is not trivial that this was also a
time when blacks were given access to jobs generally reserved for
whites. With this, gender reveals its similarity to race and ethnicity
as a factor which contributes to determine the position of individuals in the labor market (Kessler-Harris 1975; Milkman 1980). Once
the military effort was ended women as well as blacks were encouraged to return to their customary positions in society.

A third moment linked to the massive incorporation of women
into an industrial labor force is linked to the emergence of so-called
offshore manufacturing and Export Processing Zones since the end
of the Second World War. Several features characterize this trend.
Authors agree that offshore manufacturing represents a novel strategy in capital investments linked to a reorganization of the international division of labor (Frobel, Heinrichs, and Kreye 1979). During

early periods of industrial development investments from core countries in peripheral areas of the world were geared towards the exploitation of agricultural and mineral resources. Later on large capitalist firms invested in the production of consumer goods destined for internal markets in underdeveloped areas (Frank 1970; Gereffi 1979). Offshore manufacturing departs from these two trends in that it enables the transfer of "stages of production" from metropolitan to peripheral areas, with the ensuing incorporation of large numbers of women into direct manufacturing activities (Pearson and Elson 1978).

Historically the first exemplar in this current occurred in Puerto Rico during the 1950s under the rubric of Operation Bootstrap (Safa 1979). More recent manifestations are to be found in various points in the Orient, along the Mexican-American border and increasingly so in Central America and the Caribbean basin. In every one of these cases (with the exception of Puerto Rico in some aspects) offshore industrialization has been made possible by a combination of fiscal and infrastructural stimuli granted by host governments to foreign corporations (Helleiner 1973; Nayar 1977). At the same time these firms have benefitted from tax exemptions and advantageous customs provisos in core countries.

Thus, it has become normal procedure for firms based in the United States, particularly those engaged in so-called light manufacturing activities, to transfer machinery, components and raw materials to underdeveloped areas where they are assembled by native workers who are predominantely female and young. Once assembly is completed the finished or semifinished products are returned duty-free to the United States where they are marketed.

Aside from the obvious benefits derived from international wage differentials, offshore production affords corporations other advantages. By operating in various points of the world they are able to diversify political and economic risks while maximizing productivity. It is not coincidental that areas where offshore industrialization has boomed are also areas characterized by high levels of political stability (often but not always accompanied by authoritarian regimes) and low levels of unionization (Chomsky and Herman 1977).

Moreover, the fact that offshore industrialization has taken the form of massive clusters of light industries which can be dismantled with relative ease has led many observers to label them "runaway shops." Indeed much available evidence suggests that these industries are able to move to different countries when conditions for production are not optimal. However, this process does not occur as

79

easily as the term "runaway shop" suggests. Along the Mexican-American border—to give but one example—the newest expressions of this phenomenon are the subsidiaries of large corporations like General Motors, which have been accompanied by considerable capital outlays in infrastructure and machinery as well as by the intent to continue operations in that region over an extended period of time (Palloix 1973; U.N. Conference on Trade and Development 1975).

The expansion of offshore production has not been due entirely to the eagerness of host countries in facilitating foreign investment. A number of events taking place in highly industrialized countries have also acted as contributing factors. In the United States full employment during the 1960s, decreasing supplies of immigrant labor, relatively high wages resulting from labor scarcity and the strengthening of unions and the working class in general have limited the possibilities of corporations to generate maximum profits and output. Also significant in that respect have been the rise of the welfare state (which has provided women in particular with an alternative to poorly paid, manual labor) and technological changes which have generated cheaper and more efficient international transportation systems (Safa 1980, p. 7).

The expansion of offshore production linking manufacturing activities in both core and peripheral countries has paralleled in the last years the resurgence of so-called sweatshops in metropolitan countries. Piore (1979) has examined the growth in the number of small establishments dedicated to apparel manufacturing in New York, where labor conditions and organizations are pointedly reminiscent of similar industries at the turn of the century. As with offshore production plants these neo-sweatshops also employ a predominantly female labor force. This time, however, its members are Colombian, Dominican and, to a lesser extent, Puerto Rican migrants. A similar phenomenon appears to be taking place in cities like Los Angeles, where these industries hire undocumented Mexican aliens. Regrettably there is still very little information available on this trend. However, its existence must not be left unmentioned in an effort to assess the historical conditions under which women are employed for direct manufacturing activities.

The internationalization of capital investments resulting in offshore production and the emergence of sweatshops in metropolitan countries may be conceived of as facets of the same process. It is important to remember in this respect that the decline of the garment industry in the New York metropolitan area was in part caused by the flight of many industries to southern areas of the United States or to the Mexican-American border (North American Congress for Latin America 1977a, 1977b). It would appear that the loss of jobs in relatively stable unionized enterprises has been followed by the increase in the number of jobs in sweatshops and the tapping of a new labor pool. Although the form of women's employment may vary in both contexts, the trend suggests conditions under which the employment of working-class women occurs.

Gender and Labor in a Structural Framework

From the historical outline sketched above we may draw some generalizations about the circumstances under which women have been employed by industry in direct manufacturing activities.

Women's labor was a valuable resource during the early stages of industrialization as a result of several factors. Investments were still limited. Machinery, technology and raw materials required comparatively large outlays, which curtailed the availability of capital. Competition for the creation and control of markets was incipient and, therefore, fierce. This period witnessed the accumulation of capital made, in part, possible by the removal of peasants (deprived of ownership over land) from subsistence agriculture and, consequently, their transformation into urban proletarians (Burawoy 1976). Under these circumstances, wages had to be reduced to a minimum in order to insure the stabilization of industry and its continuing rationalization.

It has generally been assumed that the main reason why large numbers of women were employed in early industries was due to the fact that these originally were extensions of "traditional" female occupations such as spinning and weaving. However, this is not a self-evident proposition. While it may partly explain women's factory employment it most assuredly does not explain the employment of children up to twelve hours daily in the textile mills of Europe and America during the nineteenth and early twentieth centuries (Sacks 1975; Amsden 1979).

That tradition alone does not provide adequate answers is confirmed by evidence collected in the Mexican-American border. In Ciudad Juárez, Ica-Mex (the subsidiary of Rockwell International) employed men to perform delicate soldering of gold wire on minute metal surfaces until the plant was closed as a result of its parent firm's incorporation into the U.S. space project. According to the former manager of Ica-Mex, no decrease in either productivity or efficiency was perceived as a result of predominantly male employment in those kinds of operations.

In contrast, history shows that women have often performed labor of the most arduous kind throughout the world. An example will suffice to illustrate this point. Workers at Acapulco Fashion—one of the oldest apparel manufacturing firms in Ciudad Juárez—can remember that during the first years of operations (1968–1970) women were employed as material handlers, improvised mechanics and truck loaders. It was only later on when the plant became stable that a neat division of labor by sex was implemented.

Also there have been cases where mechanization resulted in the displacement of women from "traditionally" feminine occupations. In these instances, capitalist penetration has been linked to a change in the gender of particular work forces. Boserup (1970) describes situations in Africa and Latin America where mechanized agriculture, for example, effected the expulsion of women from food-producing activities over which they had had considerable control until the nineteenth and twentieth centuries. Thus, argumentations that explain the incorporation of women into certain manufacturing sectors only as the consequence of traditional practices or as a continuation of anteceding divisions of labor by gender fail to recognize the enormous degree of variation caused by changes in the organization of production.

Women and children were employed as early industrial workers because they maintained a particularly vulnerable position in society during the transition between agrarian and industrial capitalism in Europe and in the United States. When the services of women and children became more expensive, due to a combination of political and economic factors, other reserves were used to supply similar kinds of labor. In the United States the transition between the employment of white rural women in factories and that of migrant and/or colored women also coincided with the movement of white women into clerical employment or their withdrawal from the labor force entirely (Safa 1979).

But the labor recruitment strategies that characterized early industrialization cannot be said to be exclusively related to a sharply cut stage. Rather they are part of an ongoing process. Due to their position in the world system of production some old industries—like apparel manufacturing—and some new ones—like electronics—have constantly replicated conditions similar to the ones that coincided with early stages of industrialization (Mandel 1975, pp.

321–23). Significantly enough, these manufacturing activities fall under the rubric of "competitive" as opposed to "oligopolic." O'Connor (1973) has elaborated at length upon the features that distinguish both kinds of industries. What is important for the present analysis is to observe the links between the international constraints that impinge upon competitive industrial production and female employment.

Competition has been recognized as an inherent feature of an industrial system. Nevertheless, critical economists have questioned the validity of such an assumption. Godelier (1974), for example, points to the increased concentration of capital and control in the hands of a relatively small number of multinational firms. According to him such a concentration, as well as the penetration of multinational capital into highly diversified productive areas, has augmented the possibilities for consumer market control enabling the uniformization of the prices of production and reducing the importance of competition (Mandel 1975, chap. 11).

While this may be true for certain capital goods industries, it is important to stress the unevenness in the process of contemporary production. Competition in certain sectors of heavy industry, for example, the steel and automotive production, is undoubtedly different than competition in electronics and apparel manufacturing. What explains this difference?

In heavy industry, free competition is partly diminished by the effective formation of monopolies (and the ensuing concentration of capital in a relatively small number of firms). It is also reduced by the use of expensive machinery that places limits on the advantages derived from rapid technological change, and by the need to maintain a highly trained, stable, often unionized work force. The latter has been predominantly formed by relatively well-paid men (Gordon 1972).

Competitive industries, by contrast, are characterized by decentralization of capital, relatively low investments in machinery, and often (but not always) rapid changes in design and technology. For these reasons they rely on the use of intensive labor often provided by large contingents of unskilled and semiskilled women. In other words, competitive and oligopolic industries promote different relations in production. What these differences cause is a fragmentation of the labor force by class as well as gender (O'Connor 1973).

Therefore, the employment of women to perform certain kinds of manufacturing operations implies a more or less conscious decision, a deliberate act of selectivity which affects the social division of labor. Safa (1979) has pointed out that the large-scale incorporation of women into wage labor coincides with concrete situations related to the stages of capital accumulation and expansion.

At times of early industrialization or when industries begin to explore new areas of production and markets, women are often used to maximize the expansive potential of firms and profits. In operations (such as the ones performed under the BIP) which are based on the intensive use of human labor, it is evident that the employment of women offers the most viable means to reduce costs (Benería 1979).

Such a reduction occurs not only as a result of international wage differentials, but also as an effect of a combination of social factors which militate against women's economic gains. One of these factors has to do with the determination of skill levels and its relationship with the formation of wages (see Braverman 1974, for a discussion of the concepts of "deskilling" and "feminization" of the working class).

A good example of this is found along the U.S.-Mexican border. One of the conditions imposed by the Mexican government to allow operations under the maquiladora program has been that all unskilled and semiskilled workers must receive federally sanctioned minimum wages. Presumably, this precludes discrimination on the basis of gender.

However, other factors besides official wage policy have to be considered in a full evaluation of this theme. During 1978 the general minimum wage for Cuidad Juárez, Chihuahua was 125 pesos (approximately $5.30 a day, that is 875 pesos (about $37.10) for a forty-eight-hour work week (including full pay for Sundays and holidays). Such was the wage earned that year by all direct production maquiladora workers. These included not only those women employed to perform relatively simple assembly operations in electronics, toy manufacturing, coupon sorting, and so on, but also seamstresses, who are hardly unskilled workers. In fact, the Comisión Nacional de los Salarios Mínimos, the official organization that dictates wage policy in Mexico, classifies "seamstresses in shops and factories" as skilled (profesional) work. Therefore, in 1978, this job was assigned a minimum daily wage of 161 pesos ($6.82) (Comisión Nacional de los Salarios Mínimos 1978).

When seen in the context of other similarly defined occupations, this predominantly female activity was still one of the lowest paid. Skilled construction workers were assigned a minimum wage of 183 pesos, warehouse overseers earned 165 pesos, skilled wall painters were entitled to 174 pesos, and mechanics of various kinds had an average daily wage of 181 pesos.

Only a few categories of skilled work were given minimum wages equal to or lower than those of seamstresses. These included clerk in self-service store (158 pesos), gas station overseer (161 pesos), henhouse handler (156 pesos), agricultural machinery operator (161 pesos), plastic molding machinist (161 pesos) and watchman (161 pesos). As may be seen, seamstresses have a low position in the minimum wage hierarchy in Mexico. However, the remuneration assigned to them was considerably higher than the general minimum wage of 125 pesos.

What is surprising is not so much that female-type activities are consistently matched to lower than average wages (more than a decade of systematic research on this subject has acquainted us with this fact), but that in the case of maquiladoras, seamstresses are paid the general minimum wage rather than the wage officially assigned by the Mexican government to skilled or semiskilled laborers.

By paying the lowest possible wages sanctioned by Mexican law and by making them extensive to disparate operations, maquiladoras gain administrative expediency and (more importantly) save part of the cost of semiskilled and skilled labor necessary in particular manufacturing processes.

In this case the existence of minimum wage legislation in Mexico modifies but does not deny Pearson and Elson's proposition that women enter the labor force as bearers of inferior labor (Pearson and Elson 1978). This occurs not because the labor of women is necessarily less skilled, but because gender influences the position of labor within the no-skill/skill hierarchy. Maquiladora work is cheap because it is predominantly performed by women, not because of some objective attribute that makes it inherently inferior (Beechey 1979).

Women, Wage Labor and Reproduction

But if women constitute the most exploitable sector of the working class, why aren't they predominantly employed in all sectors of remunerated labor? Presumably, their employment should always result in the maximization of profits through the reduction of costs and of politically compromising situations. The answer to this question can only be given after an examination of women's role within the household and their relationship to wage labor.

The role assigned to women under capitalism has been that of re-producers of labor power (Hartmann 1976). Reproductive functions, however, are not confined to the biological sphere. They also entail domestic activities—such as cooking, washing, cleaning and child care—that ensure the regeneration of human energy. For several centuries, the arena where women have performed these central functions have been variously defined forms of familial organization and the physical environment formed by the household.

As stated earlier, the separation of "work" from household that followed early attempts to rationalize capitalist production brought about important changes for women. The invention of the factory, while permitting increases in output and a more efficient organization of labor, made it difficult for women to coordinate wage and domestic activities (Tilly and Scott 1978).

Gradually, women's primary role became restricted to their reproductive capacities. At the same time that production became more technified, remunerated industrial activities became male territory even in those areas of production that had originally been the domain of women. Women and children became totally dependent on men for access to resources in an increasingly monetarized marketplace.

Paradoxically, women's reproductive role and domestic responsibilities have recurrently acted as precipitants and deterrents of women's entry into the labor force. Whether they are one or the other has depended on the particular stage of capital accumulation and on the level of tensions among classes in concrete historical conjunctures (Hartman 1976; Benería 1978).

During the period of early industrialization which coincided with the massive displacement of peasant, rural-urban migration and the generalized pauperization of working people, women's employment provided an effective means to maximize profits. Because of the need of women to insure the survival of their dependents, particularly the very young and the elderly, women were prone to seek work even if only to receive the lowest possible wages. This is not unlike the situation found in the Mexican-American border, where high levels of unemployment and poverty force women to enter the labor force (International Labour Organization 1975).

However, once sufficient capital has been mustered, production rationalized and the organization of labor made more efficient, women's domestic responsibilities may become obstacles for the smooth flow of business. In particular, losses of productivity as a result of pregnancy and lactation force investors to approach wom-

86

en's employment from a cost/benefit perspective. Such a juncture has generally coincided with the enactment of protective legislation, which, under the guise of defense of the rights of mothers and wives, has limited the participation of women in remunerated work.

This process was also coterminous with the emergence and consolidation of ideologies about "woman's place," making sharper the dichotomy between domestic and wage work and sanctioning the economic dependence of women as a trait of true femininity (Ehrenreich and English 1976). The source of feminine identity became intertwined with women's confinement to the household. Convergently, masculinity became strongly tied to men's capacity to act as the sole providers of their families (Rowbotham 1974).

The particulars of this process have varied from case to case and from geographical locality to geographical locality. However, the frequency with which it has resulted in the exclusion of women from labor markets is astonishing. On the other hand, it is also true that despite ideological barriers, many women have always had to work, mainly when familial needs constrain them to do so.

But given the perceptions of and values about their proper role, when women work they are seen as invaders of an alien territory— that of men. This general proposition is frequently altered by the type of work which women do. For example, it is acceptable for women to work in jobs considered as extensions of their domestic functions. Whence the prevalence of females in elementary teaching, nursing and paid domestic work. Not surprisingly, these are poorly paid occupations. By contrast, women have been underrepresented in jobs which require high levels of "responsibility" and in those linked to high levels of technological expertise (Chaney and Schmink 1976).

Therefore, the fact that women generally earn lower wages than men (and that they are heavily concentrated in menial, unrewarding occupations) is the effect of historically determined political, economic and ideological factors which have affected the participation of both genders in wage labor in different ways.

It may be seen from the process sketched above that women's designation as the pivot of reproductive functions in the household ran parallel to the idea that men's wages should be commensurate with the costs of supporting a family. Thus, the criterion underlying the determination of wages throughout the capitalist world has been the minimal possible level required by a head of household to maintain his family (Burawoy 1976).

In this framework, the regenerative functions of women and children are denied as work and sanctioned through ideological considerations linked to the definition of romantic love and duty. The lack of recognition of domestic labor as "real work" has made it difficult to recognize the contribution of women to economic growth. It has also spared the capitalist class the need to confront the costs that the reproduction of the labor force would entail if women did not fulfill that role net of income.

Because it is assumed that women are economically dependent on men, their attempts to gain access to jobs are frequently seen as means to supplement the income of a male head of household. Therefore, the differentials in the wages earned by men and women are often a reflection of the belief that men should earn more because they have families to support, while the latter merely add to the gains of husbands and fathers.

History has proven this presumption to be erroneous in general, but its power as an underlying thread justifying and explaining discriminatory employment policies against women is undeniable. For these reasons the situation of women in labor markets bears striking resemblance to that of migrants (particularly illegal international migrants). In both cases individuals enter the labor force without a legitimizing ideology that promotes their equitable treatment. The criminalization of international migrant work and the trivialization of women's employment enable their use at the lowest possible cost and sanction numerous abuses which could not be imposed on workers protected by legal citizenship or by those who are seen as legitimate breadwinners (see Baudouin, Collin, Guillerm 1978; and Portes 1978). When workers are both female and illegal migrants, gender and the absence of citizenship combine to exacerbate inequalities even further. Because women tend to be concentrated in the most competitive sectors of capitalist production, they are the subjects of particularly acute forms of exploitation (O'Connor 1973).

Another feature in this complex set of variables must also be mentioned while touching upon the similarities between international migrant workers and women. When they acquire jobs, the members of both groups are often seen with suspicion and hostility, as it is presumed that they compete unfairly against the members of a predominantly male working class. During periods of recession or reduction of economic activity they are the first to be held responsible for the plights of workers in general. In such periods they not only bear the brunt of policies meant to assuage the fear of the "legitimate" working class, they are also frequently forced out of the labor force. Deportation and more subtle forms of voluntary repatriation may be the fate of migrants, while women are encouraged to return to their "proper" place within the home (Baudouin, Collin, and Guillerm 1978).

Again, it must be emphasized that the reasons why women (and migrants) enter the work force as bearers of inferior labor have less to do with their particular training (or lack of it) than with the fact that they are female (or migrants). That, in part, explains why universally women earn less than men when employed in jobs requiring similar levels of education, training and responsibility. In these cases, gender operates as an independent variable which explains the subordinated position of women in the labor market. Women earn lower wages than men simply because they are female.

At this point it is timely to return to the question formulated at the beginning of this section: If women's labor is generally more exploitable than that of men, why aren't they universally employed in all sectors of production? Some of the clues to answer this question have been presented in the preceding sketch. It has been suggested that the position of women in the labor force fluctuates in consonance with the requirements of capital accumulation and expansion. Women's labor may be preferred over that of men during periods of early industrialization, during times of crisis (when the availability of male labor diminishes), in situations where fierce competition in the marketplace forces industry to reduce operation costs to a minimum, and in those circumstances where women's work is attached to the reduction of costs entailing the reproduction of labor power.

A cost/benefit analysis of women's employment has led investors to sacrifice lower wages for the assurance that the reproduction of the labor force will be accomplished free of charge by wives and mothers in the confines of the household. The disruption of this scheme would be a costly venture because the circumstances do not exist under capitalism to generate a viable infrastructure for the collectivization of domestic work and for the equitable participation of men and women in remunerated labor (Beechey 1979).

These are necessary but not sufficient conditions for explaining the exploitability of women's labor. A final factor must be taken into account; that is, the contrasting access of men and women to jobs. Women are not exploitable in absolute terms; only in relation to men. Their widespread exclusion from remunerated labor merely sets up the circumstances that enable their exploitation whenever their labor is required. Why aren't women employed in all sectors of economic activity given their high degree of vulnerability? Simply because the degree of vulnerability upon which high levels of exploitation are predicated would dissipate if women were not ousted from the majority of remunerated activities and if their participation in wage labor were legitimized through ideological mechanisms (Huntington 1975).

Capitalism benefits from the exceptional. As long as women's role as wage-earners may be viewed as the exception rather than the rule (even in situations where large numbers of women work outside of the home) women will continue to be liable to sexist and discriminatory policies in wages. This is a valid proposition both in highly industrialized countries such as the United States and in peripheral areas such as the Mexican-American border.

why only Eur. historical reference pts? Marxist so assumes that the dynamics of labor are same?

CHAPTER 5

Offshore Production and
Local Labor Markets
in the International Context

The purpose of this chapter is to discuss two interrelated topics. First, I briefly outline current interpretations on labor markets. Second, I examine the part played by international capital investments in shaping local labor markets such as the Mexican-American border. As will be seen, the position of electronics and apparel manufacturing in the international scene is important when considering the question of supply and demand of labor at the local level.

In general, the movement of productive stages from highly industrialized countries to peripheral and semiperipheral areas is explained by the requirements of capital accumulation and expansion at a global scale (Nayar 1977; Frobel, Heinrichs, and Kreye 1979; Nash 1979). The degree of competitiveness and vulnerability of certain manufacturing branches in the international market, in large part explains the extent and direction of their movement beyond national borders.

As they penetrate local labor markets through industrialization programs adjusted to their needs, multinational corporations effect subtle divisions among the available labor force. Of these, the most obvious is that brought about by the use of a labor force differentiated by gender. However, gender is not the only factor that we must pause to consider. Differences in age, marital status, migratory background and educational level emerge when comparing workers employed in electronics with those in apparel manufacturing. In the first instance such differences are explained by varying recruitment policies in both sectors.

But in more general terms, employment policies are influenced by two factors: (1) the level of capital investment and (2) the type of institutional relationship existing between a parent firm and its affiliate abroad (i.e., directly owned subsidiary or subcontracted company).

Labor Markets: Current Interpretations

The Neoclassical Model

In the past, economic literature has assumed the supply of labor to be unproblematic, occurring as a rational response of individuals to given market conditions and wage rates. A variant of this model recognizes choices made on the basis of labor/leisure time (Fei 1964). It is assumed that leisure occurs within the confines of the home and family while labor takes place in the impersonal domain of institutionalized production. However, there is no current analysis in economics which articulates these two areas of choice into a coherent theory that explains household decision-making vis-à-vis the supply of labor to differentiated labor markets (Marglin 1968).

Neoclassical economic theory originally postulated a fully flexible labor market in which price adjusts to express and equate independent individual preferences regarding supply and demand of the product being traded. As with material objects, labor acquires, under this perspective, the features of a particular commodity.

In this scheme, labor demand arises from the decisions of profit-maximizing competitive entrepreneurs, who employ workers among a range of equally interchangeable choices. Choice is determined according to specific production functions to the extent that labor's marginal value product equals its price (Becker 1964).

Other factors, such as level of available technology and underlying consumer preferences shaping demand for final products also contribute to determine the marginal value of labor. Labor supply is thus assumed to result from individual choice between work and leisure for utility maximizing, taking into account wage rate, initial resource endowments and personal tastes (Marglin 1968).

Despite its apparent coherence, this model is limited in its ability to explain persistent forms of discrimination among workers by race, national origin and gender, especially when levels of skills are kept constant. Because of its reliance on the concept of a fully flexible labor market where individuals move freely, such phenomena are ultimately attributed to personal tastes and choices (of both workers and entrepreneurs) rather than to structural constraints affecting the orginization of production (Godelier 1975). In others words, discrimination by gender, race and national origin are explained by factors exogenous to the labor market itself.

One of the implications of this framework is that discrimination in the labor market will eventually disappear given its economic irrationality (Doeringer and Piore 1971). It is presumed that as education levels the abilities of workers (regardless of gender, race and national origin), their opportunities will also be equalized. However, history has proven this prediction wrong. Discrimination and occupational segregation in the labor market have been remarkably resistent to change even in highly industrialized countries such as the United States. Here, the majority of women and minorities continue to occupy the lowest echelons of the labor market independently of their level of skill and schooling (Thurow 1969).

The "New Home Economics"

Neoclassical interpretations do not take into account decision-making processes operating at the level of the household and affecting labor supply. Rather, they focus on rational free-moving individuals competing for impersonal opportunities.

To a certain extent this limitation is resolved by human capital theory or the "New Home Economics" (Becker 1964). In this framework, members of a given, fixed household optimize their work and household utility by deciding the time allocation between labor and leisure given household resources and technology. In this model, differing wage rates have a simple explanation; women don't accumulate human capital (as men do) because of the greater utility of their nonmarket work. Because of this women will tend to concentrate in occupations requiring less skill and consequently will receive lower wages when entering the labor market (Bender 1967).

Proponents of this view have the wisdom to acknowledge household decision-making as an important factor in the determination of labor supply. However, as in the previous postulates they fail to explain employment and wage discrimination. Their framework remains static by predicting women will not be found in occupations which require higher degrees of training. In fact, women (although admittedly these are in the minority) are found in highly skilled jobs and some men are often found in unskilled occupations. Moreover, women tend to concentrate in specific occupations within each skill category. This cannot be explained by this model unless exogenous variables such as individual taste are again called into play (Doeringer and Piore 1971).

In sum, the limitations found in human capital theory and broader neoclassical economic interpretations underscore the need to study the ways in which households supply labor to meet market demands. This leads to a consideration of nonneoclassical approaches, such as the labor market segmentation theories that have recently commanded attention in the social sciences.

Labor Market Segmentation

During the last decade, labor market segmentation perspectives have become a necessary reference for the study of labor in industrialized countries. According to their basic formulation there is, in such countries, a historically engendered separation between "primary" and "secondary" labor markets (Doeringer and Piore 1971). In each of these, laborers and employers operate by fundamentally different guidelines and experience varying constraints. Relatively high wages, improved working conditions, employment stability and job security, equity and due process in the administration of work rules, as well as chances for promotion, distinguish the primary labor market. In contrast, the secondary labor market is formed by jobs which are decidedly less attractive, poor paying, often hazardous and dirty, unstable, linked to harsh and arbitrary discipline and little opportunity to advance (Gordon 1972; Edwards 1976).

In the United States several factors have widened the gap between the two markets. Among these must be counted the increasing importance of skills acquired through on-the-job training. This has raised incentives for employers to create a division between these jobs and other jobs which do not require employee retention. Factors such as trade union organizations, federal welfare legislation, minimum wages laws and the income ceiling upon the tax base of social insurance programs have also accentuated the separation between stable and unstable jobs. Recently, environmental restrictions have become an important contributing factor (Piore 1974).

It may be noted, at this point, that some of these conditions, as well as pressure from organized labor and federal legislation, have contributed to prompt the transfer of productive centers from the United States to underdeveloped areas such as the Mexican-American border. Whence the term "runaway shops" given to the subsidiaries or subcontracted firms of multinational corporations operating overseas (North American Congress for Latin America 1975).

Labor market segmentation theories respond to neoclassical models by examining the nature of the demand for labor. Instead of describing labor demand as differing only by level of skill needed, these theories focus on the difference in labor demand by occupation and industry. It is, therefore, hypothesized that persistent discrimination occurs due to structural constraints in the labor market rather than to individual preferences or features (Arrow 1971).

In addition, this framework explains labor and commodity market interaction by reference to the internal dynamics of capitalism. It argues that the choice between technology and labor (especially intensive labor) is contingent on factors other than productivity. The most important of these factors is the need to control and subdue the labor force (see also O'Connor 1973). In other words, this perspective recognizes the inherent antagonism between the entrepreneurial and working classes. In so doing, it defines the structure of the labor market, its fundamental segmentation, as an expression of political contradictions. By calling into play political factors affecting the demand and supply of labor, labor market segmentation theories overcome many of the limitations of interpretations derived from neoclassical economics.

Edwards (1979), in particular, presents a coherent argument focused on the capitalist firm's need for control of its labor force through varying systems of work organization over time. These systems result in labor market segments which demand workers with different characteristics. Thus the rules that govern demand for labor in the "primary" segment of the labor market are not similar to those that distinguish its "secondary" segment.

The characteristics of workers are weighed by firms for profitability within a given control system. In certain cases, for example, in competitive industries, technical innovation in production tends to be introduced at a slow pace due to the availability of large contingents of workers labeled "unskilled" and "semiskilled" (Hodson 1978). What defines a level of skill in these cases is not so much the assortment of "human capital" features possessed by the workers in question, but the nature of the operations that they are called to perform. By strategically defining and redefining levels of skill

95

required for manufacturing, firms maximize their possibilities of control, both over the process of production and over workers (see also Braverman 1974, pp. 334–350).

Since 1976 attempts have been made to introduce considerations about the role of gender in labor market segmentation. Blau and Jusenius (1976), for example, assume that employer's perceptions of women as less dependable workers explain their predominance in the secondary segment of the labor market. However, they fall short of explaining why, even within that segment, women are hired by particular industries and concentrate in certain occupations (Hartmann 1979).

In a classic essay, Kessler-Harris (1975) explores this question by explaining women's location in the labor market as the outcome of the interaction of two distinct areas of socially relevant activity. These are relations between individuals and the family, and between families and the broader sociocultural framework. According to this view the division of labor by gender, choices between market and domestic work and the ideology that explains both phenomena (for example, in terms of taste, natural law, physiology or psychology differentiating men and women) are simultaneously shaped by the same socioeconomic and political forces.

Kessler-Harris agrees that the main features which characterize the contemporary division of labor by gender arose with industrialization. Market segmentation has increased and solidified over time through the specification of norms regarding appropriate jobs by gender. Institutional education, vocational training and specific legislation (for instance, protective legislation) have further strengthened this process (Stevenson 1975). However, questions regarding wage differentials for men and women occupying a similar segment of the labor market or akin occupations is not entirely explained by this framework.

Following the logic of the preceding ideas, it is possible to conclude that contrary to the postulates of neoclassical economics, wages do not result altogether from the natural interaction of supply and demand of labor. Rather, wage levels are decisively influenced by the definition of skill, the relative cost of technology vis-à-vis the employment of individuals and the political need to maintain at the same time control over workers and conditions adequate to the reproduction of the working class as a whole (ibid.).

Wages are calculated upon the basis of the lowest common denominator that permits the reproduction (maintenance and renewal) of the labor force according to economic and political considerations (Benería and Sen 1980). Changing circumstances (mainly derived from economic and political developments) and particularly the ongoing demands of workers (i.e., class consciousness and conflict) have historically brought about raises in wages and improvements in working conditions.

This description, however, is only partially valid for women. Women do not enter the labor market as independent wage earners (even in the limited sense that men do). Rather, women in the household have a position vis-à-vis their husbands similar to the position of the subcontracted worker vis-à-vis his contractor in the open labor market. Men are the immediate receivers of women's services. They are also women's representatives in the outer world (Cohen 1974). They mediate between women and children (the proper dwellers of the household) and the broader public institutions where power and money lie.

It has already been stated that women's services in the household are fundamental for the continuation of the productive system as a whole. Their general devaluation and their exclusion as genuine workers merely obscure the objective value of domestic labor while at the same time reinforcing its existence. The entrance of women into the wage labor force entails potential neglect of domestic services with the ensuing erosion of the circumstances that permit the expansion of the system (Fee 1976).

While these services are fundamental for the perpetuation of capitalism, they are perceived by individuals in the household as a personal matter, a question of established social procedure. When, for whatever reason, women get jobs outside the home, men may lose some of these personal services (or experience a lowering of their quality as well as reduced time allocated to them). Not surprisingly, men (including working-class men) have often opposed the entrance of women in their families into the wage labor force (ibid.).

On the other hand, the system as a whole recognizes this dilemma and uses it by conceiving women as "supplementary" wage earners, whether this definition is accurate or not. It may be suggested, then, that women primarily earn wages that compensate men for the loss of services in the household. Such wages differ from those of men (even when individuals of both genders may be occupying the same labor market segment or job) because they take into account the differing strutural position of men and women in the household. The criteria by means of which wage levels are determined for men and women differ significantly. From a structural point of view

97

women are not remunerated as independent workers. Rather, it is the men in their homes who receive compensation (in the form of wages earned by women) for home services potentially or actually lost when females enter the labor force. By looking at women as nonremunerated laborers under the tutelage and mediation of male providers, we gain insight of the varying forces at play in the determination of wages for men and women.

Wage differentials between men and women have fulfilled a twofold purpose. By maintaining women's earnings below those of men, the former always constitute a reserve labor pool which, as history has proven, may be put to use at times of economic crisis. On the other hand, lower wages for women have effectively prevented the majority of them from gaining economic autonomy. They continue to be partially or totally dependent on men for their survival. Dependence translates into the perpetuation of conditions in which women perform crucial reproductive functions almost net of cost for the system as a whole (Hartman 1979).

The New Radical Economics.

Parallel to explanations based on labor market segmentation, but broader in scope, have been recent economic studies of production and distribution in the U.S. private sector. According to James O'Connor, the U.S. private sector is composed of competitive and monopolistic industries. The former are characterized by a low physical capital-to-labor ratio and output per worker. In them growth of production depends less on physical capital investment and technical progress than on growth of employment. Production is in many cases small scale and markets are normally local or regional in scope. Because productivity and ratios of capital investment to labor are low in competitive industries, wages are also low and there is a tendency towards overcrowding prompted by the relative ease with which business can be set up (O'Connor 1973, Chap. 2).

Moreover, many competitive industries produce for (or sell in) markets that are seasonal, subject to sudden change in fashion or style, or otherwise irregular or unstable. This is the case for the most part in apparel manufacturing and, to a lesser extent, in electronics. The dominant feature in competitive firms is that their workers confront a fate of material impoverishment. In other words, they tend to have access only to jobs in the secondary labor market.

On the other hand, monopolistic industries depend on a rapid increase in the physical capital-to-labor ratio and output per worker. On account of this the expansion of production depends less on growth of employment than on increases in physical capital per worker and technical progress. Monopolistic production is typically large scale and markets are normally national or international in scope. Complex technology and work processes are required in these conditions. In turn, complex technology in combination with the need to coordinate disparate elements in production forces management to minimize arbitrary decisions. Long-term planning insures the availability of raw materials and supplies at stable prices and the maintenance of a steady market (ibid., p. 19).

For these reasons the demand for labor in monopolistic industries is relatively stable and work is available on a full-time year-round basis. The inelastic demand for labor and the physical and geographic concentration of production units facilitate the emergence of labor unions, while monopolistic product markets, even industrial structures, and large profit margins make it comparatively inexpensive for corporations to recognize workers' organizations. By and large these are industries which tend to offer jobs in the primary labor market, although workers without seniority and those in unskilled and semiskilled jobs in monopolistic industries are frequently little better off than their counterparts in the competitive sector (Rees and Schultz 1970).

To superimpose the categories developed by Labor Market Segmentation proponents and radical economists upon the conditions that exist in underdeveloped countries is a theoretically sterile exercise. Both types of analyses have evolved as analytical instruments which render their most fruitful results when applied to highly industrialized countries such as the United States. Moreover, because of its somewhat sketchy state, this perspective is undergoing constant refinements and clarifications which suggest that a simple dichotomy of the labor market is not enough to capture the complexity of the mechanisms in question even in core countries, let alone in underdeveloped areas. However, the basic assumptions of Labor Market Segmentation theory are helpful in an attempt to understand the connections between the two kinds of related labor markets within which multinational corporations operate. What is important, then, is to identify the particular *mode of insertion of local labor markets in underdeveloped areas* (such as the ones which characterize the Mexican-American border) *into a broader political and economic context that transcends national boundaries.*

For example, it seems clear that by transferring unskilled and semiskilled assembly operations abroad, multinational corporations transform foreign labor markets into an extension of the secondary sector in core countries; that is, they transfer abroad certain features present in the secondary sector of the U.S. labor market in order to embrace foreign workers. This has been accompanied by an ever-increasing fragmentation of the productive process, the uniformization of certain fractions of the international working class and a deskilling of the operations required to perform assembly work (for a detailed analysis of this process, see Braverman 1974). This has had two consequences. On the one hand, growing numbers of U.S. workers have lost jobs or seen them transformed as a result of the transfer of assembly operations abroad. On the other hand, the gap between the primary and secondary sectors of the U.S. labor market has widened as workers from underdeveloped countries are incorporated into multinational operations (Taira and Standing, 1973). This is particularly interesting when observing, for example, that along the Mexican-American border many maquiladoras are subsidiaries of large oligopolic firms which, in the U.S., tend to recruit workers through internal labor markets and offer primary sector jobs, that is, relatively stable, well-paid positions to which seniority and promotional benefits are attached.

However, as they transfer assembly operations abroad, those same firms come closer to the patterns of employment followed by competitive firms in which a simple hierarchy functions as the prevalent form of recruitment of and control over workers. That is, when these large firms operate in underdeveloped countries they tend to offer secondary jobs which are more or less temporary, poorly paid and relatively unstable, they do not offer promotional alternatives for most workers either (de Janvry 1979). In part, this is due to the fact that overseas assembly plants (maquiladoras) are not factories in the traditional sense of the term. Rather they are departments belonging to large corporations which (because of the fluidity of contemporary investments) can be relocated.

Unemployment and underemployment in areas of relocation play an important part in this process. Indeed, high levels of unemployment and underemployment in underdeveloped countries are an added advantage for multinational investment in the export manufacturing sector as they foster the availability of labor and, as will be seen shortly, ultimately precipitate the entrance of women into the labor force. The significance of unemployment as an attractive feature for relocating multinational operations may be appreciated from statements made by corporate representatives. While addressing the participants of a symposium organized by the American Chamber of Commerce in Mexico City in 1978, a prominent maquiladora manager pointed out that "thanks to the high level of unemployment, which in Ciudad Juárez reaches 30%, we are able to be highly selective with the personnel we employ."

The less than adequate working conditions and wages that characterize maquiladora operations can be justified because, when abroad, multinationals deal with mostly female "foreign" workers. Indeed, internationally, the presence of large numbers of women in certain remunerated occupations indicates their secondary nature (see Pearson and Elson 1978). This general state of affairs is further complicated along the Mexican-American border by the fact that a large number of maquiladoras depend on smaller U.S. firms which originally belong to the competitive sector. Thus, other fractures in local labor markets occur as a result of their operation in points like Ciudad Juárez.

As this case shows, it is a peculiar mode of operation of multinational corporations that they tend to benefit from and to accentuate preexisting imbalances in labor markets (Taira and Standing, 1973). As they penetrate local economies, maquiladoras enlarge the already existing labor reserve pool by employing sectors of the population which were not previously considered part of the work force (such as most women) while excluding those who were (such as men). The increase in the numbers of potential laborers (both men and women) owing to the specific employment policies of maquiladoras tends to diminish the bargaining capacity of the local working class both in areas of relocation and in core countries— whence the need to consider this process in its true magnitude, as it involves the internationalization of the industrial working class (Frobel, Heinrichs, and Kreye 1979).

In addition it should also be noticed that the transfer of secondary sector jobs from core to underdeveloped countries and the ensuing expansion of a cheap labor reserve pool affords capitalists a maximization of control, both political and economic, over laborers (in both central and peripheral countries) by employing the most manipulable sector of the working class, the one less likely to organize, demand better wages and press for improvements of working conditions.

The Electronic and Apparel Manufacturing Industries in the International Market

What is the position of manufacturing firms operating under the Border Industrialization Program in the framework outlined above and in the context of global capitalism? As pointed out earlier two branches—apparel and electronics—dominate productive activity along the Mexican-American border. Such a preponderance indicates that the advantages derived from transferring operations abroad do not affect all U.S. industries in the same way (Helleiner 1973b). Political and legislative constraints such as tariff barriers prevent certain manufacturing processes from being partially or totally exported. This is the case, for example, in capital intensive, monopolistic or "heavy" industries.

The electric/electronic and apparel industries on the other hand have different historical roots, which in part explain their contrasting features. While textile and apparel manufacturing can trace their origins to the early stages of capitalist production, the birth of the electric industry coincided with the most innovative developments of the present century. Technological advances in the former have been sparse and infrequent, making it one of the most backward of industrial activities, but the latter has confronted technological changes that stagger the imagination both on account of their frequency and imaginative content.

But although there are differences between the two industries, they also share commonalities which are worthy of mention. The first one, and perhaps the most important, is that both industries have maintained a particularly vulnerable position in the international market as a result of fluctuations, which often are difficult if not impossible to control, in supply and demand of their products. In the case of the clothing industry changes in fashion and style require constant adaptation and the exploration of new market mechanisms to enable surplus value realization. The electric industry faces similar constraints on account of rapid modifications in design and technological sophistication linked with precipitous obsolescence processes (for a more detailed analysis see North American Comgress for Latin America 1977b). Perhaps more than any other industry, electric/electronic and clothing manufacturing demand a lowering of operation costs in order to remain competitive in the international market.

A second characteristic shared by both kinds of industries is that they have a high capacity for labor absorption. In apparel production capital invested per worker amounted to little over $9,000 in 1971, that is, about half the ratio for textile production and less than one quarter the ratio for all manufacturing (Conference Board 1975). Wages have also been traditionally lower than those earned in other manufacturing activities. In combination with its relative lack of technological sophistication, the apparel industry is also character-ized by the relative ease with which it may be entered. In 1974 it was estimated that a beginning capital of $50,000 was sufficient to set up shop in it. Thus, the average size of an establishment is very small and production is highly decentralized (North American Con-gress for Latin America 1975).

In the United States roughly half of the plants in the industry employed fewer than twenty workers while only 14% employed one hundred or more. In contrast with other industries apparel manufac-turing has not spawned giants equivalent to General Motors or IBM. The sales of the industry's four largest companies account for only 5% of total industry sales, compared to 80% for the four largest firms operating in the automotive industry (Fashion Institute of Technology 1976, p. 56). From an international perspective the apparel industry's relatively backward technology makes it easy and inexpensive to start operations in any part of the world. Moreover, the acute fragmentation of its productive process, which entails the separation of administrative and marketing functions from assem-bly work, facilitates the export of certain stages of production abroad while maintaining its ties to the domestic market.

Although electric/electronic product manufacturing is also based upon intensive of human labor, some of its most distinctive features differ substantially from those of the apparel industry. For example, in 1977, the electronics industry projected sales approaching the $60 billion mark (*Electronic News*, Jan. 10, 1977, p.). Upon first glance, decentralization of manufacturing activities seems to be shared by both electronics and apparel. Six thousand firms compete in elec-tronics, nearly half of which produce components for other branches of the industry. Slightly more than half of these firms have fewer than one hundred workers each, and nearly 70% have yearly sales amounting to less than $5 million.

But in sharp contrast with the apparel industry only six electronic firms account for more than 92% of sales of all mainframe compu-ters; and one firm alone, IBM, dominated the field with a 65.5% share of the market in 1975 (*Business Week*, April 26, 1976, p. 3). The trend toward centralization is equally pronounced with respect to consumer products. In 1950, more than 140 firms assembled and sold TV receivers in the United States. At the present time there are only seven U.S. TV producers. Also, while the apparel industry experiences fluctuations due to its seasonal nature, the electronics industry operates in a nonseasonal framework. Finally—and this is a very important point—it takes considerably more capital to enter electronics than that required for entrance into the apparel industry. But entry is considerably cheaper than in many other industries (North American Congress for Latin America 1975).

Yet the electronics industry remains highly competitive in the international arena mostly due to constant changes in design and technology. The nature of competition in electronics means that industries must gear their efforts towards constant innovation. Automation must be kept to a low level because the large investments necessary for machinery would inevitably make a company dependent on a specific technology which could soon go out of fashion—whence the necessity to rely upon human labor. As opposed to the situation in which the apparel industry finds itself, in electronics it is not technical difficulties which have limited increased mechanization but rather costs within the capitalist framework (O'Connor 1973, chap. 2).

It has been stated that both the apparel and electric/electronic industries share a similar position within the international system of production, which in part explains the transfer of labor intensive operations abroad. At the local level it is possible to discern differences in employment policies between the two kinds of industries. This, in turn, is related to the interesting observation that while the majority of electric/electronic industries operate along the Mexican-American border through *direct subsidiaries* owned by large parent firms, the majority of textile garment manufacturing companies do so through one of various *subcontracted shops*. In this case the arrangement is often tenuous and it frequently involves small Mexican-owned enterprises whose owners or stockholders wish to take advantage of the stimuli granted by the government to multinational corporations. In order to achieve this, these businessmen have chosen to export part of their production while the rest is geared to the internal market. The differences in the relationship between principal firms and their subsidiaries or subcontracted firms abroad is relevant to the present analysis because they indicate various levels of capital investment abroad and, concomitantly, limits upon the criteria by which workers are hired.

Investments in machinery and infrastructural facilities have been higher in the electric/electronics industry than in apparel manufacturing, although precise information about this point is difficult to obtain. In the case of corporations which operate through subsidiaries—as in the case of electronic component manufacturing—intrafirm transactions greatly facilitate administrative functions and circulation of parts and machinery. The closeness of the relationship protects the firm from wild fluctuations in supply and demand, at least during "normal" periods of economic activity. In Ciudad Juárez, firms such as RCA Componentes de Televisión, Electro Componentes de México (General Electric) and Conductores y Componentes Electricos (General Motors) exemplify this proposition. Not only are these maquiladoras characterized by their facilities located in modern industrial parks, but they have also committed part of their investments to the training of middle-level personnel, the improvement of the skills of some of their workers and the promotion of the Maquiladora Program as a whole. Moreover, they offer relatively stable jobs and certain fringe benefits.

It should be added that it is comparatively difficult to get a job at one of these and other similar plants because of the highly selective nature of the employment policies they practice. Workers must have relatively high levels of schooling, they must be young, single and childless, they must be available for both morning and night shifts and able to document a minimal period of six months of residence in Ciudad Juárez. Some plants go so far as to establish a maximum level of schooling as a requirement for applicants. Others conduct investigations to confirm the veracity of their applicants' statements. Before getting a job, a woman must take manual dexterity tests as well as a medical examination which centers primarily on pregnancy. The numerous requirements listed above seem out of proportion with the nature of the operations performed in these plants and with the low wages earned by workers. In part these requirements can be implemented due to the abundance of women searching for jobs in an environment in which unemployment and underemployment combined reaches 30%. It should also be remembered that such a high level of discrimination in hiring practices insures the possibility of effecting tight control over workers.

By contrast, apparel manufacturing plants are smaller and all but a few operate as subcontracted firms of one or several U.S. corporations. Although brands such as Sears, the Warnaco Group and Johnson and Johnson are represented in Ciudad Juárez, the vast majority of these industries are associated with corporations that have regional rather than national visibility. Among these are Billy the Kid, Pioneer and Zenith Shirt. In combination with low capital investments and a vulnerable position in the international market, these circumstances result in hiring practices that differ markedly from those which are characteristic of the electric/electronic industry.

To put it simply, textile garment manufacturing plants tend to employ workers whose position in the local labor market is by far weaker than that of those hired by direct subsidiaries of the electric/ electronic industry. Among these workers there is a large number of older women who, solely on account of this, find it difficult to find employment elsewhere. Many are single mothers who represent the only means of support for their children. Many have sought employment after being deserted by their husbands or after losing economic support from males belonging to their households. As seen in chapter 3, the general profile of these workers also indicates that they have a lower level of schooling than that which characterizes direct production operators in the electric/electronic manufacturing sector. Because of their extreme need these women are willing to accept the less than favorable working conditions and high production quotas that prevail in the apparel industry.

In short, the important point to be stressed here is that the presence of the two kinds of industries in Ciudad Juárez effects various subdivisions within the local labor market. On the one hand, by hiring mostly women for unskilled and semiskilled assembly operations, multinational corporations establish a subdivision of the labor market by gender which deeply affects the possibilities of employment for both men and women. On the other hand, for reasons that have been outlined above, differences in manufacturing activity and in the relationship between parent firms and their associates in underdeveloped areas result in varying adaptation strategies which involve different employment policies and which, in turn, generate more subtle divisions within a predominantly female labor force.

From the perspective of workers, jobs in the electronics sector are highly desirable. Besides medical attention provided through affiliation to the Instituto Mexicano del Seguro Social, they also offer regular income earned in modern, well-organized facilities. Savings and loans programs as well as periodic bonuses and sports activities constitute added incentives. Even the fact that many of these maquiladoras have dining areas or cafeterias which spare workers the need to buy food from street vendors is often seen as an attractive feature. Although these may appear as modest benefits from the point of view of organized labor in hegemonic countries, they remain exceptional characteristics in underdeveloped areas. Thus, corporations which can afford these advantages for their workers are also in a position to hire individuals "privileged" in terms of education, marital status and age.

Subcontracting offers a markedly different picture. In this case, which dominates clothing maquiladoras, the arrangement between parent firms and their foreign associates is often tenuous. It frequently involves small Mexican enterprises whose owners or stockholders have sought the advantages of stimuli granted by the government to multinational corporations. To achieve this, many business entrepreneurs have chosen to export part of their production under the provisos of the BIP, while the rest is geared to the internal market. Others have created new companies which fully depend upon contracts from foreign firms.

Thus, management is not only responsible for the coordination of labor but also for the acquisition of contracts. Sudden cancellations may throw these firms into dangerous situations not far from bankruptcy. Thus, economic opportunism is not an untypical trait of these companies. Their vulnerability is accentuated in part by their position in an international market and by their own limitations vis-à-vis the corporations they are associated with.

The unfortunate consequence of this in Ciudad Juárez has been the proliferation of miniscule shops in which supplies are not always available on a regular basis. Work is, therefore, unstable, working conditions inadequate, equipment old-fashioned, labor requirements arbitrary and comparatively more rigorous, demands on productivity steep and abuses not infrequent. High rates of turnover accompany the need to maintain an extremely elastic work force in these plants. In short, these industries are the epitome of the competitive sector.

Because of their extreme economic need, women employed in this sector have no other choice than to accept the unfavorable working conditions and high production quotas that prevail in the apparel industry. The possibility of earning the minimum wage—even if only during relatively short periods of time—and of being incorporated into the Mexican Social Security System (Instituto Mexicano del Seguro Social), make even these plants better working alternatives than paid domestic work, employment in the petty clerical sector or in the so-called informal economy.

In the following chapters we pause to consider this broad panorama from the point of view of working women themselves.

CHAPTER 6

Maquiladoras: The View from Inside

Participant Observation, Its Use and Purpose

Shaped by more than a century of history, participant observation has become the trademark of anthropology, the feature that best distinguishes it from other social-scientific approaches. When Bronislaw Malinowski (1961) undertook the task of describing and explaining the culture of the Trobriand islanders from the lofty perspective of Western civilization, he did so from a basis of years spent as a participant observer. John Griffin (1977), on the other hand, applied a variant of the same technique when he daringly modified his physical appearance to peer directly into the experience of Afro-Americans in the United States.

As these two examples suggest, there are various forms of participant observation. A researcher becomes a participant observer when she casually mixes with the members of a group, barely uttering a word but keenly watching every gesture and behavior from the point of view of anthropological theory. While she interviews "informants" from the same group, following a previously designed questionnaire, she is carrying participant observation one step further. If she deliberately takes steps to become "one of the group" by temporarily detaching herself from her own sociocultural scene and entering the one of the people she is studying, a third variant of the same technique is being adopted (Spradley and McCurdy 1975). Much of the content of this work resulted from these forms of participant observation. However, it is with the third variant that this section is primarily concerned.

What distinguishes the three modalities described above from one another is the degree of proximity between the researcher and her subject matter. Each one has advantages and limitations, but they

108

are valuable insofar as they can yield mutually complementary information. In general, participant observation is an exploratory instrument meant to increase or deepen familiarity with specific facets of society and culture. It can be the ideal means to formulate valid research questions. But it can also be more than that; it can be the bridge between theoretical concerns and daily human experience.

Looking for a Job: A Personal Account

What is it like to be female, single and eager to find employment at a maquiladora? Shortly after arriving in Ciudad Juárez and after finding stable lodging, I began looking through the pages of newspapers hoping to find a "wanted" ad. My intent was to merge with the clearly visible mass of women who roam the streets of industrial parks of Ciudad Juárez searching for jobs. They are, beyond doubt, a distinctive feature of the city, an effervescent expression of the conditions that prevail in the local job market.

My objectives were straightforward: I was to spend from four to six weeks applying for jobs and obtaining direct experience about the employment policies, recruitment strategies and screening mechanisms used by companies in the process of hiring assembly workers. Special emphasis would be given to the average investment of time and money expended by individual workers in trying to gain access to jobs. In addition, I was to spend an equal amount of time working at a plant, preferably at one involved in the manufacture of apparel.

With this I expected to learn more about working conditions, production quotas and wages at a particular plant. In general both research stages were planned as exploratory devices that would elicit questions relevant to the research project from the perspective of workers themselves.

In retrospect, it seems odd that the doubt as to whether these goals were feasible or not never entered my design. However, finding a job at a maquiladora is not a self-evident proposition. For many women, actual workers, the task is not an easy one. This is due primarily to the large number of women they must compete with. Especially for those who are older than twenty-five years of age the probability of getting work in a maquiladora is low. At every step of their constant peregrination women are confronted by a familiar sign at the plants, "No applications available," or by the negative response of a guard or a secretary at the entrance of the factories. But such is the arrogance of the uninformed researcher. I went about the business of looking for a job as if the social milieu had to comply with the intents of my research rather than the reverse. Moreover, I was pressed for time. It was indispensable that I get a job as quickly as possible.

By using newspapers as a source of information for jobs available, I was departing from the common strategy of potential workers in that environment. As my own research would show, the majority of these workers avail themselves of information by word of mouth. They are part of informal networks which include relatives, friends and an occasional acquaintance in the personnel management sector. Most potential workers believe that a personal recommendation from someone already employed at a maquiladora can ease their difficult path.

This belief is well founded. At many plants, managers prefer to hire applicants by direct recommendation of employees who have proven to be dependable and hard-working. For example, at Electro Componentes de Mexico, the subsidiary of General Electric and one of the most stable maquiladoras in Juárez, it is established policy not to hire "outsiders." Only those who are introduced personally to the manager are considered to fill up vacancies.

Such a policy is not whimsical. It is the result of evaluations performed on a daily basis during the interactions between company personnel and workers. By resorting to the personal linkage, managers attenuate the dangers of having their factories infiltrated by unreliable workers, independent organizers and "troublemakers." This concern became particularly vivid after 1974, when several violent incidents linked to the militant activities of the Liga 23 de Septiembre resulted in the death of a maquiladora manager (Fernández 1977).

Cautiousness is also warranted given the periodic criticism to which the maquiladora program has been subjected since its inception. By adopting a watchful attitude towards their future employees managers hope to diminish the probability of conflict and disruption of business activities.

On the other hand, the resemblance of a personal interest in the individual worker at the moment of hiring enables management to establish a bond often heavily colored by paternalism. From the point of view of workers this is a two-faceted proposition. Some complain of the not unusual practice of superintendents and managers who are prone to demand special services, for example, overtime, in exchange for personal favors: a loan, an exemption from work on a busy day when the presence of the worker at home is required by her children, and so on. As in other similar cases, personal linkages at the workplace can and will be used as subtle mechanisms to exert control.

Workers, in turn, acknowledge a personal debt to the individual who has hired them. In the majority of cases, commitment to the firm is not distinct from the commitment to a particular individual through whom access to employment presumably has been achieved. A job becomes a personal favor granted through the kindness of the personnel manager or the superintendent of a factory. In the mind of the worker, particularly when she is young and female, these two angles are fused into one perception.

When asked about the reasons for her unflagging acceptance of increased production quotas without consequent remuneration, Anita offered a typical answer: "If the group leader demands more production, I will generally resist because I owe her nothing. But if the *ingeniero* asks me to increase my quota on occasion, I comply. He gave me the job in the first place! Besides, it makes me feel good to know that I can return the favor, at least in part".

Only those who are not part of tightly woven informal networks must rely on impersonal ways to find a job. In this situation are recently arrived migrants and older women with children, for whom the attempt to find maquiladora employment may be a new experience after many years spent caring for children and the home. In objective terms my own situation as a newcomer in Ciudad Juárez was not markely different from that of the former. Both types of women are likely to be found in larger numbers in the apparel manufacturing sector.

This is not a random occurrence. One of the basic propositions in the present work is that differences in manufacturing activity are related to variations in the volume of capital investments. In turn this combined variable determines recruitment strategies. (See chapters 4 and 5.) Therefore different types of persons are predominantly employed in different manufacturing sectors. Ciudad Juárez electronics maquiladoras, for example, tend to employ very young, single women. This is, in effect, a preferred category of potential workers from the point of view of industry.

Workers, on their part, also prefer the electronics sector, which is characterized by the existence of large stable plants, regular wages and certain additional benefits. In contrast, the apparel manufacturing sector is frequently characterized by smaller, less stable shops where working conditions are particularly strenuous. Because of their low levels of capital investment, many of these shops tend to hire personnel on a more or less temporary basis. The lack of even the smallest of commitments to their employees and the need to maintain an elastic work force to survive as capitalist enterprises in a fluctuating international market forces management to observe crude and often ruthless personnel recruitment policies.

One of such firms was Maquiladoras Internacionales. Throughout the year "wanted" ads for direct production workers on behalf of this factory appeared in the two main Juárez newspapers. This was but one of the indications of a permanently rotating work force and of the high rates of turnover that charactertized its operations. Its location and structure are pertinent to the present description.

Despite its flamboyant label, this assembly plant is of modest proportions and hires approximately one hundred workers. It is located in the central area of the city rather than in one of the modern industrial parks which have been established as infrastructure to foster foreign investment through the joint effort of private and state expenditures. The locale of Maquiladoras Internacionales is of difficult access by public transportation and is surrounded by unpaved streets, a not uncommon feature of the city as a whole.

More significantly, Maquiladoras Internacionales is not a maquiladora in the strict sense of the word. Rather it is a spin-off of Colchones Zaragoza, a mattress manufacturing factory founded with Mexican capital and in existence for approximately two decades. As in other similar cases, its owners have sought to take advantage of the incentives granted to foreign investment in the area of export manufacturing by gearing part of their production in that direction.

Thus, the old fashioned Singer sewing machines in need of constant repair, the shoddy one-level building where workers are crowded and the abundance of loosely disseminated cardboard boxes bearing the label of Jefferson Mills are evidence of the particular position maintained by this firm in the context of the maquiladora program.

The obsolete machinery as well as the imported precut fabric contained in the boxes has entered the country "in-bond." The precariousness of the construction and its impoverished nature suggests the awareness of investors about the slightness of their venture.

Attached to the tent-like factory where women work from 7:30 A.M. to 5:00 P.M. from Monday to Friday there is a tiny office. I entered that office wondering whether my appearance or accent would elicit the suspicion of my potential employers. The personnel manager looked me over sternly and told me to fill out a form. I was to return the following morning at seven to take a dexterity test.

I tried to respond to the thirty-five questions contained in the application in an acceptable manner. Most of the items were straightforward: name, age, marital status, place of birth, length of residence in Ciudad Juárez, property assets, previous jobs and income, number of pregnancies, general state of health, and so on. One, however, was unexpected: What is your major aspiration in life? I pondered briefly upon the superfluous character of that inquiry given the general features of the job sought.

At the same time a doubt struck me. Would several years of penmanship practice at a private school in Mexico City and flawless spelling give motive for suspicion? When trying to modify a writing style and idiosyncrasies one comes face to face with the meaning of participant observation, its pitfalls and limitations.

The following morning I was scheduled to take an on-the-job test. I assumed that this would consist of a short evaluation of my skills as a seamstress. I was to be proven wrong. At 7 A.M. I knocked at the door of the personnel office where I had filled out the application the day before. But no one was there yet. I peeked into the entrance of the factory in a state of moderate confusion. A dark-haired woman wearing false eyelashes ordered me to go in and promptly led me to my place. Her name was Margarita and she was the supervisor.

I had never been behind an industrial sewing machine of the kind I confronted at this time. That it was old was plain to see; how it worked was difficult to judge. An assortment of diversely cut denim parts was placed on my left side while I listened intently to Margarita's instructions. I was expected to sew patch-pockets on what were to become blue jeans. Obediently, I started to sew. The particulars of "unskilled" labor unfolded before my eyes.

The procedure involved in this operation required perfect coordination of hands, eyes and legs. The left hand was used to select the larger part of material from the batch next to the worker. Upon it, the pocket (swiftly grabbed by the right hand) had to be attached. There were no markers to guide the placement of the pocket on its proper place. This was achieved by experienced workers on a purely visual basis. Once the patch-pocket had been put on its correct position, the two parts had to be directed under a double needle while applying pressure on the machine's pedal with the right foot.

Because the pockets were sewed on with thread of a contrasting color, it was of peak importance to maintain the edge of the pocket perfectly aligned with the needles so as to produce a regular seam and an attractive design. Due to the diamond-like shape of the pocket, it was also indispensable to slightly rotate the materials three times while adjusting pressure on the pedal. Too much pressure inevitably broke the thread or resulted in seams longer than the edge of the pocket. Even the slightest deviation from the needles produced lopsided designs which had to be unsewed and gone over as many times as necessary to achieve an acceptable product. According to the instructions of the supervisor, once trained, I would be expected to sew a pocket every nine to ten seconds. That is, between 360 and 396 pockets every hour, between 2,880 and 3,168 every shift.

For this, velocity was a central consideration. The vast majority of apparel manufacturing maquiladoras operate through a combination of the minimum wage and piecework. At the moment of being hired, workers receive the minimum wage. During 1978 this amounted to 125 pesos a day (approximately $5.00). However, they are responsible for a production quota arrived at by time-clock calculations. Workers receive slight bonus payments when they are able to fulfill their production quotas on a sustained basis throughout the week. In any case they are not allowed to produce less than 80% of their assigned quota without being admonished. And a worker seriously endangers her job when unable to improve her level of productivity.

At Maquiladoras Internacionales a small blackboard indicated the type of weekly bonus received by those able to produce certain percentages of the quota. These fluctuated between 50.00 pesos (approximately $2.20) for those who completed 80% to 100.00 pesos (about $4.40) for those who accomplished 100%. Managers call this combination of steep production quotas, minimum wages and modest bonuses, "incentive programs."

I started my test at 7:30 A.M. with a sense of embarrassment about my limited skills and disbelief at the speed with which the women in the factory worked. As I continued sewing, the bundle of material on my left was renewed and grew in size, although slowly. I had to repeat the operation many times before the product was considered acceptable. But that is precisely what was troubling about the "test." I was being treated as a new worker while presumably being tested. I had not been issued a contract and, therefore, was not yet incorporated into the Instituto Mexicano del Seguro Social (the National Security System). Nor had I been instructed as to working hours, benefits and system of payment.

I explained to the supervisor that I had recently arrived in the city, alone, and with very little money. Would I be hired? What was the current wage? When would I be given a contract? Margarita listened patiently while helping me unsew one of many defective pockets, and then said, "You are too curious. Don't worry about it. Do your job and things will be all right." I continued to sew aware of the fact that every pocket attached during the "test" was becoming part of the plant's total production.

At 12:30 during the thirty-minute lunch break, I had a chance to better see the factory. Its improvised aura was underscored by the metal folding chairs behind the sewing machines. I had been sitting in one of them during the whole morning, but until then did I notice that most of them had the well-known emblem of Coca-Cola painted on their backs. I had seen this kind of chair many times in casual parties both in Mexico and in the United States. Had they been bought or were they being rented from the local concessionary? In any event they were not designed in accordance to the strenuous requirements of a factory job, especially one needing the complex bodily movements of sewing. It was therefore necessary for women to bring their own colorful pillows to ameliorate the stress on their buttocks and spines. Later on I was to discover that chronic lumbago was, and is, a frequent condition among factory seamstresses.

My curisoity did not decrease during the next hours, nor were any of my questions answered. At 5 P.M. a bell rang signaling the end of the shift and workers quickly prepared to leave. I marched to the personnel office with the intent of getting more information about a confusing day. But this time my inquiry was less than welcome. Despite my over-shy approach to the personnel manager, his reaction was hostile. Even before he was able to turn the disapproving expression on his face into words, Margarita intervened with energy. She was angry. To the manager she said, "This woman has too many questions: Will she be hired? Is she going to be insured?" And then to me, "I told you already we do piecework here; if you do your job you get a wage, otherwise you don't. That's clear isn't it? What else do you want? You should be grateful! This plant is giving you a chance to work! What else do you want? Come back tomorrow and be punctual."

This was only the first in a number of application procedures that I underwent. Walking about the industrial parks while following other job-seekers was especially informative. Most women do not engage in this task alone. Rather they do it in the company of friends or relatives. Small groups of two or three women looking for work may be commonly seen in the circumvicinity of the factories. Also frequent is the experience of very young women, ages between sixteen and seventeen, seen in the company of their mothers. "We've been coming every day for a week," a woman told me. "I sell burritos at the stadium every weekend and her father is a janitor. But we don't earn enough money for the six children. Elsa is the eldest although she is only sixteen. I can't let her go alone into the parks. She's only a girl and it wouldn't be right. Sometimes girls working at the plants are molested. These *chavalillas* are too young. It's a pity they have to work. But I want to be sure she'll be working in a good place."

At the times when shifts begin or end, the industrial parks of Juárez form a powerful visual image as thousands of women arrive in buses, taxi-cabs and *ruteras* while many others exit the factories. During working hours only those seeking jobs may be seen wandering about. Many, but not the majority are "older women." They confront special difficulties due both to their age and to the fact that they often support their own children. These are women who, in most cases, enter the labor force after many years dedicated to domestic chores and child-care. The precipitant factor that determines their entry into the labor force is often the desertion by their male companions. The bind they are placed in at that time is well illustrated by the experience of a thirty-one year old woman, the mother of six children: "I have been looking for work since my husband left me two months ago. But I haven't had any luck. It must be my age and the fact that I have so many children. Maybe I should lie and say I've only one. But then the rest wouldn't be entitled to medical care once I got the job." Women often look for jobs in order to support their children. But being a mother is frequently the determining factor that prevents them from getting jobs.

In early June, 1978, Camisas de Juárez, a recently formed maquiladora was starting a second (evening) shift. Until then it had hired approximately 110 workers operating in the morning hours. As it expanded production, a new contingent of workers had to be recruited. Advertisements to that effect appeared in the daily newspapers. I responded to them. So did dozens of other women.

Camisas de Juárez is located in the modern Parque Industrial Bermúdez. On the morning that I arrived with the intent of applying for a job, thirty-seven women had preceded me. Some had arrived as early as 6 A.M. At 10 the door which separated the front lawn from the entrance to the factory had not yet been opened. A guard appeared once in a while to peek at the growing contingent of applicants, but these were given no encouragement to stay on, nor was the door unlocked.

At 10:30 the guard finally opened the door and informed us that only those having personal recommendation letters would be permitted to walk inside. This was the first in a series of formal and informal screening procedures used to reduce the number of potential workers. It was an effective screening device: Thirteen women left immediately, as they did not have the letter of recommendation alluded to by the guard. Others tried to convince him that although they had no personal recommendation, they "knew" someone already employed at the factory. It was through the recommendation of these acquaintances that they had come to apply for a job.

One of them, Xochitl lacked both a written or a verbal recommendation but she insisted. She had with her a diploma issued by a sewing academy. She was hopeful that this would work in her favor. "It is better to have proof that you are qualified to do the job than to have a letter for recommendation, right?" I wondered whether the personnel manager would agree.

Indeed her diploma gave Xochitl claim to a particular skill. But academies such as the one she had attended abound in Ciudad Juárez. For a relatively small sum of money they offer technical and vocational courses which presumably qualify young men and women for skilled work. However in an environment lacking in employment opportunities, their value is in question. In many cases maquiladora managers prefer to hire women who have had direct experience on a job or those who are young and inexperienced but who can be trained to suit the needs of a particular firm. As one manager put it to me, "We prefer to hire women who are unspoiled, that is, those who come to us without preconceptions about what industrial work is. Women such as these are easier to shape to our own requirements."

With hesitant pride Xochitl allowed me to read her diploma. It was a glossy document which showed the imposing figure of an open-winged eagle clutching a terrestrial globe. An undulating ribbon upon which the words, "labor, omnia, vincit" were etched served to complement the design. Beneath it there was certification of Xochitl's skills:

The Academy *Mi Corte Universal* certifies that there exist filed in the secretariat of this institution documents which verify that according to its established program and the corresponding laws, Miss Xochitl González Luna has completed in an entirely satisfactory manner the course on cutting. Thus, she is accredited to exercise her specialization free of restraint.

A preoccupied expression clouded Xochitl's face while she glanced at her certificate. On its left margin there was an oval picture of a young girl with shiny eyes who barely resembled the prematurely aged woman with whom I was speaking.

Xochitl was now thirty-two and the mother of four children. Her husband, a peddler of home-made refreshments, did not earn enough money to support his family. That was the reason why Xochitl had taken up sewing at home. For every beach dress finished on her old Singer sewing machine she received 22 pesos ($0.80). She was generally able to complete three of these garments every hour. Her day was highly structured. When there was work available (which was not always) she was accustomed to sew from 6 A.M. until 3 P.M. In the afternoon she cooked, cleaned the house, washed clothes and went shopping.

Xochitl didn't like doing piecework, especially when the earnings were so small and irregular. She knew that each one of the dresses she sewed was sold in the market for approximately 150 pesos ($8.00), a figure that entailed a sizable profit for her contractor. She resented this, but need had compelled her to combine home and wage-earning labor. She had no other choice. Most of her income was spent on food, clothing, and in feeble attempts to furnish her two-room adobe house. Her husband owned it and thus they didn't have to pay any rent. That, at least, was some source of relief. Her husband was convinced that their property was worth at least thirty-thousand pesos but Xochitl doubted it. How could such a small and shabby lodging in the middle of an unpaved street be worth that much?

As she waited in line, Xochitl thought about her children. All but one had been left alone at home. She had already been standing outside of the factory for three and a half hours; longer than she had expected when she put on her shoes that same morning determined to find a job. All this while she could have been sewing at home and minding the children. Her husband didn't even know she was away. Perhaps he wouldn't approve of her escapade. He was proud. It was one thing to sew at home, but another to work in a factory. Almost four hours had been spent already, and if she didn't get the job her time would have been entirely wasted.

We waited upon the benevolence of the guard who seemed unperturbed by the fluctuating number of women standing by the door. To many of us he was the main obstacle lying between unemployment and getting a job from someone inside the factory in a decision-making position. If only we could get our foot in, maybe there was a chance. . . . The young man dressed in uniform appeared to the expectant women as an arrogant and insensitive figure. I asked him how long had he worked there. With the air of one who feels he has gained mastery over his own fate he answered, "Uy! I've been working here for a very long time, I assure you: almost two years."

To me his words sounded a bit pathetic. But Beatríz and Teresa, two sisters of twenty-three and nineteen years of age, respectively, were not pleased by his attitude. Their patience had been exhausted and their alternating comments were belligerent: "Why must these miserable guards always act this way? It would seem that they've never had to look for a job. Maybe this one thinks he's more important than the owner of the factory. What a bastard!" But their dialogue failed to elicit any response. Guards are accustomed to similar outbursts.

Teresa wanted to know whether I had any sewing experience. "Not much," I told her, "but I used to sew for a lady in my hometown." "Well, then you're very lucky," she said, "because they aren't hiring anyone without experience." The conversation having begun, I proceeded to ask a similar question, "How about you, have you worked before?"

Yes, both my sister and I used to work in a small shop on Altamirano Street in downtown Juárez. There were about seventy women like us sewing in a very tiny space, about twenty square meters. We sewed pants for the minimum wage, but we had no insurance.

The boss used to bring precut fabric from the United States for us to sew and then he sold the finished products in El Paso. When he was unable to get fabric we were laid-off; sent to rest without pay! Later on he wanted to hire us again but he still didn't want to insure us even though we had worked at the shop for three years.

When I was sixteen I used to cut thread at the shop. Afterwards one of the seamstresses taught me how to operate a small machine and I started doing serious work. Beatríz, my sister, used to sew the pockets on the pants. It's been three months since we left the shop. Right now we are living from the little that my father earns. We are two of nine brothers and sisters (there were twelve of us in total but three died when they were

119

young). My father does what he can but he doesn't have a steady job. Sometimes he does construction work; sometimes he's hired to help paint a house or sells toys at the stadium. You know, odd jobs. He doesn't earn enough to support us.

I am single, thanks be to God, and I do not want to get married. There are enough problems in my life as it is! But my sister married an engineer when she was only fifteen. Now she is unmarried and she has three children to support. They live with us too. Beatríz and I are the oldest in the family, you see, that's why we really have to find a job.

I also used to work as a maid in El Paso. I don't have a passport so I had to cross illegally as a wetback, a little wetback who cleaned houses. The money wasn't bad. I used to earn up to thirty-five dollars a week but I hated being locked up all day. So I came back and here I am.

At that point Beatríz intervened. I asked whether her husband helped support the children. Her answer was unwavering: "No, and I don't want him to give me anything, not a cent, because I don't want him to have any claim or rights over my babies. As long as I can support them, he won't have to interfere." I replied, "But aren't there better jobs outside of maquiladoras? I understand you can make more money working at a *cantina*. Is that true?"

Both of them looked at me suspiciously. Cantinas are an ever present reminder of overt or concealed prostitution. Teresa said,

That is probably true, but what would our parents think? You can't stop people from gossiping, and many of those cantinas are whorehouses. Of course, when you have great need you can't be choosey, right? For some time I worked as a waitress but that didn't last. The supervisor was always chasing me. First he wanted to see me after work. I told him I had a boyfriend, but he insisted. He said I was too young to have a steady boyfriend. Then, when he learned I had some typing skills, he wanted me to be his secretary. I'm not stupid! I knew what he really wanted; he was always staring at my legs. So I had to leave that job too. I told him I had been rehired at the shop although it wasn't true. He wasn't bad looking, but he was married and had children. . . . Why must men fool around?

At last the guard announced that only those with previous experience would be allowed to fill out applications. Twenty women went

120

into the narrow lobby of Camisas de Juárez, while the rest left in small quiet groups. For those of us who stayed a second waiting period began. One by one we were shown into the office of the personnel manager where we were to take a manual dexterity test. The point was to fit fifty variously colored pegs into fifty similarly colored perforations on a wooden board. This had to be accomplished in the shortest possible time. Clock in hand, the personnel manager told each woman when to begin and when to stop. Some were asked to adjust the pegs by hand, others were given small pliers to do so. Most were unable to complete the test in the allotted time. One by one they came out of the office looking weary and expressing their conviction that they wouldn't be hired.

Later on we were given the familiar application form. Again, I had to ponder what my greatest aspiration in life was. But this time I was curious to know what Xochitl had answered. "Well," she said, "I don't know if my answer is right. Maybe it is wrong. But I tried to be truthful. My greatest aspiration in life is to improve myself and to progress."

I was to remember Xochitl's words months later during a conversation with a representative of the El Paso Chamber of Commerce. I had been invited by this gentleman to see an audiovisual presentation, whose purpose was to promote the twin-plant program among potential investors. The narration as well as the sequence of colorful slides portrayed the benefits accruing to Mexican workers from foreign investment. Smiling women in neat uniforms stood beside conveyer belts while a recording extolled the merits of Mexican border industrialization. It appeared to me that some of the information used for that purpose was either innacurate or out of context. Certainly none of the daily squalor, deprivation and exhaustion that characterize the life of many maquiladora workers were present.

At the end of the presentation Mr. M asked for my opinion. I willingly admitted that this would be an effective promotional device. Then he asked for an altogether different evaluation. "Tell me," he said, "with a basis on your study, what is it that these women really want? What makes them tick? Do they really want to move ahead? Do they have aspirations? The words of hundreds of women like Xochitl who I had known while doing research came to mind. "Yes," I replied, "they have goals similar to yours or mine, but they don't have as good a wage."

After completing the application at Camisas de Juárez there was still another test to take. This one consisted of demonstrating sewing skills on an industrial machine. Again many women expressed doubts and concern after returning to the lobby where other expectant women awaited their turn. In the hours that had been spent together a lively dialogue had ensued. Evidently there was a sense that all of us were united by the common experience of job seeking and by the gnawing anxiety that potential failure entails. Women compared notes and exchanged opinions about the nature and difficulty of their respective tests. They did not offer each other overt reassurance or support, but they made sympathetic comments and hoped that there would be work for all.

At 3:30 P.M., that is, seven hours after the majority of us had arrived at the plant, we were dismissed. We were given no indication that any of us would be hired. Rather we were told that a telegram would be sent to each address as soon as a decision was made. Most women left disappointed and certain that they would probably not be hired.

Two weeks later, when I had almost given up all hope, the telegram arrived. I was to come to the plant as soon as possible to receive further instructions. Upon my arrival I was given the address of a small clinic in downtown Ciudad Juárez. I was to bring two pictures to the clinic and take a medical examination. Its explicit purpose was to evaluate the physical fitness of potential workers. In reality it was a simple pregnancy test. Maquiladoras do not hire pregnant women, although very often these are among the ones with greater need for employment.

Especially during the first years of its existence, the maquiladora program confronted some difficulties in this respect. Many pregnant women sought employment at the plants knowing that once there they would be entitled to an eighty-two-day pregnancy leave with full pay. Not seldom women would circumvent plant restrictions by bringing to the clinics urine specimens of friends or relatives. As a result, potential workers are now subjected to more careful examinations. Although extreme caution is exerted, managers complain that even at present, undetected pregnant women sometimes get hired. The largest and more stable plants are generally compliant with the law. But in small subcontracted firms where working conditions are bad and employment more or less temporary, women are often fired as soon as managers discover they are pregnant.

Having been examined at the clinic, I returned to the factory with a sealed envelope containing certification of my physical capacity to work. I was then told to return the following Monday at 3:30 P.M. in order to start work. After what seemed an unduly long and complicated procedure, I was finally being hired as an assembly worker. For the next six weeks I shared the experience of approximately eighty women who had also been recruited to work the evening shift at Camisas de Juárez. Xochitl, Beatríz and Teresa had been hired too.

On weekdays work started at 3:45 P.M. and it ended at 11:30 P.M. At 7:30 P.M. a bell signaled the beginning of a half-hour break during which workers could eat their dinner. Some brought homemade sandwiches, but many bought their food at the factory. Meals generally consisted of a dish of *flautas* or *tostadas* and carbonated drinks. The persistence of inadequate diets cause assembly workers numerous gastric problems. On Saturdays the shift started at 11:30 A.M. and it ended at 9:30 P.M. with a half-hour break. We worked in total forty-eight hours every week and earned the minimum wage, that is, 875 pesos per week; 125 pesos per day; an hourly rate of approximately $0.60.

According to the statutes of the Mexican labor law, maquiladoras are expected to pay their laborers the federally sanctioned minimum wage. With the exception of Zone 1 where the state of Baja California is located, Zone 09 to which Juárez belongs offers the highest minimum wages in the country. Many migrants flood the city for this reason, but as may be seen workers' earnings are very small by comparison to those of U.S. laborers performing similar kinds of operations. However, maquiladoras are also compelled by the Mexican government to affiliate their workers to the National Security System (Instituto Mexicano del Seguro Social), and to the National Housing Program (Instituto de Fomento Nacional a la Vivienda). As a result, investment per work-hour reached $1.22 in 1978. Although this is a small sum, it is comparatively high when seen in an international context.

From the perspective of workers, medical insurance is as important as a decorous wage. This is particularly true in the case of women who have children in their care. Thus, it was not surprising to find out that some new workers at Camisas de Juárez were there mainly because of the *seguro*. Maria Luisa, a twenty-nine-year-old woman told me, "I don't have a lot of money, but neither do I have great need to work. My husband owns a small restaurant and we have a fairly good income. But I have four children and one of them is chronically sick. Without insurance medical fees will render us poor. That's the main reason why I am working."

As do the majority of garment maquiladoras, Camisas de Juárez operates by a combination of piecework and the minimum wage. Upon being hired by the plant every worker earns a fixed wage. However, all workers are expected to fulfill production quotas. On the first day at the job I was trained to perform a particular operation. My task was to sew narrow biases around the cuff-openings of men's shirts. As with other operations I had performed before, this one entailed coordination and speed.

On my left side were placed the batches of precut sleeves. On my right were the minute pieces of colorful bias. With one hand I was to select a sleeve and place it underneath the needle. With the other I had to insert the bias along a special apparatus attached in close proximity to the sewing needle. Once the two parts had been matched, pressure had to be applied on the pedal for just long enough as to bring the bias to the end of the sleeve opening. Afterwards, the needle had to be lifted and the sleeve had to be rotated in order to position the bias along the other side of the opening. Then pressure was applied on the machine's pedal again in order to complete the operation.

As for the production quota, I was expected to complete 162 pairs of sleeves every hour, that is, one every 2.7 seconds, more than 1,200 pairs per shift. It seemed to me that to achieve such a goal would require unworldy skill and velocity. In six weeks as a direct production operator I was to fall short of this goal by almost 50%. But I was a very inexperienced worker. Sandra, who sat next to me during this period, assured me that it could be done. It wasn't easy, but certainly it could be done.

Sandra had worked at various maquiladoras for the last seven years. Every time she got too tired, she left the job, rested for a while and then sought another job. She was now twenty-five, the divorced mother of two children. The children were under the custody of their father who worked at a boat manufacturing factory in Azcárate. Sandra had left them when she left her husband. They didn't get along. He wanted her to stay at home all the time although she tried to explain to him that with the two of them working there would be more money and they could live better. But he didn't understand. One night he dared beat her and she had to leave. She was hopeful that as soon as she had enough money, the children would come to live with her. Now she was living with her parents and trying to have a good time.

She was a very speedy seamstress and she acted with the self-assurance of one who is well acquainted with the particulars of factory work. She was also hard to impress. During the first days of our acquaintance she responded to my friendly approaches with nothing else but monosyllabic utterances. At the same time she deliberately showed us her considerable sewing ability. It was difficult not to admire her skill and aloofness, especially when I was being continuously vexed by my own incompetence.

But one evening all resistance was broken. She thought my complaints and mode of speech were funny, and we proceeded to have a lively conversation at the end of which she admitted liking me. I was flattered. Then she stared at my old jeans and ripped blouse with an appraising look and said, "Listen, Patricia, as soon as we get our wage, I want to take you to buy some decent clothes. You look awful! And you also need a haircut." So much for the arrogance of the researcher who wondered whether her class background would be detected!

Sandra became my most important link with the experience of maquiladora work for the next few weeks. During that time I had a chance to visit her parents' house where she lived and where she expected to bring her children as soon as possible. The house was situated in *las lomas* in the outskirts of the city. The area was rugged and distant, but the house itself conveyed an aura of modest prosperity. There were four ample rooms, one of which was carpeted. All essential and some unessential gadgets were present. There were two sinks in the kitchen as well as a refrigerator, a blender, a beater and a brand new washing machine "made in the U.S.," which was not in use due to the lack of running water in the area. The family believed that this service would soon be available. Then they would be able to use the washing machine. Besides the numerous family pictures which decorated its walls, the living room was further embellished by an American-made television and a comfortable set of chairs.

Sandra's father was a butcher who had retained his job at a popular market for many years. Although in the past when his three daughters were small, it had been difficult to stay out of debt, better times were at hand. He only had two regrets: a failing health and Sandra's divorce. He felt both matters were beyond his control. And Sandra was indeed a good daughter. She never failed to contribute to the expenses of the household and she was also saving to be able to support her own children.

The conversations with Sandra and occasional visits to her house alternated with my efforts to become an efficient worker. Only by taking work at the factory seriously would it be possible to glimpse, at least superficially, into the experience of thousands of factory women laboring in Ciudad Juárez. The nature of research demanded total identification with the role of the direct production worker. But there was more to it than that.

The factory environment was all-embracing, its demands over-whelmed me. Young supervisors walked about the aisles asking for higher productivity and encouraging us to work at greater speed. Periodically their voices could be heard throughout the work place: "Faster! faster! Come on girls, let us hear the sound of those machines!" They were personally responsible before management for the efficiency of the workers under their command.

Esther, who oversaw my labor, had been a nurse prior to her employment in the factory. I was intrigued by her polite manner and her change of jobs. She dressed prettily, seeming a bit out of place amidst the heated humdrum of the sewing machines, the lint and the dispersed fabric that cluttered the plant. She told me it was more profitable to work at a maquiladora than at a clinic or a hospital.

Esther saw her true vocation as that of a nurse, but she had to support an ill and aging father. Her mother had died three years earlier, and although her home was nice and fully owned, she was solely responsible for the family debts. Working at a factory entailed less prestige than working as a nurse, but it offered a better wage. She was now earning almost one thousand pesos a week. As a nurse she had earned only a bit more than half that amount. From her I also learned, for the first time, about the dubious advantages of being a maquiladora supervisor.

As with the others in similar positions, Esther had to stay at the plant long after the shift ended and the workers left. Very often the hours ran until one in the morning. During that time she verified quotas, sorted out production, tried to detect errors and, not seldom, personally unseamed defective garments. With the others she was also responsible for the preparation of shipments and the selection of material for the following day's production. In other words, her supervisory capacities included quality control and some adminis-trative functions.

When productivity levels are not met, when workers fail to arrive punctually or are absent, or when there is trouble in the line, it is the supervisor who is first admonished by management. Thus, supervisors occupy an intermediary position between the firm and the workers, which is to say that they often find themselves be-tween the devil and the deep blue sea.

As with the factory guard, supervisors and group leaders are frequently seen by workers as solely responsible for their plight at the work place. Perceived abuses, unfair treatment and excessive demands are thought to be the result of supervisors' whims rather than the creature of a particular system of production. That explains, in part, why workers' grievances are often couched in complaints about the performance of supervisors.

But while supervisors may be seen by workers as close allies of the firms, they stand at the bottom of the administrative hierarchy. They are also the receivers of middle and upper management's dissatisfaction, but they have considerably less power and their sphere of action is very limited. Many line supervisors agree that the complications they face in their jobs are hardly worth differences in pay. At RCA a young woman told me that "since I was promoted to a supervisory capacity I feel that my workmates hate me. We used to get along fine. I would even go so far as to say that we shared in a genuine sense of camaraderie. Now, they resent having to take orders from me, a former assembly worker like themselves. They talk behind my back and ask each other why it was I and not one of them who was promoted."

For some months this woman labored under considerable stress. Her problems were compounded when she had to decide who among her subordinates would have to be laid off as a result of plant adjustments. Caught between the exigencies of management and the resentful attempts of workers to manipulate her, she came close to a nervous breakdown. A short time afterwards she asked to be transferred to her old job. From her point of view, it was more convenient to sacrifice pay and be equal to the rest of the workers along the assembly line than to be, in her own words, "a sandwich person."

The Organization of Labor in the Factory

The pressures exerted by supervisors at Camisas de Juárez were hard to ignore. Esther was considerate and encouraging: "You're doing much better now. Soon enough you'll be sewing as fast as the others." But I had doubts, as she was constantly asking me to repair my own defective work, a task which entailed an infinite sense of frustration. I began to skip dinner breaks in order to continue sewing in a feeble attempt to improve my productivity level. I was not alone. Some workers fearful of permanent dismissal also stayed at their sewing machines during the break while the rest went outside to eat and rest. I could understand their behavior; their jobs were at stake. But presumably my situation was different. I had nothing to lose by inefficiency, and yet I felt compelled to do my best. I started pondering upon the subtle mechanisms that dominate will at the workplace and about the shame that overwhelms those who fall short of the goals assigned to them.

The fact is that as the days passed it became increasingly difficult to think of factory work as a stage in a research project. My identity became that of the worker; my immediate objectives those determined by the organization of labor at the plant. Academic research became an ethereal fiction. Reality was work, as much for me as for the others who labored under the same roof.

These feelings were reinforced by my personal interactions during working hours. I was one link in a rigidly structured chain. My failure to produce speedily had numerous consequences for others operating in the same line and in the factory as a whole. For example, Lucha, my nineteen-year-old companion, was in charge of cutting remnant thread and separating the sleeves five other seamstresses and I sewed. She also made it her business to return to me all those parts which she felt would not meet Esther's approval. According to her she did this in order to spare me further embarrassment. But it was in her interest that I sewed quickly and well; the catch in this matter was that she was unable to meet her quota unless the six seamstresses she assisted met theirs.

Therefore, a careless and slow worker could stand between Lucha and her possibility to get a weekly bonus. The more a seamstress sewed, the more a thread cutter became indispensable. As a consequence, Lucha was extremely interested in seeing improvements in my level of productivity and in the quality of my work. Sometimes her attitude and exhortations verged on the hostile. As far as I was concerned, the accusatory expression on her face was the best work incentive yet devised by the factory. It was not difficult to discern impinging tension. I was not surprised to find out during the weeks spent at Camisas de Juárez that the germ of enmity had bloomed between some seamstresses and their respective thread cutters over matters of work.

Although the relationship between seamstresses and thread cutters were especially delicate, all workers were affected by each other's level of efficiency. Cuffless sleeves could not be attached to shirts. Sleeves could not be sewed to shirts without collars or pockets. Holes and buttons had to be fixed at the end. Unfinished garments could not be cleaned of lint or labeled. In sum, each minute step required a series of preceding operations effectively completed. Delay of one stage inevitably slowed up the whole process.

From the perspective of the workers, labor appeared as the interconnection of efficiently performed individual activities rather than as a structured imposition from above. Managers are nearly invisible, but the flaws of fellow workers are always apparent. Bonuses exist as seemingly impersonal rewards whose access can be made difficult by a neighbor's laziness or incompetence. As a result, complaints are frequently directed against other workers and supervisors. The organization of labor at any particular plant does not immediately lead to feelings of solidarity.

On the other hand, common experiences at the workplace provide the basis for dialogue and elicit a particular kind of humor. In this there is frequently expressed a longing for relief from the tediousness of industrial work. One of Sandra's favorite topics of conversation was to reflect upon the possibility of marriage. She did so with a witty and self-deprecatory attitude.

She thought that if she could only find a nice man who would be willing to support her, everything in her life would be all right. She didn't mind if he was not young or good-looking, as long as he had plenty of money. Were there men like that left in the world? Of course, with the children it was difficult, not to say impossible, to find such a godsend. Then again, no one kept you from trying. But not at the maquiladora. All of us were female. Not even a lonely engineer was to be found at Camisas de Juárez. One could die of boredom there.

However, the fact that there weren't men around at the plant had its advantages according to Sandra. At many factories men generally occupied supervisory and middle- and upper-management positions. Sandra knew many women who had been seduced and then deserted by engineers and technicians. In other cases women felt they had to comply with the sexual demands of fellow workers because they believed otherwise they would lose their jobs. Some were just plain stupid. Things were especially difficult for very young women at large plants like RCA. They needed guidance and information to stay out of trouble, but there was no one to advise them. Their families had too many problems to care.

Common knowledge had it that during the first years of the maquiladora program irregular situations had arisen. There were ingenieros who insisted on having only the prettiest workers under their command. A sort of factory harem mentality had been at work. If you were not attractive, you didn't get hired. She had known a man ("Would you believe this?") who wanted as much female diversity as possible. He had a crew formed of women all of whom had—upon his own request—eyes and hair of a different color.

Another one took pride in boasting that every woman in his line had borne him a child.

There had been several scandals, widely covered by the city tabloids, about the spread of venereal disease in certain maquiladoras. There were too many single mothers working already at the plants. And even if these were exaggerated accounts, it was clear that men working at the factories entailed covert and overt dangers. Sandra knew how to take care of herself, but she still thought it was better to have only female fellow workers. The factory was not a good place to meet men.

Fortunately, there were the bars and the discotheques. Did I like to go out dancing? She didn't think so; I didn't look like the kind who would. But it was great fun; we should go out together sometime (eventually we did). The Malibú, a popular dancing hall, had good shows. But it was tacky and full of kids. It was better to go to the Max Fim, and especially the Cosmos. The latter was always crowded because everyone liked it so much. Even people from the other side (the United States) came to Juárez just to visit Cosmos. Its décor was inspired by outerspace movies like Star Wars. It was full of color and movement and shifting lights. They played the best American disco music. If you were lucky you could meet a U.S. citizen. Maybe he would even want to get married and you could go and live in El Paso. Things like that happen at discotheques. Once a Jordanian soldier in service at Fort Bliss had asked her to marry him the first time they met at Cosmos. But he wanted to return to his country, and she had said no. Cosmos was definitely the best discotheque in Juárez, and Sandra could be found dancing there amidst the deafening sound of music every Saturday evening.

The inexhaustible level of energy of women working at the maquiladoras never ceased to impress me. How could anyone be in the mood for all-night dancing on Saturdays after forty-eight weekly hours of industrial work? I had seen many of these women stretching their muscles late at night, trying to soothe the pain they felt at the waist. After the incessant noise of the sewing machines, how could anyone long for even higher levels of sound? But as Sandra explained to me, life is too short. If you don't go out and have fun you will come to the end of your days having done nothing but sleep, eat and work. And she didn't call that living. Besides, where else would you be able to meet a man?

Ah, men! They were often unreliable, mean or just plain lazy (wasn't that obvious from the enormous number of women who had to do factory work in Ciudad Juárez?) but no one wanted to live alone. There must be someone out there worth living for; at least someone who didn't try to put you down or slap you. Sandra couldn't understand why life had become so difficult. Her mother and father had stayed married for thirty years and they still liked each other. There had been some difficult times in the past, but they had always had each other. She knew a lot of older folks who were in the same situation. But it was different for modern couples.

Not all maquiladoras in the Parque Industrial Bermúdez worked the evening shift. After 8 P.M. ruteras and buses did not go into the area seeking clients. By 11:30, when the bell signaled the end of the shift at Camisas de Juárez, the park was entirely deserted and dark. In a state of euphoria women prepared to go home. At 11:15 workers had to interrupt their operations and swiftly clean up their working area. Each worker was held responsible for two spools and a pair of scissors. These had to be removed from the plant every night lest they be stolen by workers the following morning.

As soon as the bell rang we would begin a disorderly race to be first to check our time cards. Then we would stand in line with our purses wide open in order that the guard could check our belongings. Management feared that workers would try to steal material or the finished products. Women resented this nightly examination with vehemence. From their point of view it was an unnecessary form of humiliation. It was like being treated as potential thieves until proven innocent by the guard's inspection.

Once outside of the factory women walked towards the entrance of the park which led to the main avenue where public transportation could be reached. They laughed and screamed teasing one another and often exchanging vulgarities. On most occasions we would board an almost empty bus as soon as we reached the main avenue. Sometimes the wait was longer and we became impatient. In jest women pushed one another to the forefront suggesting provocative poses so as to attract a passerby from whom, presumably, a ride could be obtained. However, when a car stopped, women moved away in haste. They joked a lot, but to accept a ride from a man, especially late at night, was to look for trouble. As far as they were concerned only whores did that.

Individually these women bore an aura of vulnerability, even shyness. As a group they could be a formidable sight. One time an unlucky male happened to board the bus when we were already in it. His presence exacerbated the level of euphoria. He was immediately subjected to verbal attacks similar to those women sometimes experience from men. They chided and they teased him, feeling protected by anonymity and by their numercial strength. They offered kisses and asked for a smile. They exchanged laughing comments about his physical attributes and suggested a raffle to see who would keep him. To all this the man responded with silence. Curiously, he adopted the outraged and embarrassed expression that women often wear when they feel victimized by men. When he left the bus, he did so followed by the stares of whistling women.

Although this was the only time I had an opportunity to witness such a phenomenon, I was often told that this sort of behavior was not uncommon among factory workers. "It is pitiful," an acquaintance told me, "those girls have no idea of what proper feminine behavior is." This person assured me that he had seen cases where women had gone so far as to paw or pinch men while traveling in buses and ruteras. According to him, factory work was to blame: "Since women started working at the maquiladoras they have lost all sense of decorum." But from what I was able to observe these were hardly the expessions of moral turpitude. Rather they were harmless games fostered by the temporary sense of membership in a group. As Sandra liked to remind me, "Factory work is harder than most people know. As long as you don't harm anybody, what's wrong with having a little fun?"

CHAPTER 7

Maquiladoras and Cultural Change in Ciudad Juárez

Factory Work, Sex Roles, Consumption and Leisure

If one lends credence to a common opinion voiced by the media in Ciudad Juárez, the maquiladora program has effected a kind of "emancipation" by affording women the opportunity to earn their own income. Much is made of the fact that women can now spend money on clothes, cosmetics, jewelry and entertainment. The proliferation of clothing stores, discotheques and bars favored by maquila workers seems to support this observation. The frequency of newspaper advertisements encouraging them to purchase a diversity of services and commodities in modern shopping malls financed as part of the National Border Program (PRONAF), further confirms this belief.

It is only necessary to walk along the crowded streets of downtown Juárez to notice the extent to which offshore production has transformed the commercial texture of the city. Many stores announce in earnest and graphic terms their willingness to cash maquiladora checks and to extend to their possessors the benefits of credit and lay-away plans. The preference of factory workers for Avon cosmetics and Stanley costume jewelry has acquired legendary reputation in this environment.

Especially on paydays, petty merchants and taxicabs flow to the factories hoping to get their share of the presumed affluence enjoyed by maquiladora workers. A common scene at such times is formed by the numerous men who wait outside the plants for workers to exit. Some of these men are relatives waiting to escort women to their homes and thus decrease the likelihood of assult or theft. But many others are opportunists hoping to obtain invitations to bars or dancing halls. They are adept in the arts of seduction.

Because in many cases daughters and wives earn more than fathers or spouses, some believe that a peculiar role reversal which undermines traditional patterns of male authority in the family is already in existence. It is assumed that as women spend more hours in the factory, men are forced to take more responsibility for domestic chores (especially when they are unemployed or underemployed) with deleterious effects upon their sense of manhood. Donald Baerresen (1971) points out, for example, that "some families are suported almost entirely by the income of . . . a daughter. Certainly male egos of fathers and would-be boyfriends must suffer some deflation from this dramatic change in the economic influence of these young women."

The flippancy with which Baerrensen subsumes a complex problem into the sentence cited above is not untypical of the way in which the impact of women's employment upon family and male-female relationships has been viewed. Two opposed but interrelated perspectives have gained prevalence in this regard. On the one hand, there are those who praise female industrial employment as an instrument which strengthens women's autonomy and bargaining power both in the household and in the marketplace.

As in earlier times, industrialization is equated with modernization, and the participation of women in the work force is seen as a positive force facilitating the elimination of residual or archaic cultural patterns. Many promoters of the maquiladora program adhere to this view. Thus, they see multinational corporations, whose entrance into Mexico they have aided, as harbingers of progress in a context whose obsolete cultural practices they see with a measure of contempt. As a prominent maquiladora manager explained to me, "The first industrial revolution took place in England during the nineteenth century and it changed the world. We have brought the second industrial revolution to the Mexican-American border. We are again transforming the world by bringing progress to all people, but especially to women."

Interestingly enough those who share this perspective also commend the virtues of maquiladoras as instillers of discipline, punctuality and efficiency among the members of a formerly disorganized and apathetic working class. In particular they point to the fact that women have profited from the existence of a constructive employment option where formerly they could only choose among petty clerical work, domestic unemployment or prostitution. As one government official expressing a commonly held impression told this author during an interview: "Since there are maquiladoras in Ciudad Juárez, there are fewer prostitutes."

On the other hand there are those who see the influence of maquiladoras upon family life and composition from a critical point of view. They deplore the negative effects that women's work outside the home may have upon the welfare of children. They believe that as women gain economic power, the integrity of the family is threatened. Daughters are prone to challenge the authority of parents. Wives may refuse to comply with the demands of their husbands and disrespect for traditional values may become a daily occurrence.

A major preoccupation stems from what is interpreted as growing promiscuity and moral looseness among maquiladoras workers. Many see evidence of this in the large numbers of single mothers, and what is said to be an increase of illegitimate births among women working at offshore production plants. Stories about indiscriminate sex, venereal disease and forced abortions among maquiladora workers are periodically reported by the city's tabloids. Occasionally scandal is caused by the discovery of a fetus in the rest rooms of a plant.

Those who see these occurrences as symptoms of moral decadence also tend to view factory work as a cause—not a palliative—of prostitution. A well-known doctor at the service of one of the largest plants in Ciudad Juárez, expressed the following view: "The problem is that because these little women lack information and experience they are easily misguided. Their recently acquired affluence makes them prey of all sorts of irresponsible opportunists. Others deliberately look for a good time without considering the consequences. They need guidance to preserve their moral integrity."

Albeit in a different way, the concern over moral behavior is shared by many maquiladora workers. A young woman working at an electronics plant told me, "I constantly worry about this because many people, especially men, treat you differently as soon as they know you have a job at a maquiladora. They surely think that if you have to work for money, there is also a good chance you're a whore. But I assure you that my friends and I are decent women." As may be seen, a facile one-to-one casual relationship between factory work and prostitution is often drawn. However the relationship is complex and difficult to evaluate.

Public relations managers and maquiladora promoters have countered accusations based on the preceding frame of reference by pointing to specific policies which have been implemented by maquiladoras to reaffirm the value of femininity and a stable family life. Some firms offer courses on human sexuality, birth control and home economics to their workers. Incentives are given, such as annual beauty contests in which workers are encouraged to participate. In many plants, operators receive red carnations as tokens on Saint Valentine's Day. It is the conviction of many managers that women's work does not have to result in a debilitation of the positive aspects of tradition. Rather, through their employment, women can contribute to improve the material, educational and spiritual welfare of their families.

Indeed, a permanent concern over the integrity of the family and the moral improvement of workers pervades many plants' propaganda and labor relations strategies. Weekly newsletters distributed among employees include constant reminders of the individual and collective benefits that accrue to those who value family life. Much effort is directed towards the promotion of sports activities and competition. A prominent spokesman of the Asociación de maquiladoras in Ciudad Juárez explained that "most of our newspaper clipping collection contains reports about athletic competitions among maquiladora teams. We are proud to promote these activities. It's a simple question of good public relations. Sports keep our workers happy and they provide an effective way to bring families together."

Impressionistic judgments and the lack of empirical information have combined to generate a particular mystique around maquiladora work to the point where women have become the object of a nascent folklore. What distinguishes these perceptions is their profound ambivalence towards female employment and its consequences.

This is particularly evident in the way connections are made between factory work and prostitution. In this sense these ideas reveal the concerns of the local middle class and not necessarily the reality lived by maquiladora workers. They form the ideological framework within which conflicts, fears and resolutions are articulated and made explicit despite the underlying confusion.

To move beyond these ideological constraints it is indispensable to differentiate between myth and the objective material circumstances that surround offshore production in Ciudad Juárez. It has been one of the purposes of this essay to demonstrate that the employment of women in multinational assembly plants does not inevitably lead to gains in autonomy on the part of women. Rather,

136

the employment of daughters, wives and mothers in maquiladoras frequently stems from the vulnerable position that they and their families have in an enfeebled labor market.

With rare exceptions fathers are the holders of authority. They are responsible for the most important decisions affecting family life and for discipline imposed on wives and children. Mothers, on the other hand, are the principal administrators of the home. Thus, they are the direct recipients of a large portion of their daughters' earnings. The case of the young woman who promptly transfers all of her weekly wage to her mother—who, in turn gives her a small allowance for essentials—is not uncommon among maquila workers.

As shown in preceding sections of this work, forms of employment have an impact upon the organization of families and households. However, maquiladora workers' families, in general, conform to the model outlined before. Indeed, in a very small number of cases, other housing arrangements are found. Young women may live with other single friends or acquaintances with whom they may share expenses. Whether these households have resulted from a fragmentation of intact domestic units due to tensions caused by women's employment or whether they signal a trend is not evident at this time. What is clear is that they are exceptional.

Neither has women's employment diminished their responsibility for domestic chores. Quite the contrary. Of all married women interviewed by this author as part of a sample of maquiladora workers, only one lived in a home where her husband had taken full charge of housework and children while she acted as the sole provider. None of the single women interviewed reported having fathers, brothers or other male relatives who share domestic work to any significant extent; in the majority of cases women perform double work loads.

This is important because domestic labor in houses where maquiladora workers live is, in the majority of cases, not aided by sophisticated mechanical gadgets. Less than half of the women interviewed had washing machines. The vast majority of the remaining group reported using washing boards regularly. Only a few make use of the few public laundromats that exist in Ciudad Juárez.

While some working women (16% of my sample) hire the help of relatives or acquaintances, the majority have sole responsibility for central duties. It was found, for example, that mothers with young children who are also maquiladora operators have working days that extend over an average of fifteen hours daily.

Single women with or without children who live with parents and siblings enjoy a more relaxed situation. Although most of them are responsible for at least some household chores, the burden is shared among all females living under the same roof. According to single women interviewed, the time they allocate to housework averages 1.5 hours daily.

With more time on their hands and at least some increased affluence derived from the wages earned at maquiladoras, women have become the target of market propaganda, and it appears from the available evidence that they are indeed developing distinctive patterns for consumption. In particular, products having to do with personal embellishment and entertainment are popular among maquiladora workers. On the average, women reported spending 75 pesos a month on clothes and entertainment (or entertainment related purchases) every week. This figure, however, varies significantly in accordance with marital status and number of children among married women, and with family size and composition for single women.

An extremely high number of maquiladora workers interviewed (82) reported having recently purchased a combination of stereo record player and radio (consola). Of 510 cases studied, only 90 lived in houses where there weren't televisions present. Although these objects may appear out of context in homes such as the ones described in other sections of this work, they are an important feature in the lives of maquiladora workers. Their houses may be small and fragile, they may lack some indispensable public services like plumbing and running water, but seldom are TV's and stereo systems not found (as status symbols) in them.

Besides the consumption of certain popular products, certain sectors of the entertainment business have flourished in Ciudad Juárez in recent years, thanks in part to the patronage of maquiladora workers. In particular, discotheques, dancing halls, restaurants and various kinds of bars are favored by women who often arrive in them unescorted.

Gathering for conversation on Friday evenings at the *cervecería* Cruz Blanca (a local beer manufacturer in Ciudad Juárez) is a popular form of entertainment among factory workers. At those times, male presence is uncommon, some say for fear of ridicule inflicted by groups of women who monopolize the area.

What impresses the observer attending these gatherings is an animated sense of conviviality. Women laugh, joke and talk loudly while they drink frequently until the late hours of night. "I really like it here," a woman told me. "although my husband doesn't know that I come every Friday. I always tell him I've been visiting friends, otherwise he would beat me up for sure. Factory work is hard and tedious. You know there is no future there, but in the cervecería you can forget your troubles and enjoy yourself with other women who are just like yourself."

While meeting at the cervecería has a familiar local flavor to it, discotheques eptiomize the degree to which cultural penetration from the United States has been achieved at the border. Their extravagent décor, blinking lights and high levels of sound create a dream-like atmosphere; a space and time greatly detached from the ordeal of daily living. Most of the music heard in Ciudad Juárez discotheques is foreign. Dancing styles and style of dress are similar to those found in any metropolitan spot in the U.S. or Europe. To many, discotheques and the possibility to enjoy them are certain symbols of modernity. In effect they are a symptom of transculturation, that is, the transposition of cultural patterns to suit the adaptive needs of local communities and individuals.

But, as with everything else, women working at maquiladoras have established preferences and hierarchies among various discotheques and dancing halls. As Sandra, my work fellow at Camisas de Juárez told me once, "You have to learn what the best places are. When I was younger, the Malibú was all right. They have good shows once in a while but it's sort of sleazy. It has no class. The Max Fim and expecially Cosmos are the best. Now, if you really have money and an international crossing card the place to go is Smuggler's in El Paso."

Because of a number of reasons having to do primarily with employment opportunities, there is some disproportion between the size of the male and the female population in Ciudad Juárez, the latter being larger than the former. This allied with the increased consumptive power of some maquiladora workers when compared to that of their male counterparts has resulted in a peculiar phenomenon. By and large those who attend discotheques are young women rather than men. They arrive in small groups and sit patiently waiting for an invitation to dance. Occasionally, women friends dance with one another although this is still the exception rather than the norm.

From all my conversations with maquiladora workers it is difficult to reach the conclusion that significant changes have occurred in sex roles. While the material realities in men's and women's lives have been modified by the advent of border industrialization, expectations and norms remain untouched. As a result certain tensions, already discernible, may accentuate over time.

Adela, an unmarried twenty-three-year-old woman is torn by some of these conflicts. She started work at seventeen as the second born in a family of five.

My parents have always been very strict especially my father. For four years I didn't spend a single penny of my own earnings. My mother took my whole wage. I had to beg every time I needed a new dress. It was pitiful. And they still accused me of wanting to have money to be free and loose. Two years ago I started keeping part of my wage for personal expenses. I wanted to be able to do the sorts of things that my friends do, but I was still helping my family. In a fit of rage, my father demanded that I get out of his house. I was tempted to follow his orders just to teach him a lesson. I didn't leave because I don't have anywhere to go and marriage is certainly not the answer. What is the use of spending your whole life being a housewife like my mother and not even getting credit for it? I am getting old and what I want is to live my own life, have my own hard-earned money. But people think you are a bad woman if you admit to having these ideals.

More difficult to evaluate is the connection that some see between a change in sexual mores and maquiladora work. Extensive interviews with maquiladora workers conducted by this author indicate that their perceptions, attitudes and aspirations in this area conform to traditional feminine definitions. Women often see their working status as temporary. They eagerly anticipate the prospect of marriage and motherhood linked to their retirement from the work force. More importantly, they share a conventional differentiation between "decent" and "indecent" female behavior. To be confused for a prostitute is cause of grave preoccupation.

However, "decency" defined in conventional terms may be a difficult asset to preserve. Subtle and overt forms of seduction sometimes interfere with the work routine. Although its extent is difficult to judge, sexual harassment on the job is not uncommon. In many cases women complain that middle management and supervisory personnel members are inclined to ask for sexual favors in exchange for job stability.

In other instances, women themselves see their sexuality as the only viable means to gain access to employment. Therefore, they "offer" themselves to men in decision-making positions. Mr. Ruíz, a maquiladora manager, has received some of these offers. "One morning when I arrived for work, there was a very young woman waiting at the entrance. She told me she had applied for a job at the plant and wanted to be sure to get it. 'Just tell me when and where you want me to meet you for a good time and I'll come.' Then she added that she wouldn't be offering me sex if it weren't because she was desperate to get a job. I explained to her that things didn't happen like that in our plant, but I still saw to it that she got the job. I shudder to think what would have happened if it had been someone else and not me who got the offer."

In general, women are particularly vulnerable to advances made by men who have a superior status in the professional, economic and educational hierarchy. Some evidence indicates that loyalties won through romantic entanglement can be fruitfully used to insure efficiency and docility on the job.

Women often find themselves in situations where they have to resort to their sexuality to gain a sense of precarious power in the labor market—for example, to insure access to or stability of employment. Only in exceptional cases is this true for men. Thus, sexual behavior among maquiladora workers is frequently more than a moral issue. It is a vivid expression of the feeble political position that women have in society.

The question is not whether workers have attained increased control over their bodies and sexuality, thus challenging established norms and eroding the basis of female subordination. In an environment characterized by ignorance, fear and superstition on sexual matters, this is an unlikely prospect. Rather, the issue at stake here is the manner in which the particular position of women in the labor market in combination with conventional sexual mores is used to reinforce control over women.

It is in the nature of ideology to articulate conflict in manners that do not threaten the structural foundations of social organization. The phrasing of political and economic asymmetries in moral terms has two corollaries. On the one hand, fears about loss of control over a particular group are made explicit, albeit in a distorted manner. On the other hand, the members of the group in question are hard pressed to act aggressively when they too fear the possibility of their involvement in moral corruption.

In this case women's incorporation into the industrial work force has elicited concerns about the extent to which their direct access to wages might result in loss of control over them. At the same time accusations about improper moral behavior precipitate defensive responses from working women and prevent solidarity on the basis of class and gender.

The Question of Factory Work and Prostitution

These propositions acquire full meaning when the relationship between prostitution and factory work is examined. Mague's experience provides a suggestive illustration in this respect:

> I was seventeen when I got the job at the plant. It was not my first job, however. During the two previous years I had worked as a counter clerk at an ice cream parlor, but it was more a hobby than real work. I didn't make much money and had none of the benefits that go with factory employment.
>
> At the time I began work at the maquiladora I was living with an aunt, my mother's sister, because my parents were divorced and remarried when I was still a child. I didn't want to be a stepdaughter. I was afraid I would be mistreated. Work gave me a chance to stand on my own. It was good to earn money and be able to help my mother. But I had few responsibilities and could use most of my earnings to suit my needs. I felt lucky. Other women at the factory had a hard time making ends meet.
>
> One day the superintendent at the plant invited me to go out dancing. I was very flattered; it was like a dream come true. He was handsome and distinguished and took me to a fine place. We became very involved. But at eighteen, when I found out I was pregnant, he said he couldn't marry me. He had never told me before he had a wife and two children! It was a very scary situation, but I had to face it alone. My aunt couldn't be told; I didn't have the courage to make her suffer after all the kindness she had given me. So I left her house and rented a room by myself.
>
> The personnel manager wasn't happy to learn about my condition, but I didn't care. I had job tenure (contrato de planta). By law I was entitled to an eighty-two-day leave with full pay. After my baby was born I went back to work but I was soon laid off because I had anemia. This time I was only entitled to half-pay.
>
> Believe me, those were hard times with the baby and all. I

didn't have enough money to pay for food, the rent and milk for the child. So I found a way. I started inviting male friends to my house. Some were old acquaintances from my hometown. We had known each other when I was younger. I had sex with them and when they didn't understand my intentions, I explained my needs and those the baby. It didn't take them long to catch on, and they helped out.

I guess you could say I became a prostitute, but I didn't see myself as one. Most of the time I was too tired to care or too busy with the baby to think about it. In general, men were kind to me. I did what I had to do to survive. When I got well and the baby was older, I went back to work. All is fine now.

If I was the only woman who had restored to prostitution to support herself and her child, maybe I would feel bad about my past. But the truth is that many women at the factory do the same once in a while. Even some married women see one or two clients a week. People may say what they want, but for some women it's the only way to increase their earnings. I'm not saying everybody does it, but it is not as unusual as you might think.

As for me, I have no regrets. I would have preferred things to be different. I would have liked to get married and have a nice home of my own. But now that is unlikely. Who would want me with a child, and why would I ever impose a stepfather on my own son when I didn't want to have one myself. My fate is to live alone, so I take it easy, one day at a time.

Although Mague's story contains unique personal features, the sequence of events that led her to practice prostitution as a means of supplementing her earnings suggest the limits of public opinion on this issue. Rarely is prostitution a full-time occupation. Frequently it is an alternative chosen by women at times of personal economic crisis. More than a moral choice, it is often a condition imposed by the material circumstances that individuals confront.

Although no systematic research has been attempted on this subject, it is possible to assert that there is not a direct connection between factory work and the practice of prostitution. It would be possible to hypothesize that by providing women with employment alternatives, maquiladoras remove the need to sell sexual services. However, as may be seen from the previous accounts, factory work offers wages and benefits that keep women only a step removed from the circumstances that can lead to prostitution.

Moreover, some new situations related to factory employment expose women to special forms of pressure, which may, in turn, lead to covert forms of prostitution. The transformation of sexuality into a commodity is necessarily attached to power differentials among men and women. Prostitutes are, in the majority of cases, in a most vulnerable political and economic position with respect to their clients. Maquiladoras do not remove the conditions that make women vulnerable. Thus it should not be surprising to find that in some cases prostitution and factory employment are compatible.

Cases like the ones described above do not substantiate allegations in the sense that women's employment under the conditions described in this work leads to emancipation of any kind. Nor do they confirm simplistic judgments about moral decay.

Mague herself summed up the predicament that Ciudad Juárez's maquiladora workers confront on a daily basis: "No matter how you look at it, we are in a bind. Either as husbands, lovers or managers, men have power over us. They can't be trusted. But when you have to live you can't afford to be too fussy about these things. And you may even end up having some fun!"

Maquiladora Work and Unionization

Among the many factors that have led multinational corporations to set up operations along the Mexican-American border must be counted the tranquil political atmosphere that prevails in the area and the amiable disposition of workers' organizations in Mexico. Although recent years have seen the advent of attempts to consolidate an independent trade union movement in the country, it is still the case that the majority of official organizations function hand in hand with the interests of the most powerful sectors in the Mexican state.

The predominance of women among maquiladora workers along the Mexican-American border makes study of the impact of trade unionism in that sector a particularly difficult task. While the Mexican government has required firms to pay federally sanctioned minimum wages to maquiladora workers, it has not imposed unionization in any form. Whether to incorporate workers into official unions has been left as an option for maquiladoras. Thus, in Ciudad Juárez, less than one-third of assembly workers (approximately 24%) are unionized.

From testimonies gathered among factory managers, it is possible

144

to conclude that the decision in favor or against workers' unionization is determined by the needs and preferences of the firm rather than by the requirements of workers themselves. Although there are no rigid rules in this regard, certain criteria appear to be widespread.

On repeated occasions managers, industry spokespersons and official representatives explained to me that the number of workers employed by a given firm may be a decisive factor when deciding in favor or against unionization. The personnel manager of an electronics firm which hires approximately three hundred workers offered the following opinion: "We are like a big family here. Almost everyone knows everyone else; I personally know all my workers by name. There are no problems, we don't need a union. Unions have their own interests, and they are a source of conflict among workers and employers."

But maquiladoras which have a large work force (ranging between nine hundred and six thousand employees) have found that unionization may be an effective tool in labor-management interactions. For large firm representatives this is an administrative question rather than a concession to the demands of workers. The manager of a multimillion-dollar operation in Ciudad Juárez voiced a common opinion: "To us this is a matter of maintaining control over a huge mass of employees without any detriment of their rights. We have found that Mexican unions are very cooperative and understanding. Their leaders share our conviction that it is important to generate more maquiladora jobs. They don't want to kill the 'hen that lays the golden eggs' (which is in fact what the maquiladora industry is). Therefore they help us in the bargaining process between labor and management."

There are only a few studies which address the issues of female participation in maquiladora unions. One of these studies examined trade union activities in the electronics sector in Nuevo Laredo during the period between 1973 and 1975 (Peña 1980). Its most interesting conclusion was that the series of strikes, protests and demonstrations which occurred during that time were generated primarily by alleged abuses and corruption among the representatives of the Confederación de Trabajadores Mexicanos (CTM). The same study reported that workers' protests were not solely intended as a way to gain wage raises but as a means to force firms to improve working conditions. Another reason was the desire to participate in a general unionizing effort that would offer an alternative to the corrupt practices of established organizations. The research also suggested that female rank-and-file members were moving into the

145

leadership positions of both official and independent maquiladora unions.

Research carried out by Peña on the subject of trade unionism in border maquiladoras suggests that there have been four major periods of strike activity in the Border Industrialization Program. The first one (occurring in 1973 and 1974) was characterized by four different but interrelated strikes. During this period several walkouts and demonstrations at some plants developed in response to previous strikes taking place at other factories.

The second cycle, which took place during 1974 and 1975, developed in the midst of a recession that deeply affected the electronics sector. At the same time unions demanded compliance on the part of firms to the stipulations contained in the Mexican labor law. A third cycle occuring during 1975 was precipitated by the full effects of the recession. After approximately three years of relative calm, a fourth cycle of union activity took place between 1978 and 1980. It should be noted at this point that the focuses of unionism have, in every case, been located in Nuevo Laredo, Mexicali and Tijuana.

What has distinguished these four periods of union turmoil has been a variation in the demands of workers vis-à-vis employers. For example, during the first cycle requests for wage increases paralleled demands for better working conditions, collective bargaining rights and the replacement of "corrupt" union officials. Later on, issues of solidarity with other workers, protests against the implementation of "temporary" contracts, demands for inspection of health hazards at the work place and the investigation of sexual offenses by plant supervisory personnel have taken precedence.

Peña reports that most of these strikes have occurred in electronics manufacturing maquiladoras. Seven of the nine strikes covered by this study have been in electronic sector operations. The other two occurred in the garments sector. Interestingly enough, the same researcher has looked at the connection between what he calls the organizational status of firms (i.e., the formal position and marketing relations of maquiladoras with respect to their parent firms) and the incidence of unionization and strike activities.

With respect to organizational status, Peña distinguishes between direct subsidiaries and subcontracted operations. He agrees with the present work by noting that subsidiaries generally provide higher earnings for workers, produce greater outputs and offer relatively stable, long-term production schedules. Subcontracted firms, in contrast, tend to pay lower wages, being also characterized by smaller outputs, seasonal fluctuations and interruptions in production schedules.

A survey of strike activity shows that despite the comparative advantages they offer workers, subsidiary firms have been the hardest hit by trade union activities. Eight of the nine strikes reviewed took place at subsidiary plants. All but one of these subsidiaries operate in the electronics sector. The only subcontracted firm affected by the strikes was a garment factory in Mexicali. A subsidiary garment factory in Tijuana had also been struck.

Another aspect of the firms' organization status reviewed by Peña has to do with the type of ownership of the capital invested in maquiladora operations. Among the plants surveyed in his study all electronic subsidiaries were 100% U.S. owned. Of the remaining two operations, one was a garment subsidiary fully controlled by U.S. capital and the other one a subcontracted firm with 75% U.S. and 25% Mexican investment. Thus, it also turns out that from the scant evidence collected firms fully controlled by foreign capital are more likely to be struck and to confront turmoil among their work force.

The findings outlined above are important in the context of this work for several reasons. Given the differences in wages, benefits, stability and general working conditions between direct subsidiaries and subcontracted firms in the maquiladora sector, it would be reasonable to expect that workers' discontent (translated into unionizing attempts and militancy) would be more prevalent in the latter than in the former. Indeed, if degree of militancy were directly related to the level of exploitation in any particular industry, then we would expect competitive firms to confront protests and strikes on a regular basis while oligopolic firms would remain relatively unaffected by such events.

However, we are told that it is precisely the opposite that occurs among maquiladoras. What are the factors that explain this apparent contradiction? The answer to this question must not be sought only in the manner in which production is organized but also by giving attention to the composition of the work force in both kinds of industries. It is this respect that some of the preceding sections in this work can be used most fruitfully. A few examples will suffice to clarify these ideas.

The willingness to particpate in unionizing efforts and to seek the vindication of workers' rights is tightly allied to the possibilities for developing class consciousness and action (Safa 1976). Historically

147

these features have emerged only after workers accumulate labor experience over relatively long periods of time. In this sense, the relative youth of the maquiladora program in Mexico precludes the formation of solid independent workers' organizations in the immediate future.

However, more important than the question of accumulated labor experience for facilitating the creation of genuine labor movements are some of the features that characterize maquiladora operations. For example, the relative youth of workers and the high rates of turnover that prevail in the plants militate against successful attempts at organizing the labor force. Finally, the issue of gender must be considered again when reflecting upon the likelihood of effective unionization.

Indeed, it is commonly admitted that women are particularly difficult to organize. From the point of view of the entrepreneurial sector this has been an important incentive for the generalized employment of females in poorly paid, unrewarding jobs. From the point of view of unions, on the other hand, the issue of women's presumed docility and their reluctance to actively participate in workers' organizations is not easy to explain.

The fact is that unions in general have been reticent to include in their agenda issues that are particularly relevant to women. In other words, in their attempt to deal with worker's problems and grievances from the point of view of class (often conceived in a narrow sense) they have neglected the potential of gender—specific concerns as tools for effective organization. This allied to the circumstance that most union leaders continue to be men, even in places where a large part of the work force is female, has contributed to deflate the potential for unionism in maquiladora plants.

As may be seen from these considerations, unionization among maquiladora workers is limited. Nevertheless there are reasons why strike activity is more prevalent in electronics plants than in garment shops.

When looking closely at the characteristics of workers in both industries one feature emerges: The majority of workers in the clothing industry are simply not in a position to take unionizing activities seriously. Their situation as workers and members of distinctly organized households precludes them from taking directed political action. From here part of the significance in noting that almost one-third of workers laboring in Ciudad Juárez garment maquiladoras are heads of household. Their grave responsibilities as sole providers of their dependents and the need to maintain jobs that are highly unstable and temporary by nature acts against the possibility of their organization.

Impressed by numerous abuses inflicted upon workers at a particular apparel manufacturing plant, I discussed the possibilities of unionization with some of the workers. A bit annoyed with my explanations, one of them told me, "Look, if I had an alternative, I would take it as fast as lightning strikes the ground. But I don't. I know I'm being exploited, but with this job I pay for the livelihood of my whole family. What is a woman going to do when she is twenty-eight years old and has five children to support? You may think I have nothing to lose by making demands, and yet I assure you that I do."

Workers in the electronics industry are in a somewhat different situation. Most are single, with few or no children, and they generally live with their parents and siblings. Although the vast majority of them contribute to their families' support, they often live in households where there are other income earners. It is also among the members of this group that a significant number (103 in a sample of 510) continues to study at the same time that they work. These women, in particular, appear to have gained a clearer consciousness of the merits of unionization.

Although still bounded by family needs, these women often enjoy a measure of independence which may lead them to consider action on behalf of workers' interests. However, even these women continue to be extremely skeptical about official unions' disposition to address the problems of maquiladora workers. These are seen as corrupt organizations at the service of company interests. Leandro Benítez, a local union leader disagrees: "The majority of unions genuinely look out for the interests of the workers. It was the union that first suggested that sports competitions be held in this plant. It was the union that organized a savings program, and it was the union that convinced management to install a cafeteria adjoining the working place. When people criticize the unions they are just letting out steam; we can't please everybody."

One final point should be stressed before concluding this section. The preceding considerations, although still based on scant empirical evidence and research, have a practical dimension. Where unionization is concerned this information suggests that efforts will be more fruitful when directed towards the workers of the electronics industry. As long as union leaders and organizers continue to ignore the questions posed by gender their attempts will be limited. The preceding analysis suggests that in organizing efforts it is as important to consider gender (and even family ties) as to appreciate the broad theoretical issues derived from the process of production itself.

CHAPTER 8

Maquiladora Work and Household Organization: An Ethnographic Account

Household Organization and Labor Supply

One thing is to speak about the general structural conditions which determine the movement of production centers from core countries to underdeveloped areas and to examine the factors that explain the existence of phenomena such as the Border Industrialization Program. Another one is to examine the conditions that precipitate the entrance of a particular sector of the population (e.g., women) into the work force. This cannot be achieved by looking exclusively at the requirements of capital accumulation and reproduction. It is also necessary to take into consideration supply channels which result from the particular position of individuals—endowed with personal characteristics—within the household and labor market (Kessler-Harris 1975).

In other words, a study of offshore assembly plants, must include an analysis of the broad structural conditions which have determined the movement of productive centers from hegemonic countries (such as the United States) to underdeveloped geographical areas (such as the Mexican-American border). It must also investigate the concrete conditions found at the household and community levels (see also Schmink 1979).

As stated earlier, a number of factors distinctive of the present stage of capitalist development have contributed to a growing fragmentation of productive processes, a redefinition of skill levels and an accentuated fluidity of capital investments throughout the world (Braverman 1974. chap. 4). These factors have, in turn, re-sulted in the feminization of growing contingents of workers (Braverman 1974, p. 323).

But while the requirements of capitalist accumulation and repro-duction determine the *demand* of labor, this alone sheds little light upon the issue of labor *supply*. In strict terms what matters from the point of view of capitalist rationality is not that the workers have a specific gender or nationality, but that they can be used to yield maximum profits and productivity under the least politically com-promising circumstances.

Why then do women increasingly become the bearers of labor so defined? Contrary to what may appear at first glance, the answer to this question is not self evident. It requires a thorough examination of the position of individuals—endowed with certain personal char-acteristics—within the domestic units to which they belong (Scott and Tilly 1975). In other words, only through the analysis of house-hold organization and structure is it possible to move beyond the reductionism inherent in all-encompassing concepts such as "re-serve industrial army" and "cheap labor."

This is a difficult point to approach because it is too often assumed that small-scale reproductive units such as the family and the household are inexorably shaped through complex historical processes to fulfill the needs of the capitalist class (Engels 1972; Hartmann 1979). This may be a valid proposition at the general level, but when taken literally it may result in an unduly simplistic and mechanical interpretation of a complex phenomenon.

Some authors, for example, have documented the role played by the family as a bastion of resistance against the impositions of capital (Zaretsky 1973; Caulfield 1974). Others have stressed the relative autonomy of household organization in relation to capital demands. In general it should be acknowledged that there is consid-erable variation among the internal organization of households even when they share a similar class background. Households to which Ciudad Juárez's maquiladora workers belong are not the exception to this proposition.

In the following section two ethnographic accounts are presented. The first one centers on the experiences of a cluster of individuals living in Zaragoza Street, a proletarian neighborhood in Ciudad Juárez. Many of these are maquiladora workers, and all have been substantially affected by border industrialization. Emphasis is placed upon the connections existing between local labor markets, informal economic activities, international migration and factory employment. As will be seen, maquiladora workers are enmeshed in an extensive network of informal support mechanisms at the household, neighborhood and community levels.

The second ethnographic account presents the contrasting cases of three maquiladora workers. Two of them, Florencia and Francisca, are young women who labor at electric maquiladoras of varying sizes. The third one, Sylvia, has worked at apparel manufacturing plants for nearly a decade.

The importance of considering the relationship between the insertion of individuals into particular sectors of the labor market and household organization becomes apparent through careful ethnographic observation. Although there are central residential areas in Ciudad Juárez where there is a heavy concentration of maquiladora workers, the work force employed in the in-bond plants is widely dispersed. Participation of women in industrial labor has tended to give a particular flavor to neighborhoods and to alter the features of family and community living. More significantly female industrial employment coexists with other forms of labor force participation both in Ciudad Juárez and across the border, forming a configuration of networks and survival strategies that has received little scholarly attention until now. Ciudad Juárez provides a quasi-experimental setting where it is possible to observe the interaction of international migration, female employment in industry and work in the so-called informal sector of the economy.

The following examples are offered as illustrations of the preceding points. Although they are limited in their scope and in their capacity to substantiate broader generalizations, they suggest particular ways in which families group and regroup in order to adjust to wider economic constraints. Such adjustments result in modified versions of household organization. They also determine the use of space and time, giving neighborhoods and communities their distinctive features. As will be seen, family organization and household composition forms a variegated rather than a uniform reality. In a relatively small physical space, many forms of family and household organization exist. The factors that explain such differences must ultimately be related to labor market conditions.

Calle Zaragoza: Maquiladoras and Neighborhood Living

María de Jesús Sánchez, "Chuy," became nineteen years old in January 1978. For the preceding three years her life in Ciudad Juárez

153

had been characterized by repeated but unsuccessful attempts to find a job in maquiladora. Her periodic peregrination to the industrial parks of Juárez had alternated with two other kinds of experience. Chuy often worked as a maid and baby-sitter in the neighborhood where she lived with her mother, an older half-sister, Emma, and Emma's three children. For relatively extended periods of time Chuy had also been an undocumented worker in the United States. As an illegal alien Chuy had been employed in a cannery in Texas, a food-processing plant in Chicago, two different laundries in Arizona and several private homes in El Paso.

She agreed with most undocumented migrants that higher wages earned *al otro lado* made worthwhile the risk of detention and harassment by immigration and naturalization service officials. But Chuy also admitted that life as an illegal alien was hard. On five different occasions she had been deported. Once she had been detained at the customs office for almost two full days.

Unfortunately, Chuy had few choices. Her intent to become employed in a maquiladora had been frustrated by her low schooling level. "When I came to Juárez," she told me, "the plants required six years of school (primaria); now many are asking for nine (secundaria)." Although Chuy knew how to read and write, she had only attended school in her hometown for three years. Why hadn't she continued her education? Chuy had been born out of wedlock in a small village in Jalisco. Her mother, Elisa, was a young widow; the mother of two older children, Emma and Raul, whose father had died of a cardiovascular disease. Emma had fond memories of her father, but Chuy had never known hers. Three years after the birth of her third child, Elisa had become the common-law wife of a small sharecropper, Manuel. Their only child, Inocencio, had died at the age of three of typhoid.

Life at the farm had not been easy for Chuy. As an "illegitimate" child and a female, she had endured special abuses at the hands of her stepfather.

> He never saw me as a daughter. To him I was more like a servant and field-hand. He started teaching me how to clean a patch of land when I was seven years old. From him I also learned how to milk a cow and take care of the henhouse. But he was a violent man. Sometimes when he got drunk he used to beat me hard so that I might grow up to be a good woman. According to him it was better to end up crippled in heaven than whole in body in hell. Such were his ideas about discipline.

154

He also used to punish my mother once in a while, but where I was concerned she always took his side. I think she was grateful to him for having taken her in with someone else's child. He resented having to support both of us, although God knows we earned our food through hard work. I always thought of myself as a burden on my family. My stepfather could have thrown me out of the house at any time. He often threatened to do so.

As a member of a rural household where she was never fully accepted, Chuy started work at an early age. She worked both in the field and in the house. In many ways her early training was a mixture of sex-typed occupations. Because of this her experiences differed from the experience of other girls in the area. When she was still in school she found it easier to befriend boys than girls. With them she used to play hookey and roam the countryside. She found true delight in this, although later on she regretted not having finished her elementary education. She learned to climb trees, and to play *rayuela*. Before the age of thirteen she was skillful at betting games. Shortly afterwards she became a habitual smoker. She adopted a determined and aggressive posture. Her masculine demeanor enabled her to hustle in the outer world and to resist the petty cruelty of household life.

As an adolescent, Chuy's life had been complicated by changes in her stepfather's hostility. On occasion she would find him staring at her in a drunken stupor. The flaccid smile on his face had frightened her, but she had no words to describe her feelings and no one to seek out for shelter. One Sunday morning while her mother was attending mass, Manuel had tried to rape her. When she had resisted he had beaten her furiously and torn her new blouse to shreds. It wasn't long before her mother returned carrying a bag of fresh vegetables purchased at the market. She had been startled to see her shaking daughter, hair unbraided, her eyes swollen from the crying. Manuel, who only minutes before had threatened her with murder if she snitched on him, explained what had happened. He had found Chuy trying to steal money away from him. Curiously, Chuy had felt shame rather than anger at his words. Elisa believed him and proceeded to slap her daughter a little more. That night, Chuy took her few possessions and thirty pesos that were hidden in the kitchen and she came to Juárez where Emma had been living for twelve years. When Chuy arrived at the door of her sister's house, she was penniless. She hadn't tasted food for more than a full day.

Elisa's oldest daughter had married Anselmo, a *jornalero* from her hometown when she was sixteen and he eighteen. Anselmo wanted a good life for himself and his family. He was hard-working, willing to do almost anything honest to earn a living. His father Luis had once owned some land but even while Luis was growing up, he saw the fields producing less and less. In the end, the land had been sold and the six children in the family had been sent out to work. Anselmo found that occupational opportunities in the countryside were scarce and low paying. First he took Emma and their baby daughter Estela to Guadalajara where he had a cousin. After a few months in that city, his meager savings exhausted, he began contemplating the idea of crossing the border. If he could work hard in the United States for four or five years, then maybe he might return to Encinitas and buy himself a house. With this goal in mind he moved his family to Ciudad Juárez.

Although the first two months in the city had been rough (ever morning he had to find odd jobs, never knowing whether they would be enough money to eat that day) he had been lucky. One day while he was doing construction work, the boss had noticed him. He knew a man who was hiring workers for a dairy farm in the outskirts of El Paso. It was a good deal, as the farm's owner, Mr. Roy Paterson, knew how to get his workers green cards.

When Anselmo started work at the plant milking cows, he did so without any legal rights. In this he had to trust Paterson and that worried him. But he had to take a chance. Ten years later he felt that he had made the right decision. Although during that time his occupation had not changed much (he was still milking cows) he had earned a stable minimum wage. In 1978 he was making $2.90 an hour.

Of course he had had to make some adjustments. When he had started work in the United States, Anselmo had decided that it would be more convenient to live on the Mexican side of the border for two reasons. First, it would have been difficult to move the family to the United States at a time when his residential status was still in doubt. Having a family in the proximity of El Paso was also reassuring, especially if anything went wrong and he was deported. Second, life in Juárez was cheaper than in El Paso. Anselmo wanted to save as much as possible.

But commuting to the outskirts of the U.S. city on a daily basis, he soon found out, was impractical and costly, especially for someone without a car. Thus, he had started living in the farm's quarters. Roy Paterson leased clean rooms in the adjoining areas for what appeared to be a very reasonable fee. Emma and her children remained in Ciudad Juárez, living in the centrally located neighborhood where I met them in 1978. Their house was small but clean. On one of the walls of the main room, which served both as parlor and as dining room, hung a large painting of tigers on velvet. An assortment of cheap china collectibles decorated the top of a cabinet. Plastic flowers alternated with small gilded mirrors and posters in a montage which combined small-town taste with urban paraphernalia.

The house had two bedrooms and a kitchen. In one of the bedrooms there was a middle-size black-and-white television and a *consola*, that is, a gaudy combination of stereo system, record player and radio. There was also a refrigerator in the kitchen. Anselmo had bought the television and the refrigerator but, as I was to find out, Chuy had paid for the consola. Aside from these few luxuries there was little more that could be shown for eleven years of work at the dairy farm.

Anselmo visited his family at Juárez every other week. The rest of the time he lived alone in El Paso, although sometimes Emma wondered somewhat guiltily whether her husband kept another woman *al otro lado*. But even if he did, he was a good man. He had never failed to support her and her three children, Estela, Luis and Francisco. He could be counted upon to give guidance and discipline to the youngsters. He was a good man and he got along well with Elisa, her mother. Two years after Chuy had come to live with Emma, the former had persuaded their mother to leave Manuel and move in with them. Elisa's health had deteriorated in the last years. Although she was still a handsome woman at sixty, her eyesight was failing and she experienced periodical nervous breakdowns. Emma and Chuy believed that Manuel had cast an evil spell on her, and at times she certainly acted as a woman possessed.

In 1978, Anselmo was leasing the house for a monthly rent of 250 pesos plus a small additional amount that entitled them to the use of water and electricity. Besides this house, his landlady, Chela, owned two other small houses in the same lot. One, a single-room adobe house, she leased to Rubén and Margarita Suárez and their two preschool children. When I met them, both of them were working in CENTRALAB, one of the largest maquiladoras in Ciudad Juárez. Rubén was a repairman, Margarita an assembly worker. Chela, who lived in (and also owned) the third house, was a woman with initiative. The small quarters which she shared with her husband also held a tiny grocery store, La Nueva. Chela and her store were in many ways the pivot about which much neighborly life flowed.

As with many such corner stores, La Nueva offered a variegated assortment of canned foods, refreshments, staples, toys and sweets. At all hours of the day small children, running errands for their mothers, would stop by holding empty bottles of milk and soda. They would stare for minutes on end making Chela lose her patience while trying to decide whether to buy bubble gum or a colorful *pirulí*, a conic-shaped delight which could be licked for hours making their lips and fingers sticky.

One of the reasons why La Nueva was popular among the families living in this proletarian neighborhood was that it offered easy credit. With the most scrupulous efficiency Chela recorded her debtors' names and the quantities they owed the store on a lined notebook. Individually these were small debts, but in bulk they amounted to a small capital. Chela calculated that at any particular time during 1978, her clientele's debt amounted to four thousand pesos. So even though business was always slow, the steady flow of money resulting from partial payment on the debt, kept La Nueva alive.

On the other hand, profits were very small and towards the end of 1978 Chela was losing heart. Her enterprise had not become as rewarding as she had originally expected. According to Chela the problem was an abundance of competition. Hers was not the only corner store in the neighborhood. She had to share her clientele with five other establishments. In all of them prices were and had to be fairly uniform.

In general, all canned goods were more expensive at these stores than at the closest supermarket, Futurama. But then again, Futurama did not offer the kind of credit that was accessible at the corner store. Although individuals paid more for certain goods in them, the difference in expense was made up by their proximity. You could walk to La Nueva, whereas you had to take a bus or a *rutera* in order to get to Futurama.

This was an important feature from the point of view of La Nueva's patrons, who were mostly women. Many of these women were assembly plant workers or had daughters working at the plants. Many had husbands or fathers whose wages were not stable or regular. During periods of unemployment, La Nueva could be relied upon to provide at least the most essential means of survival.

Besides a steady flow of income through the maintenance of her patrons' debts, Chela derived additional benefits from her position as a storeowner and creditor. In order to supplement her earnings she had obtained a concession as a saleslady from Avon, the cosmetics manufacturing firm.

Sales and purchases of Avon products have become an almost legendary feature of proletarian colonies in Ciudad Juárez. At first glance it appeared unusual that in these impoverished environments such an exchange was as highly favored. Many of Chela's clients periodically organized meetings at each other's houses in order to introduce new products and persuade friends to buy them. Thus most of their transactions took place within the neighborhood. Only occasionally were they carried out during visiting trips to friends and relatives (in this Chela was also exceptional; she had a few clients in the fairly distant town of Guadalupe). And that was precisely the crux of the matter. In this proletarian barrio everyone appeared to be indebted to everyone else. Women purchased a jar of facial cream, a bottle of cologne or a lipstick not only because they were interested in the products but also because in buying they felt they were doing the seller a personal favor. They knew the favor would be returned when the opportunity arose. As Chuy said, "hoy por ti; mañana por mi" (your turn today; tomorrow mine).

Lack of reciprocity in these transactions was a breach of etiquette which could lead the guilty party into isolation from the neighborly network. Few could afford to be in such a situation. As may be seen, these exchanges operated as a redistributive mechanism by means of which the limited earnings of neighbors were widely and legitimately shared. The secret was to maintain a steady flow of money among the participants. This involved selling, purchasing and extending credit. In addition, Avon representatives received a commission proportional to the sales achieved. This too enhanced the flow of money. Redistributive mechanisms exist in all societies, an abundant assortment of anthropological writings teach us. In this, the barrio was not alone. However, what made it unique, as an example of present living in Ciudad Juárez, was the intervention of a highly impersonal modern commercial firm in the process of neighborhood living. Avon, an enterprise whose primary purpose is to peddle superfluous luxuries, was one of the links by means of which poverty could be evened out in the barrio.

Such being the case, it was difficult for any particular woman in the neighborhood to refuse Chela's insistent approaches as an Avon seller. Chela was the woman thanks to whom food was easily available even at the end of the week when wages had been severely depleted by the expenses of daily living.

159

Chela's virtues as a bonafide entrepreneur contrasted with her calm and quiet manner. She was thirty-seven and childless. At twenty she had met Genaro, her husband. Chela found it hard to believe that they had been married for almost seventeen years, especially when considering that Genaro had never been able to support her for extended periods of time. On the wall of her living room hung her wedding picture, showing a very young and slender Chela. She remembered having had great illusions about what her future life would be like. Things hadn't quite worked out as expected.

Every summer for the previous five years, Chela had worked at a *caneria* (a cannery) in El Paso without any documentation, earning the minimum wage. Her task consisted in sorting green and red peppers which were swiftly moved by a conveyor belt. It was a very tedious job only made bearable by the ongoing conversation with other Mexican workers also hired by the plant. Chela found pleasure in stealing the largest and most beautiful peppers. It took some skill to conceal them without altering the pace of work. Some ended up in her kitchen, others were sold at the store. It was difficult to tell what benefit Chela derived from her thefts. Although far from wealthy, she was not hungry or needy. In fact, by neighborhood standards she had a privileged position.

However, Chela had her motives. She deeply resented the monotony of her job. For eight hours every day she wasn't able to sit down. It was even hard to get permission to go to the toilet. Her feet were always swollen when she returned to her home in Juárez every evening. The cannery didn't even have air conditioning. According to Chela, the boss was a slave driver who couldn't hide his dislike for Mexican people. It made her feel good to know that she had this edge on him. Every day she took revenge. After all, some of the best peppers never saw their way into the cans.

Genaro, Chela's husband, spent much of his time gambling, drinking and involuntarily terrorizing the children in the block with his reckless driving. His prize possession was a 1967 Ford truck. Whether he or his wife would drive the *troca* was often a motive for heated argument. Chela needed it to go shopping and to visit clients. During the summer it was her most expedient means of transportation across the border, and although her husband claimed otherwise, she remembered paying most of what it had cost. Genaro, on the other hand, needed the truck to look for jobs, a task he was perpetually engaged in with little success.

Occasionally, he too worked at the cannery but only during the summer months. Chela was accustomed to his periodic absences. When he went on a binge, he would disappear for days. But he always came back looking ashamed and repentant. It was no use to try to break up with him. Chela had long before accepted the fact that she would have to support both of them. But she was bitterly glad they had never had any children, although that too had been disappointing. Sometimes Chela wished Genaro had been more like Rubén Suárez, her other tenant and Margarita's husband. He was young but responsible. He had been employed at CENTRALAB for almost four years and he had almost never missed a day's work.

Every morning at five-thirty—one hour before their shift started—Rubén and Margarita awakened and prepared for work. At twenty-five he was a skilled repairman: at twenty-two, she was an assembly worker. Although the two had been hired almost at the same time, their employment status differed markedly.

Rubén had been hired on a permanent basis, that is, he had a contrato de planta. This afforded him stability on the job and seniority privileges, which, in Mexico, are especially important in case of dismissal. Laid-off workers with a permanent contract can claim a three-month indemnity payment from their employers and additional compensation proportional to the length of time worked at a particular firm. As a repairman, Rubén earned 184 pesos a day.

Margarita, on the other hand, had never been issued a contrato de planta. Rather, for the length of her employment at CENTRALAB she had been periodically given temporary contracts. "Every three months, the personnel manager calls some of us into his office and he asks us to sign resignation sheets. I always sign immediately, because I want to stay out of trouble. The next morning he rehires me for another three months. I'm a nervous wreck, I never know when my resignation will be final!" As an assembly worker, Margarita earned 125 pesos a day.

She and Rubén had been married for five years. They were, indeed, a handsome couple. But at twenty-two Margarita felt she was growing old too quickly. She wanted to build a future for her children. Astrid, a miniature replica of her beautiful mother, was four years old. Rubén was almost three. Her eldest child, a son, had died when he was six months. It was painful for Margarita to remember the circumstances that had surrounded her baby's death.

Of my three children, he was the best. His skin was as white as ivory (whereas Astrid is much too dark) and he was a boy too. He never gave me a day's worry until the week of his death. At

161

first I thought he had a simple cold, but after a while it was clear that he had great difficulty in breathing. I took him to the Seguro, where they treated him. They told me I could take him home after a day and a half. So I did. That night he died. The doctors at the Seguro never agreed on what the reasons for his death were. Rubén went crazy when he found out. He held me responsible for my own child's death. That was the first time he laid a hand on me. I left him and went to live with my mother. We were separated for six months, but we couldn't stay away from each other for long. It was too painful.

Since they had started working at the factory, Rubén and Margarita had been trying to save enough money to build a house. Her parents had given them a small plot of land in the outskirts of the city. At first Rubén had refused to accept such an expensive gift. He was a proud man and he resented being indebted to his in-laws. In fact, since their temporary separation, they too looked at him with suspicion. They simply didn't get along. But reason had prevailed. They had to think about the children. To build a house, to have a piece of property, was a step in the right direction.

Even with the two working, Margarita found it difficult to save. Most of her earnings were used to buy food and clothing and to pay Elisa, her neighbor and Emma's mother for her services. Elisa took care of Astrid and Rubencito during the day. Sometimes, she also cooked and cleaned house for Margarita. Margarita, however, did her own laundry by hand and cooked most of the time. Every afternoon after work at the maquiladora, she stopped at La Nueva to buy groceries and to chat with Chela. And it was Chela who had suggested that she become an Avon saleslady. Margarita promptly took her advice. She had a special advantage; she could sell cosmetics at the factory. She knew many women who did, although management frowned on these activities.

As a young girl, Margarita had studied to become a beautician. She did that while at the same time finishing her secondary school education. She had hoped to be employed by a beauty parlor, maybe even own one someday, but then she had married Rubén and at first he hadn't wanted her to work at all. It was all for the better Margarita felt, because most beauticians that she knew were out of work. Beauty parlors had been driven out of business by "stylists" and "unisex" hair cutters. Indeed, she knew at least five beauticians who were working at CENTRALAB.

But her skills had not gone to waste. She had a small clientele among her neighbors. Every Saturday morning and afternoon she put her knowledge to practice with encouraging results. The cash was welcome. Late in the day she took care of the laundry, to her a most unpleasant job. Besides her other efforts at saving, she was also trying to put money away for a downpayment on a washing machine; nothing big, just something to ease the burden of that weekly chore. Rubén didn't know she hid small sums in the kitchen cabinet. If he found out he would probably beat her up.

Neither Rubén nor Margarita liked their job at the factory. It wasn't only the fact that she was not hired on a permanent basis that upset them. Working conditions were far from adequate. Common knowledge had it that CENTRALAB was one of the most polluted maquiladoras in Ciudad Juárez. Its manufacturing process required the use of graphite, a soft, black lustrous form of carbon that irritates the eyes and skin. When inhaled, graphite dust can also induce a myriad of respiratory diseases. On several occasions, local inspection agencies had instructed management to implement more effective safety measures and to provide employees with suitable protection. However, according to workers' testimonies, very little had been done. The majority were still not even provided with face masks to filter out polluted air.

With rising costs of living and the limited capacity of minimum wages to forward individual advancement, Rubén became restless during the course of 1978. Two years earlier he had bought a 1960 aquamarine Chevrolet. But now most of his earnings were being saved for the house. Margarita took care of the daily expenses, including food and rent. Rubén paid for gas and occasional diversions for them and the children. After three years of effort, however, they still didn't have enough money to start building a home. While it was true that Rubén had lost frequently at betting games with Genaro and his friends, he felt these transgressions (sorely resented by his wife) were not the reason for their present situation. There was no future in his job. Therefore he began considering other alternatives.

He knew that if he was fired by CENTRALAB, he would have a claim to a three-month indemnity compensation plus twenty days of wages per year worked at the plant. That amounted to more than nineteen thousand pesos; from his perspective, a very desirable sum. The point was to get fired, otherwise a voluntary resignation would leave him penniless and, worse, without a job. With this in mind, Rubén started to look for the right opportunity to enact a strategy. Rubén was a union worker. That had advantages and disadvantages. On the one hand, if he could prove that the plant had fired him unfairly, the union would back him up in his demands. On the other hand, if management could prove the opposite, he would be helpless. Power is not on the side of the worker. However, he knew the union leader well. It could almost be said that they were friends. It was through him that he had got the job in the first place; they knew each other from way back. Surely he would support him in his demands. Maybe he would invite him to become his *compadre*.

These thoughts gave Rubén confidence. He missed a couple of days of work, knowing that he was stepping on thin ground. Three absences within a month were followed by a managerial admonishment. Repeated unjustified absences are considered to be legitimate cause for dismissal without compensation. From Rubén's perspective the goal was to cause enough of a problem to be fired but not to become a problem so great as to lose all claim to compensation. Although he continued working, he reduced his level of efficiency, he became indolent, spending hours at tasks that normally had taken him a few minutes in the past. Because he was a repairman he had relative power. His sluggishness could paralyze activities along the assembly line. At the same time it was hard for his supervisor to tell whether his behavior was deliberate or not. Rubén complained that the equipment was antiquated or the parts used for repair defective.

Throughout the ordeal he remained courteous, even servile. The supervisor's attitude, on the other hand, shifted gradually from mild suspicion to outrage, especially after confronting middle management complaints. Management intervened at low levels when there were noticeable decreases in productivity. Rubén's deliberate incompetence was beginning to cause problems in that area. He was warned that his behavior would bring him serious difficulties. His presumed friend, the union leader, emphatically suggested that he adopt a more cooperative attitude. But Rubén assured him (and everyone else who asked) that he was being subjected to a great injustice.

According to his version of the events, management was trying to get rid of him because "he had been with the firm for too long a time." The firm already owed him a large sum of money in benefits, and management knew that the debt would increase if he continued working there. Management didn't want to keep long-term workers. That explained why he was being given defective parts. That's why he was accused of trying to upset the manufacturing process. If they found a legitimate cause to fire him, he would be thrown out without a penny. This had happened to a lot of people he knew. The plant was trying to frame him. The union leader didn't know who to believe.

Five months after he had begun his concerted effort at defeating the interests of the plant, Rubén was called into the personnel manager's office.

He told me they had noticed changes in my behavior and a lowering in my efficiency. They were convinced that I was unhappy with the job, but they didn't want to create trouble for either of the parties. Therefore they were letting me go, and they offered a settlement of four thousand pesos if I resigned voluntarily. I didn't want to accept that offer; they owed me much more than that! They're always ripping off the worker. Why shouldn't I have wanted to fight for my share? I told him I would file a complaint at the Junta de Conciliación y Arbitraje (the official mediating agency). He only smiled at me. He told me to remember that those procedures took a long time and workers were almost never on the winning side. If I wanted to do that I wouldn't even get the four thousand pesos. Later on when I discussed my problem with the union leader, he gave me the same advice and he didn't even know who was telling the truth! He was on the side of the plant right from the beginning. Now I know I didn't have a chance. I had to take the measly four thousand pesos and give up the job.

Rubén's dismissal from CENTRALAB caused great distress among those who were close to him in the barrio. Elisa, who baby-sat for his children, wondered whether he would be able to find another job without a letter of recommendation from his previous employer. Margarita, his wife, became the sole support of the family. Now she became even more concerned about her temporary employment status at the plant. Her weekly debt at La Nueva grew considerably during the following week. She hoarded as much as she was able to.

Reluctantly Rubén searched for a new job. After three weeks he started working at another maquiladora. It was the same kind of job as the one he had had before. It was like starting from scratch, except that now he was four years older. He lasted in it for less than two weeks. Afterwards he became sullen and got drunk two times, something he had rarely done in the past. He felt there was no future for him. But something kept him going. "I swear I'll go down fighting."

It was during that period that Rogelio, his friend, discussed with him the possibility of moving to the United States. To be sure it was a gamble, but the worst that could happen was that they would be deported and that wasn't all that bad, was it? So Rubén sold the car (leaving Margarita having to take the rutera to go to work) and on a Wednesday morning in November 1978 the two of them crossed the river at Azcárate, with the water reaching their shoulders.

Once on U.S. territory, they had two alternatives, either to stay in the El Paso area or to go inland. Rubén felt that staying in El Paso meant a higher probability of detention and deportation. For the same reasons, the further inland they went, the safer they would feel. Because neither of the two friends had enough information to arrive at a decision, instinct rather than experience impelled them to continue their journey. First they boarded a crowded bus, then they walked for a quarter of a mile until they reached the El Paso airport. There they purchased tickets to go to Phoenix, Arizona, and during three hours they waited anxiously for the departure of the aircraft.

At the airline counter a clerk stared at them suspiciously, observing their features, the color of their skin and their sparse luggage. On three different occasions she had asked for their address in El Paso and for the purpose of their trip. She had been courteous, knowing that she had no right to press the inquiry. The third time Rogelio had answered impatiently. He spoke a broken English, but his attitude was unmistakably defiant: "I told you before, me and my friend live in El Paso and we're going to visit friends. What's the matter lady? Don't you believe me?" As he expected, the clerk remained silent. Rogelio had learned from others with more experience than him that in similar cases it is better to act outraged and determined than to adopt a meek attitude. Clerks can't tell the difference between a legal resident and a wetback. The risk of scandal and potential lawsuits for impinging upon citizens or legal residents' rights are often powerful deterrents for further inquiry.

Despite some inconvenience, it appeared to Rogelio and Rubén, as they looked back, that everything had run smoothly and according to plans. No one had bothered them at their arrival in Arizona where, indeed, one of Rogelio's compadres lived. They stayed with him and his family until they found a job. Afterwards they moved into a leased furnished room. Only one week after their arrival in Phoenix, the two friends had been hired at a factory to perform janitorial and maintenance work. Rubén was earning $3.20 an hour, the highest wage he had ever earned. He kept the job for a little longer than three months.

Back in Juárez, Margarita took full responsibility for the maintenance of her children. Some time would pass before Rubén was able to send her money. Her anxiety grew as the days passed without a word from her husband. When, at last, a letter arrived saying he was well and had a job, she was elated. However, life was expensive in the United States, and he still had no money to send back; she would have to wait longer for that. Knowing that her unreliable job was, for the moment, the only means of support made Margarita nervous. Moreover, separation from her husband caused her some additional concerns. Maybe he wouldn't come back at all. Some men never did. They crossed leaving their families behind to fend for themselves. Perhaps Rubén would marry a *gringa* and become a legal resident. He had nothing to lose by forgetting her and the children. Only time would tell.

In late September, almost two months after Rubén had left, something happened that altered the monotony of factory and house chores. Margarita was working on a special project. Astrid, who had recently started school, was to participate in a United Nations Parade, a local commemoration of Columbus Day. The event required that each child in school wear a different national gown. Astrid had been selected to represent Albania. The children's parents had to provide the outfits. Because this was the first social event to which Astrid had been invited, it acquired in Margarita's mind an exaggerated significance. She saw it as a first step in a series of attempts to provide her child with all the opportunities she herself had not had. She decided Astrid would be the best outfitted child in the parade. Everyone, parents and schoolmates alike, would be equally impressed. She was only sad that neither Rubén nor herself would be able to attend the celebration. She had to work at the maquiladora, and her husband was still in the United States.

With her mother's help and much patience, Margarita set about the odd but gratifying task of sewing an Albanian gown, having only the faintest idea of what it should look like. Surely, she didn't even know where Albania was located. But the school provided some guidelines; the dress was to be white, long, and sheer with colorful ribbons embellishing its hem and headdress. Margarita had taken the additional liberty of sprinkling glittering sequins on the gown's bodice, an original touch having more to do with a Mexican woman's desire to create beauty than with Albanian tradition.

167

Three days before the parade Margarita wanted me to see the almost-completed gown. For this reason she invited me into her tiny home. The dress had been sewed entirely by hand after working hours. Now it laid in full display on the bed while the woman explained with almost reverent pride how she had arrived at her beautiful design. Only a few finishing touches were left. It had cost more than five hundred pesos, an extravagant sum, especially when considering that the gown would probably only be worn once. But from Margarita's point of view both the hard work and the expense were well worth the satisfaction. There was nothing like knowing that your children had a chance to shine because of you. No one would look down upon Astrid.

But there was an additional reason for joy. Only an hour earlier one of Rubén's friends had come knocking at the door. He was visiting his family in Ciudad Juárez after almost a year of work in the United States. Rubén had asked him to bring greetings and an impressive assortment of gifts for his family. There were toys and clothes for the children and for Margarita there was a medium length vinyl jacket "assembled in Taiwan." The young woman beamed with delight as she pointed out to me how the material looked like real leather. And how surprised she had been to get it, especially from Rubén who never seemed to pay any attention to her demands and wishes. Months before, while the two were walking down a street, she had longingly glanced at a similar jacket in a windowcase. Now she knew he would come back. Too bad he wouldn't be there for the Columbus Day celebration.

The morning when the parade was to take place, Margarita woke up earlier than usual, her heart pounding with excitement. After five minutes of compulsive misbehavior and two exasperated slaps from his mother, Rubencito was sent to Emma's house. This allowed Margarita to give full attention to her daughter. She bathed and dressed her with the care of a collector about to display her finest possession. Astrid's hair was braided, her fingernails and lips enhanced by a touch of pink. As she looked at her daughter, Margarita wondered whether Albanian women had brown skin.

A few minutes after six Elisa brought Rubencito back into the room. She was to take Astrid to school at seven, half an hour earlier than usual. The parade would begin at nine. As Margarita left for work she hoped aloud that the event had as much meaning for her daughter as it had for her. She wanted Astrid to remember; "When you get old, all you have got are memories."

Exactly two weeks later Rubén came back without notice. He had saved two hundred dollars but he had deserted the job in Phoenix. The point was that he had proven to himself that he could survive in the United States; his faith was renewed. But there were problems too. Without a woman, life can be hard and more expensive. You have to work all day and then come home to a sparsely furnished room without a kitchen. If you eat out, your hard-earned savings are quickly undermined. Ruben missed his family and in coming back his intents were clear: The four would have to move to the United States.

Margarita was unhappy with that prospect. Her parents and relatives had always lived in Ciudad Juárez. Having a family living close by meant a lot to her. You can always seek your family for support when everything else fails. Besides, she didn't speak English. Rubén had comforted her with respect to this. There were many parts in the United States where English was almost not spoken; such was the size of the Spanish-speaking population. He had friends in Phoenix who could be relied upon while they adjusted to the new environment. Margarita could stop working and take better care of her home. There was a future in the United States, especially for the children. But Margarita remained skeptical. With the perspective of moving abroad, her less-than-satisfactory job suddenly became desirable. She had finally saved enough money to make a down payment on a washing machine. She was proud of this achievement, but now she would have to send it back and she would be totally dependent on Rubén. It would be like becoming suddenly blind and relying upon someone else for everything.

But there were no adequate options. Rubén's mind was made up, and after a few enthusiastic attempts at persuading his wife he had announced that if she didn't want to follow him he would still go. He was fed up with Juárez. There were no assurances that he would return. Things moved speedily thereafter. Rogelio was to take them in his old truck to a relatively isolated area near the border where the river was shallow. They would walk across carrying the children. At the other end, a "coyote" would be waiting. He would drive them and two other people directly into Phoenix. It was as simple as that. They couldn't take much with them. Therefore their few possessions would be left in the care of Rubén's mother. She had a house in Colonia Durango. If things went well, they would come back to Juárez in a few years and buy a house of their own.

Margarita followed her husband's orders in silence. She gave notice at the factory that she was leaving and returned the washing machine. But while she was saddened and preoccupied with the prospect of their departure, Astrid was excited. Not that she knew what exactly was happening. She merely reacted to the sense of expectancy that permeated her parents recent behavior. Very seriously she told me that they were going to "Fini."

One Sunday morning, a few neighbors assembled at the Suárez house to help pack and move out the furniture. It didn't take very long for the family's belongings to be piled on top of the truck. Margarita paid off her debt at La Nueva with her last weekly wage. Rubén, in turn would pay the "coyote's" fee—three thousand pesos, a considerable investment in their future life. He only hoped that they wouldn't be deported, for the fee was not redeemable. If successful, they would arrive in Phoenix almost penniless, but then he was sure to find a job soon. He hoped.

Their neighbors agreed that moving to the U.S. with the whole family was riskier and more difficult than doing so alone, but then again it wasn't as hard as people thought to cross the river. Amelia, one of Margarita's friends, had been doing so periodically on weekends with her children. They weren't looking for jobs or anything like that. They just liked to spend time at the Plaza de los Lagartos in downtown El Paso. It was fun and they had never been detained. If you kept a cool attitude and knew what you were doing nothing inconvenient would happen. She advised Margarita never to panic.

Chuy agreed. She had many stories of her own to tell amidst laughter and smoking. With the Suarez's departure her own desire to migrate was reawakened. If she hadn't gone away recently it was only because her mother Elisa had asked her to stay in Juárez. Her health was worse than ever, and she worried too much. But Chuy was far from satisfied with her life in Mexico. Since her arrival in Juárez, five years earlier, she had had several jobs both in the U.S. and in Mexico, but they weren't good. She wanted to become a maquila worker, but as soon as they knew that she only had three years of schooling, her application was not paid further attention. She thought of herself as a grown woman. It was unthinkable to go back to school with young children. And besides she had to work, for she had no one to support her. Her most recent job was as a babysitter and maid at Ofelia's service.

Ofelia Mendoza lived two blocks away from Chuy's house. She worked as a seamstress at Acapulco Fashion, one of the largest maquiladoras in Ciudad Juárez. Her husband, a self-employed mechanic, and she had a three-year-old child. When Ofelia had started working one year and a half earlier, she had considered leaving the youngster at one of the two day-care centers in Ciudad Juárez. But she soon found out that this was not a very practical idea. She didn't have a car and for reasons unknown to her, both day-care facilities were at a considerable distance from where the maquiladoras were located. Because she had to start work at 6:30 A.M., the child had to be taken by rutera or bus to the *guardería* very early in the morning. Especially during the winter months this was a risky task. Ofelia was afraid for her child's health. She didn't like the idea of him spending day after day in the care of strangers. It was better for him to be near people Ofelia knew. Thus she had hired Chuy as a maid for a weekly wage of 60 pesos.

It was an odd situation, because long before Chuy had become Ofelia's maid, they had been equals. The houses where they lived were not very different from one another. There were also many similarities in their backgrounds. The two came from poor families with many mouths to feed, and they were roughly the same age. Chuy felt that the only important differences between them were that Ofelia was married and had a job at a maquiladora, while Chuy was a maid and single. But since she had started working for her, Ofelia had adopted a distant and superior attitude. Chuy resented her demeanor; nor did she appreciate the smallness of her wage and the fact that she had few choices with respect to employment. She was outspoken in her complaints.

It is a strange thing to see how much people change when they get money, especially women; all because of the maquiladoras. Ofelia and I went to many parties together. She used to confide in me when Pedro was courting her. Now she acts as if she were a real lady. She is just a factory worker who can't even look after her own child. She may not want to admit it, but we are made of the same stuff, the same flesh and blood. I can't understand what is the matter with her; we belong to the same class. I wish she wouldn't put on airs.

On the other hand, Chuy loved the child she had in her care and staying close to home saved her money and effort. She rarely went far from the neighborhood. During the day she would often bring the toddler to her mother, Elisa, while she went grocery shopping or cleaned Ofelia's house. But she had a restless spirit; she felt life had been unfair to her in many ways, and she was not resigned. As Rubén and his family prepared to leave for the United States she experienced a renewed urge to do the same. Very few things held her back in Ciudad Juárez. Besides her mother, she had no one else she cared deeply for in the city. Living in her sister's house was often stressful, and in many ways she felt everybody would be better off if she left.

In late December Chuy borrowed six hundred pesos from her brother-in-law to pay a "coyote" woman for smuggling her into the United States. Her intent was to go to any city in northern Texas. But as they drove down a road their vehicle was detained by the state police who promptly transferred them into the hands of the migra. Twenty-four hours later Chuy was safely back in Ciudad Juárez. Her journey had lasted exactly three days.

As for the six hundred pesos, they weren't recovered; their loss was part of the risk taken when trying to cross the border illegally. Looking sullen and tired, Chuy returned to her job as a maid. For some time, all that she could think about was how to pay her debt back to Anselmo. She wanted to salvage part of her wounded pride. But he didn't mind all that much. When he had given Chuy the money, he had considered it more as a gift than as a loan. Anyhow, he felt sorry for the girl; she had always been unlucky.

From the point of view of the anthropologist the manner in which individual experiences intertwine to form distinct and unique patterns is a continuous source of fascination. But the lesson to be apprehended from related isolable lives should go beyond the limits of personalism. All human beings are an end product of specific historical processes. Life, even when dissected into intelligible parcels, is still conditioned by broader sociostructural conditions. There was much to be learned from the manner in which people living in the Juárez barrio related to one another. The most important of these lessons had to do with the way in which individuals, as workers and household members, adjust to an environment in which opportunities are limited and modest survival is a quotidian task.

All those living in Zaragoza Street had been directly or indirectly affected by the geographical proximity of the United States and by the mirage of opportunities perceived across the Rio Grande. As the preceding account indicates, international migration is part and parcel of everyday existence in Ciudad Juárez. In Anselmo's case legal residence in the United States had provided him with access to a stable working situation and, by Mexican standards, relatively attractive earnings. The cost had been to give up daily cohabitation with his wife and children. His was a good example of the ways in which families expand and contract in order to meet the needs of its members.

172

For Chuy and Rubén, illegal migration was a desperate step which followed the exploration of numerous alternatives in the Mexican city. Neither of the three individuals or their relatives saw life in the neighboring country as a permanent goal. Their intent, in every case, was to accumulate enough earnings to live comfortably in Mexico. From the available evidence on the subject, it is known that many Mexican migrants in the United States long for the time when they will be able to return to their country of origin. Not all, however, fulfill this intent. Many continue to enlarge the files of low paying jobs in the U.S. for the rest of their lives. They are a vivid symptom of the particular economic and political relationship between a central highly industrialized power, the U.S., and a semi-peripheral country, Mexico.

In recent years, the majority of those living in Zaragoza Street had also felt the impact of maquiladora production. Women, in particular, had grown increasingly conscious of the availability of factory work as an independent source of income destined, in the majority of cases, to the maintenance of their families. In general these women saw maquiladora work as the best alternative in the midst of few suitable working options. Pondering upon the future of her thirteen-year-old daughter, Emma, Chuy's sister, Anselmo's wife, looked forward to the time when she would be able to support herself.

Time does pass on quickly. In two years Estela will be having her *fiesta de quince años*. She will then be a young woman, but I don't want her to get married soon. She should have a better chance than I did to be on her own and enjoy life. With marriage come the babies and with children great responsibilities which make you old before your time. The women in my generation were taught only one thing: to be mothers and wives and to humor and respect men. My father used to say that educating a woman is a waste of time. They don't teach you how to be a good wife in school.

But times have changed. Girls should go to school long enough to have a good opportunity in life. As you can see it is impossible to get a good job even at a maquiladora unless you have a primary school certificate. Estela should complete secondary school or attend a commercial academy before she tries to get a job. Now, we are still a poor family, but we can support our children until they are strong enough to make it on their own. But by all means Estela should work when she is ready. I will try very hard to persuade her father to let her work. The best jobs are in the maquiladoras, especially in those which manufacture electric products. I definitely wouldn't want her to be a seamstress, that kind of work is too exhausting.

Estela should work so that she can buy the clothes and things she wants. Many young women support their families by working at the maquiladoras. That's very noble, but in many cases their parents, especially their fathers, take advantage of them. I know a family with seven children. The father doesn't work at all; he lives off the earnings of his three eldest daughters, all of whom are spending the best years of their lives at the maquiladoras. What a pity! Estela should work for herslf. If she wants to help her family once in a while, that's all right, but parents shouldn't exploit their daughters. Let her work for a few years and have fun while she gets married. Later, if she finds a good man, she may have a home and children of her own, as all women should.

There are few desirable jobs for women outside of the maquiladora sector. Besides its obvious economic impact, having a job at an assembly plant has had other subtle but not less important effects upon the lives of women and their families. Consider the case of Ofelia and Chuy. They embody two distinct female experiences found among the members of the same social class. It has been suggested in earlier chapters that maquiladoras employ a relatively well-educated female contingent to perform repetitive "unskilled" and "semiskilled" operations. Therefore there is no direct correspondence between level of schooling and the level of skill required to perform maquiladora operations. But while education may not have a clear relationship with respect to the abilities necessary for work in an assembly plant, it continues to have political and ideological functions. That is, level of instruction is an effective screening device for regulating the size of the maquiladora work force.

For these reasons, the emphasis upon a given level of schooling (no matter how arbitrarily it has been determined) decisively influences the mode of insertion of potential workers into a particular labor market. With only three years of education, the choices for Chuy were clear cut: illegal migration, paid domestic work and some other "informal" activities, including prostitution. With a primary school certificate, Ofelia, Chuy's former friend and present employer, had been able to get a factory job. Her relative affluence enabled her to hire a woman of similar class background to help with household chores and child care. With minor variations, Rubén's wife was in a similar situation.

While relative affluence through factory employment may enable the purchase of domestic services, the need to fulfill two distinct and often contradictory roles ultimately explains this phenomenon among some maquiladora workers. Ofelia's experience is a case in point. The nonexistence of properly located day-care facilities and a rational transportation system makes it very difficult for mothers working in maquiladoras to combine wages and domestic labor. Hiring the services of neighbors who are very young, elderly and/or unemployed has become the preferred option to resolve a persistent contradiction.

In some circumstances, when women lack the proper networks, they are forced to resort to strategies reminiscent of those employed during early stages of industrialization in Europe. I knew several women whose children were literally farmed out while they worked to support them. One, for example, religiously sent most of her earnings to her mother (in whose care her three children lived) in Santa Barbara, a small Chihuahuan city. Another one, lacking even a distant relative to resort to, had placed her young daughter in a boarding school while she lived alone in Ciudad Juárez. However, these were unusual cases. Most maquiladora workers rely on their female kin and/or neighbors to reconcile the contradiction between paid work and child care.

Multinational offshore production in the form of maquiladora operations has combined with informal economic activities at the household, neighborhood and community levels. Small grocery stores such as La Nueva are important sources of credit, food and other essentials. Because many women employed at maquiladoras have male relatives who are without permanent jobs, access to small establishments such as La Nueva (in as personal a manner as possible) is indispensable. During periods when women themselves are seeking jobs, and therefore lack a regular income, they must rely upon familial and neighborly networks to survive.

Informal economic exchanges at the level of the household and the neighborhood facilitate the daily maintenance of actual and potential workers. Because these workers' wages continue to be smaller than the cost of living, such exchanges are fundamental for subsistence. They extend purchasing power beyond what the natural limits of wages would be otherwise. The articulation of informal transactions into the broader national (and international) economy has importance for capitalists and for workers. From the point of view of the latter, they operate as part of a strategy to maximize resources. From the vantage point of capitalists informal economic transactions among workers contribute to maintain wages at low levels. In this sense they are a form of subsidy for the extraction of surplus and the generation of profit (see Portes, 1982).

Thus, contrary to "modernization" perspective assumptions, the so-called informal sector economy is not a residue of archaic systems of production destined to disappear under the effect of further industrialization. Rather, capitalist industrialization continuously reproduces the social and economic circumstances within which informal economic activities occur as a support mechanism for the effective surplus extraction and profit maximization. They are the lowest echelon in a vertically integrated system of labor and production. It is important to notice, as some authors have done, that women have a vigorous participation in informal economic activities as the description of Zaragoza Street suggests.

But what was especially interesting in that case was the odd combination of transactions surrounding the sale and purchase of cosmetics and jewelry among those living in the barrio. Modern luxury item firms such as Avon and Stanley have found among the poverty-stricken inhabitants of Ciudad Juárez neighborhoods an expanding clientele. The apparent contradiction of women engaging in transactions which would seem better suited for the members of more affluent sectors may be explained by centering attention upon the short-term functions they play.

Sales and purchases occurring among neighbors afford women several advantages. First, they enable them to increase their income without neglect of their responsibilities as wives and mothers. Because these are transactions that fall outside the formal labor market, they are seen with leniency by men. While husbands and fathers often object to their wives' and daughters' employment outside of the home (even when they are forced into acceptance by need), they seldom disapprove of activities which do not threaten common notions of femininity and women's place in society. Second, as indicated in the description of Zaragoza Street, an important element of reciprocity permeates neighborly transactions. These could summarily be described as mechanisms for maintaining a perennial debt among their participants. Their purpose was not to expand personal profits on a regular basis but to make modest supplementary earnings. In turn customers were able to obtain products which otherwise would have been beyond their needs by relying upon credit extended to them by salesladies. Partial payment of individual debts enabled the latter to receive commissions from their respective firms.

Finally, the same transactions served as opportunities for sociable contact in an environment in which the purchase of leisure and entertainment is beyond the means of the majority. Periodic gatherings at neighbors' homes with the purpose of introducing a new product or demonstrating the beautifying effects of another product had become major events in the neighborhood. Such gatherings were often accompanied by lively conversation; they were a way to approximate the imagined life-style of well-off women who are also in a position to purchase more expensive commodities. In this sense informal transactions such as the ones described contain an important ideological component.

The purpose of this section has been twofold. On the one hand, an ethnographic description of Zaragoza Street, a Juárez barrio where a large number of maquiladora workers live, provides a scenery to understand the interaction of factory work with other sorts of economic activities in which women, as well as men, have vigorous participation. It is not possible to understand the participation of women in the maquiladora work force without some understanding of their life as members of families and neighborhoods.

On the other hand, the analysis of ethnographic materials informed by larger socioeconomic considerations provides the first step for explaining the relationship between men's and women's participation in labor, illegal international migration, informal economic activities and family organization. As seen earlier, these connections are central for the question of labor supply and the manner in which men and women participate in the social division of labor. Too inflexible or static a definition of family precludes any possibility for insight in concrete circumstance. As seen from the materials contained in this section families are extremely flexible units which expand and contract to meet needs determined by broader economic and social realities.

Francisca, Sylvia and Florencia: A Profile of Maquiladora Workers

Francisca Lucero is nineteen years old and has worked for three years at the largest electronic assembly plant in Ciudad Juárez, a subsidiary of a U.S. multinational corporation. Born in Santa Barbara, a town in the interior of the state of Chihuahua, Kika (as she is known to friends and family) was brought to Juárez at the age of three. With her came two brothers and her parents to swell the ranks of the hopeful that constantly migrate to the Mexican-American border.

Earlier, her father, who once had owned a small parcel of promising farm land, was forced to sell it and join other displaced agricultural workers who had been driven out by large agribusiness. It is not that Kika's father wanted to move from the Santa Barbara area or that he was lured by the mirage of urban opportunity and progress, as some migration students believe. Rather he knew, even then, that suffering was to be expected in a big city, for cities are often cruel to newcomers. He had heard that life was expensive. But he had no choice. It was either further impoverishment in a small town or the gamble for a better life in Ciudad Juárez. At that time he placed his faith in two somewhat encouraging signs. First, Ciudad Juárez was growing. There had to be work in a big city like that for a man willing to do virtually anything to earn a living. Besides, Valente, his uncle, had migrated to Juárez five years earlier and was willing to help him for as long as it took to find a house and settle down. Second, Juárez was very close to the United States, only a few minutes away from El Paso, Texas. If things became too difficult he could cross into U.S. territory. Many were doing so in spite of the ever-present danger of la migra, and he might also try. He was not afraid.

Kika can still remember those early days in Juárez. The city turned her father from an impoverished migrant into an unskilled general worker with no stable or regular income. In time he did have to cross the border and toiled in the fields of Arizona as an "illegal alien." The *gringos* treated him well, but the ordeal was trying. Eventually, he came back to Juárez, a more silent and older man. It was fortunate that he returned. Many men don't; they find ways to remain in the United States while their families are left behind to fend for themselves.

Francisca can vividly describe, amidst sighs of regret and nervous laughter, the hardships of living with seven other persons of various ages in a one-room adobe house in las lomas, an area on the outskirts of the city with no paved streets, no electricity and no piped water. Three younger brothers and two sisters were born there. For ten-odd years her mother worked as a maid in order to help support the family. But the most she ever earned was one hundred pesos a week (about $8). Occasionally, she would wake up

earlier than usual, brush away from her face the signs of discourage-
ment and cook *burritos*, *empanadas* or *gorditas*, which she later
sold at the local stadiums. There were only a few assembly plants or
maquiladoras in Juárez at that time, although people hoped their
presence would change the city; they were seen as a sign of progress.
Kika's mother tried to get a job at one of the new factories, as it soon
became clear that they hired mostly women. However, they required a primary school diploma. Having attended school irregularly
for only four years, she didn't have one.

Their situation improved, however, when Kika's oldest brother
turned sixteen and was able to supplement their father's income by
becoming an unskilled construction worker. Kika too had to help
but not before completing six years of schooling. By then her parents
knew that without a primary school certificate her chances of
finding work at a maquiladora would be poor. And the consensus is
that assembly plants, which operate as subsidiaries of multinational
corporations, offer the best employment alternative in Ciudad
Juárez. Maquiladora workers regularly earn the minimum wage
stipulated by Mexican law and, more significantly from the perspective of the workers, they insure medical care through the participation of their personnel in the Instituto Mexicano del Seguro Social
(the Social Security System). These are benefits which unfortunately cannot always be obtained by working in other sectors of the
economy.

Kika had been a good student. She would have liked to attend
secondary school and to become a nurse. But familial duties dissi-
pated her hopes. Although she doesn't remember any sort of direct
parental pressure, she felt partly responsible for the well-being of
her family. The needs were many and the earnings scant. When her
father ruefully encouraged her to continue studying, she refused by
arguing that school was boring. At fourteen she went to work as a
clerk in a grocery store. Hours were long, the wage small and she
was excluded from the benefits that the Mexican Labor Law requires, but nothing could be done. She knew it would be impossible
to get a better-paying job until after her sixteenth birthday. Patiently, she waited.

At fifteen, however, she started looking for employment at the
largest industrial park in Ciudad Juárez. She had learned about
young women who lie about their ages and alter birth certificates in
order to qualify for work in the plants. She was willing to do
whatever was necessary to become an *operadora* (line worker). As
time passed, the industrial park acquired formidable dimensions in

179

Kika's mind. She began to admire the geometric profiles of factories aligned by the side of carefully manicured lawns and the design of multi-national emblems. In particular she learned to contemplate, in awe, the sharp contrast between the industrial park—a symbol of modern opportunity—and the drab neglect visible throughout Ciudad Juárez.

In 1975 Kika and one of her best friends would regularly arrive at the industrial park at six-thirty in the morning. Wearing their best clothes, hungry, expectant and shy, the two would walk from plant to plant in search of precious job applications. It wasn't easy to get one. Signs reading *No hay solicitudes* (no job applications) or *No hay vacantes* (not hiring) hung on the doors of many maquiladoras. At one of them a young and smartly dressed secretary looked them over and told them to come back next week. At another a guard with an air of solemnity about him asked if they had letters of recommendation and, after receiving a negative response, triumphantly stated that a personal recommendation was indispensable to apply for a job at an assembly plant.

After two months of similar experiences, Kika was confused. She felt belittled and impotent; incapable of gaining control over a situation that deeply affected her life and that of her family. If, as common knowledge has it, there are so many opportunities for women in Juárez, why was she having difficulty finding a job? She did not know that for every production operator working along the assembly lines, behind the sewing machines, or attached to welders and wire cutters, three other women with similar economic need and similar abilities constantly search for employment. Those who are older, who support children or who have not completed primary school find it particularly difficult to get a job. Many are driven across the border and work illgally as domestics in El Paso. Women, single or married, of different levels of education and age who roam the streets and industrial parks in need of jobs, have become a distinctive feature of Ciudad Juárez. It is part of the irony of their quest that until the maquiladora program appeared, the majority were not members of the labor force. Fourteen years later these women have become urban proletarians.

Kika may have despaired at her difficulty to find a job in an environment where the only viable employment opportunities were geared to women almost exclusively. But the apparent paradox in which she found herself obscured many of the advantages of relocation from the point of view of multinational corporations. Women who are forced to compete against one another for a limited number of jobs turn out to be efficient and docile workers when competition occurs in a social milieu devoid of occupational opportunities for men.

"We hire mostly women because they are more reliable than men; they have finer fingers, smaller muscles and unsurpassed manual dexterity. Also, women don't get tired of repeating the same operations nine hundred times a day." Such was the explanation offered by Kika's personnel manager when asked why 90% of the plant's workers are women. His was a lucid articulation of the ideology that justifies the employment of women (particularly young women) in low-paying assembly operations by referring to presumed biological and emotional differences between the sexes.

By distorting and over-simplifying complex phenomena, ideology obviates the need to center attention upon economic and political realities. To the social scientist, statements like the one recorded above may appear as trivial, irritating or quaint manifestations of "false consciousness," but they should not be taken lightly; they make social events understandable to members of the managerial sectors as well as most workers. Kika certainly agrees that women tend to be more responsible, patient and dexterous than males. But she doubts that men would be willing to perform the sort of exhausting and repetitive work that she does for the kind of wage that she earns. Also, Kika feels women are more shy and submissive, more used to following orders. They can be easily intimidated and forced to obey. Here lies the economic and political crux of the matter. As Kika herself explains, "I would prefer to stay home and not do factory work. But my family needs my earnings. My father cannot support us, my brothers and sisters are young. I *have* to be efficient and patient at my job."

Until recently, when her seventeen-year-old sister was able to get a similar position at another plant, Kika provided the only source of stable income for her family. Earlier her older brother had left to become one of the countless wetbacks, or *mojados*, sporadically working on the ranches of the U.S. Southwest. With three younger brothers and one sister still in school, Kika feels obliged to give at least five hundred pesos ($22), that is, half of her weekly wage, to her mother who uses it to buy food and pay other household expenses. Thanks to her and her sister's contribution a younger brother will be able to attend secondary school.

Of the half wage she keeps for herself, about 17% is spent in transportation and meals at the factory. With what is left she attends to personal needs. She would like to furnish a room for

181

herself. She is tired of sharing her bed with other members of her family. Also, she is fond of fashionable clothes, cosmetics and, much to the dismay of the city's moralists, she enjoys disco dancing. True, she sometimes has to treat a male companion unable or unwilling to pay the entrance fee at the Malibú, one of the many popular dancing halls in Ciudad Juárez. But more often she may be seen sitting alone or in the company of other female friends waiting to be approached by a young man. Her relative affluence has been a mixed blessing in a context in which men are expected to take the initiative in most areas of social life. The dancing and the euphoria of discotheques provide Kika with the only means of release in an uninterrupted cycle of monotonous work and domestic problems which remain unresolved day after day.

After four years of tedious labor at the plant, Kika admits she is exhausted. More discouraging than monotony is the realization that promotions are hard to come by and wages are forever shrinking. Since she began work, she has put in at least forty-eight hours each week for an average of 58 cents an hour. She has worked from 6:30 A.M. to 3:15 P.M. on weekdays and from 6:30 A.M. to 11:30 A.M. on Saturdays. From Monday to Friday she, like the rest, is allowed ten minutes in the morning to have breakfast and thirty minutes in the afternoon to eat lunch.

The rest of her time is filled by attempts to fulfill production goals set up by Mexican industrial engineers who have been recruited by U.S. management. Quotas are high to the point that the loss of a few minutes at the beginning of the day may create confusion and delays along the assembly line throughout the rest of the shift. The conveyor belt never ceases to move at the same exasperating speed, and operations are minute and complex. They demand undivided attention. Even basic needs like going to the bathroom require special permission from the supervisor.

Transportation is also a problem. Although 90% of Ciudad Juárez is covered by public transport, the quality is inadequate at best. During the rush periods which precede the entrance of workers at the factories, it is possible to see hundreds of women crowded like cattle inside rundown ruteras and buses. To arrive punctually at the plant, Kika must take two ruteras every morning (one from her house to the downtown area and another one to the industrial park), because she lives in one of the colonias in the periphery of the city, where the majority of working people are concentrated. The neighborhood where she lives still has no paved streets, although electricity and sewerage were recently provided. Usually it takes Kika between forty-five minutes and one hour to get from her home to the plant.

In this respect, as in many others, hers is a situation markedly different from that of managers who, almost without exception, live in the U.S. El Paso suburbs. Every morning, shortly after the ruteras have delivered the women to the plants, the managers may be seen commuting from the United States to Ciudad Juárez (a thirty-minute ride, at the most). The proximity of the industrial parks to El Paso enables management and their families to enjoy the advantages of the "American way of life." What better example may be found to illustrate the convergence of two different styles of life in an international setting which lays bare the contradictions of a gender differentiated labor division?

The personnel manager at the plant where Kika works often reflects that "maquiladoras have brought about an industrial revolution to the Mexican border. They have taught an otherwise inexperienced work force about the merits of punctuality and industrial discipline." Maybe! But Kika has experienced another aspect of this story. In the last three years she has learned what it is like to work as an appendage of a machine. She knows about the boredom bred in dark surroundings filled by lead vapors due to defective ventilation. She has often felt the nerve-racking effects of continuous high levels of noise and the nausea induced by glues and solder.

Kika must go on working because she has no choice. She longs for the day when she will be able to get married, leave the work force and have a home of her own. Being a member of a generation of female factory workers that is barely a decade old, Kika does not see herself as a member of the proletariat, but as a potential wife and mother. Novels and soap operas have instilled and reflect romance in her mind. But marriage is a hazardous prospect in a context characterized by economic constraints that keep men in her circle from performing their traditional role as providers.

To promoters of the In-Bond Manufacturing Program, maquiladoras may represent a success, but Kika knows she lives in a painful bind. And is that not what the terms underdevelopment and dependency mean in a most precise manner? Cut from their abstract embellishments, they describe a social reality in which persons like Kika and the members of her family must always move perilously between destitution and mere subsistence, even while surrounded by the glitter of "progress." Kika agrees with her personnel manager that maquiladoras are the best thing that ever happened to Ciudad Juárez. That, indeed, describes the real paradox.

183

* * *

In November, 1978, Sylvia had been working for five months at Trimex, a small subcontracted apparel manufacturing shop whose finished products bear the labels of Sears and Devon. She was then thirty-one, married to a kind but irregularly employed thirty-three-year-old man, and the mother of six children ranging in ages from two to fourteen years.

Sylvia and her family live in a two-room adobe house in the Colonia Mariano Escobedo, one of the peripheral zones where poverty-striken workers and recently arrived immigrants from the interior of Mexico concentrate. The house, which lacks plumbing and running water, is surrounded by an intricate mesh of unpaved roads which valiantly cross over semi-arid hills. It takes Sylvia an hour every morning to get from her home to the maquiladora where she works from Monday to Saturday (forty-eight hours a week) for an hourly wage of less than $1.00.

Sylvia was the fourth-born in a family of seven. Her father, an intermittent agricultural worker had for some time been an illegal alien in the U.S. Southwest. Her mother—much to the pride of her daughter—had always been a housewife. Survival was difficult, but Sylvia's father did not approve of married women who worked outside of their homes. Mostly due to scarcity, Sylvia started work as a maid in Ciudad Juárez at thirteen. Thus, she was never able to complete her elementary education. At fifteen, she married Jose and shortly afterwards their first daughter was born.

Soon afterwards, facing the increasing costs of child support, Sylvia began crossing the border illegally in order to work as a maid in the neighboring city of El Paso, Texas. This was before the Border Industrialization Program became a reality. When the first maquiladoras began to operate in Ciudad Juárez rumor quickly spread that jobs were available for women. Requirements were then extremely lenient and crowds flowed to the factories in search of employment. In 1969 Sylvia got a job at Acapulco Fashion, one of the subcontracted firms of Figure Flattery International and one of the oldest maquiladoras in Ciudad Juárez. Many of her life's memories are linked to factory work.

Of course I can remember what it was like when maquiladoras began operating in the city! They hardly even asked whether you were married or not, or whether you had an education or didn't know how to read and write. They were hiring anyone who showed up to apply. Things are very different now. Now it matters whether you have finished your primary education or not. And, as you know, many maquiladoras don't want to employ women who have children to support. They prefer the chavalillas because they are easier to handle. Ten years ago things were altogether different.

We had rough beginnings. Women were hired to do everything, including the handling of material and the loading of trucks. Operators were hired without the assurance of a wage, because, as management stated, "this company is giving workers free training." Later on we were paid by the piece, but only when there was enough material to be sewed. Still, this was better than having to cross the border three or four times a week.

I worked at Acapulco Fashion for nearly ten years. During that time the company became better organized and larger. Currently it has five plants, one of which works for Johnson and Johnson under contract. For most of the time I worked there, I was able to earn more than the minimum wage, although management kept on raising production standards. [Acapulco Fashion, as with the majority of clothing producing maquiladoras, has always operated through a combination of minimum wages and bonuses given to workers if they fulfill established production quotas.]

I used to arrive at the shop half an hour before the shift started to make sure my production quota would be completed by the end of the week. I was so efficient that I started getting a reputation. Once the personnel manager singled me out among the rest of the workers. She congratulated me publicly for the quality of my work and productivity. I was very proud.

During the time I worked at the factory, I had four babies and on every occasion I was granted an eighty-four-day leave with full pay. You may think this was a great benefit and in a way it was, but the truth is that I didn't want to have more than two children. When I knew that I was pregnant for the third time, I was desperate. I used to cry all the time, not because I didn't like the idea of being a mother, but because we've never had the means to support a large family.

When my third baby was born, I asked the doctor at the Seguro Social to help me. I wanted a tubal ligation, but birth control programs were not yet fashionable in Mexico, and I was too ignorant to know about other alternatives. The doctor said I was young and healthy and could bear many more children. He said Mexico's wealth laid in its abundant population. I felt guilty not to want to be a mother. I've had three other children and the last one nearly killed me.

After nine years of work at Acapulco Fashion, I became ill with chronic lumbago. The doctor said that this was a work-related condition and suggested that I either resign or ask my supervisor to employ me in a different operation—one not requiring sitting behind a sewing machine for eight continuous hours a day. Naturally, I couldn't resign because I had a family to support. But management did not want to give me a simpler job. Instead, they wanted me to continue being as productive as I had been in the past. And they didn't want to fire me, because I had been at the company for too long. They knew I was entitled to seniority and indemnity benefits at the time of dismissal.

Management had to find a way to get rid of me, but I was determined to stay on the job. After nearly a decade of efficient work, I began to have problems. First, I was accused of pretending to be ill in order not to get the job done. As a result of that, I asked the physician at the Social Security clinic for a letter certifying the work-related nature of my ailment, but he refused. He said he didn't want to get into trouble and that it was better for everyone concerned when medical personnel collaborate with the factories. Again, he advised me to resign and give more time and attention to my family.

Later on they started giving me different new operations and demanding that I fulfill production quotas after a few days. No longer was I able to earn a wage above the minimum. Finally, I was called into the personnel manager's office and invited to resign. "You are tired," she said, "and you are making us very unhappy. Resign and we'll give you a 4,000 peso settlement." I couldn't believe it: 4,000 pesos after ten years of work. I was entitled to ten times that amount.

One morning, my supervisor ridiculed me before the other workers. That was too much. I left the factory immediately with the intent of filing a complaint at the Junta de Concilia-cion y Arbitraje. They heard me all right but they offered no advice. They said I should have accepted the settlement. After-wards, the company denied all responsibility. They said I had deserted the job voluntarily and I didn't even get the 4,000 pesos. The worst part of this story is that workers at Acapulco Fashion are unionized. The union did not lift a finger to defend my case. Because I was not aware of the correct legal proce-dures, I was unable to fight back.

At thirty and with a family to support, Sylvia faced particularly harsh limitations in a labor market where young, single, childless females with comparatively high schooling levels are preferred for assembly work. Two months of uncertainty, credit at the grocery store and borrowed money passed. Finally Sylvia got a job at Trimex, a small garment shop that employed two hundred direct production workers of whom only twelve had a permanent status. The rest were laborers without any right to seniority or compensation in case of dismissal. Many had been working for the company since it had started operations in the autumn of 1974 but they had never been granted job tenure. Instead, every three months each of these workers was asked to sign a resignation and immediately afterwards was issued a new temporary contract. Of the two hundred workers, eighty-seven had been hired during the six months prior to Sylvia's employment. Working conditions were dismal and discipline arbitrary. Moreover, management effected a weekly discount upon the weekly wages of the workers.

For Sylvia, employment at Trimex represented a step downward in the occupational scale—a common fate shared by older women who have worked as maquiladora operators for some time. As younger women are incorporated into the ranks of assembly work, older women are squeezed out of the least exploitative positions and cornered into situations such as the ones that prevail at Trimex.

*   *   *

Florencia's experience differs to a large extent. At the time Sylvia was hired by Trimex, Florencia had completed her third year as an assembly worker at Electro Componentes de Mexico, the subsidiary of General Electric in Ciudad Juárez. She was then twenty years old and single. She and her family have lived in the same house for the last four years. Her parents and seven brothers and sisters aged fourteen to twenty-six share four ample bedrooms and a modest but well-equipped kitchen and living room. Zaragoza, the area where the house is located has been transformed in the last years into a suburb of Juárez. Not long ago it was still an independent cluster of extended cotton fields. Its recent rural past is apparent amidst the contrast created by rough unpaved streets and disco music heard daily at its central square. It takes Florencia only fifteen minutes to get from her home to the modern Parque Industrial Juárez where Electro Componentes de Mexico is located. Two older sisters aged twenty-one and twenty-three are also employed in maquiladoras. One works at Juarmex, a subsidiary of the Warnaco Group, the other one is a supervisor at Sylvania. Her twenty-five-year-old brother has been a print setter for a local newspaper for four years. Florencia sees her life as a struggle for upward mobility.

My father is an "independent" photographer. He works hard trying to get as many odd jobs as possible. Business is good on weekends because of the many weddings and christenings. But weekdays are slow. Three or four times every week he sells candy outside of a local school to make ends meet. Things were harder when my brothers and sisters were younger.

When my brother was old enough to work he quit school and started giving money to my mother. Then my two sisters got jobs in maquiladoras and things improved. It was thanks to them that I was able to finish secondary school. I also attended a commercial academy. I wanted to be a secretary, but because I don't speak English I'll never be able to get that kind of a job. At first my father didn't want me to work. Only because our family needed the money did he allow my sisters to look for jobs, but by the time I was sixteen he felt our situation was much better. Fortunately, he changed his mind; he has become less strict, more modern.

I wanted to work to have money of my own and to furnish a bedroom all to myself. As a child I always had to share my bed with two sisters. I was lucky to get a job at Electro Componentes. Assembly work is hard and boring, but the wage is better than average. In fact there are few worthwhile jobs in Juárez outside of the maquiladoras, especially for women. I give half of my weekly wage to my mother and the rest I keep for myself. I spend most of my money in clothes, and once in a while I enjoy an evening at a discotheque. A girl should have fun. Things will change when I get married. Then I will settle down, quit my job and take care of my home and children. In that respect, I agree with my father: Married women should stay at home, like my mother did all of her life.

* * *

It is always risky to generalize from individual case histories. Personal experience is unique and difficult to make fit the harness of rigid descriptive models. On the other hand, the fate of a household and its members is, to a large extent, determined by the economic and political composition of a given social environment. It is at the point of convergence between a broad analysis and personal experience that anthropology can yield its most fruitful results. Sylvia's and Florencia's experience in assembly work, their personal characteristics and future prospects are representative of two distinct groups of women whose labor is indispensable for the expansion of the maquiladora industry. Although in many ways the two groups overlap and share many commonalities, their degree of vulnerability and position within the labor market are significantly different. Their insertion into a labor force linked to the demands of international capital can only be understood by understanding the evolution of households and families over time. The absence of employment alternatives for the male population plays a significant role in this respect. In environments where women are socialized mainly to fulfill the functions of mothers and wives, the existence of thousands of female industrial workers indicates the importance of these considerations.

CHAPTER 9

Epilogue

Exploratory studies do not end with a period but with a question mark. Such is the case with this book. A constant motive for frustration, from the point of view of the researcher, is the length of time that must elapse between active data collection and the moment when information can be made available to a wide audience for analysis and discussion. In the field, every perception, every new finding, every puzzling observation commands intense attention. At every step of the way there are poignant reminders of the theoretical and political concerns that guided research in the first place. Months afterwards, unanswered questions and new points of interest haunt consciousness as harbingers of the task that must yet be undertaken. Therefore, the reader should consider this effort as a first step in an ongoing inquiry. It is to be hoped that this pioneer study will provide the basis for analysis and debate of issues whose importance in the contemporary world cannot be exaggerated.

The contribution of the present work lies in its description of circumstances which have led to the formation of a new working class under the effect of rapid corporate industrialization. That this new proletariat is differentiated by class and national background, as well as by gender, is regarded as a symptom of the continuing socioeconomic and political tendencies of capital investments at an international scale.

In this sense the present study is more than the examination of a localized phenomenon because it focuses upon one of many similar and interrelated developments taking place in distant countries. Women employed in Ciudad Juárez's maquiladoras are bound to working women in Export Processing Zones (EPZs) located in Singapore, Hong Kong, Mauritius, Southern Italy, Puerto Rico, the United

States and the Caribbean by their inclusion in what some authors have labeled "the global assembly line." For them, as never before, there is now the possibility for international solidarity on the basis of shared objective economic experiences.

Global assembly lines have been the consequence of trends that began after the end of the Second World War. Since then a growing portion of international capital has been invested in the transfer of manufacturing stages—particularly those involving labor-intensive operations—from industrialized countries (such as the U.S., Germany and Japan) to developing areas (such as the Orient and the Mexican-American border). In the United States this economic tendency began as factories moved operations from locales such as New York and Massachusetts to the American South. Later they transferred operations to Southwest Indian Reservations. Currently, this southbound flux has spilled over the border into Mexico and expanded westward, crossing the Pacific and extending to Asia. Under such trade marks as RCA, Sony, General Motors, United Technologies, General Electric, Mattel, Chrysler, American Hospital Supply, and so on, workers linked halfway around the world are assembling electronic calculators, digital watches, clothing, toys and electrical transmission systems.

This has had a momentous impact in areas of the world where industry has relocated. Underdeveloped and developing countries are experiencing profound changes as a result of the rapid incorporation of large contingents of young, formerly "unemployable" women into the work force. In the Orient, Latin America and the Caribbean, between 75 and 90% of those working in EPZs are female. Moreover, it has been estimated that over 3 million workers are directly employed by multinational assembly plants in the U.S. and abroad. Nearly 300,000 (almost half of the total labor force) are in Asian electronics factories located in EPZs and more than 150,000 Mexican women work in electronics and garment industries.

As we have seen, the impact of the Maquiladora Program has been considerable. Between 1970 and 1975 imports from Mexico under the 807 tariff provision grew from $261 million to $915 million, an increase of 25%. Imports under 806.30 increased by 950% from 1971. While in 1968 there were but a few plants scattered along the border employing less than 5,000 persons, as of 1979 the program included 531 plants with 476 of these in the frontier zone and 55 in the interior. In 1982 the number of plants operating in Ciudad Juárez alone reached 120 with a work force of over 40,000 persons.

191

Moreover, goods produced under the auspices of this program during 1979 represented 24% of Mexico's total manufactured exports and 10.5% of total exports. At present it is the fastest-growing economic sector (including petroleum-related activities). Therefore it comes as no surprise to learn that Mexican public officials see the Maquiladora Program as an integral part of their development strategy. For them this is a glowing example of progress, which other countries would do well in emulating. Nevertheless, their opinions represent only one facet of a complex reality. While maquiladoras have brought about employment alternatives for women and expanded their potential for economic participation, they have also generated social tensions and painful dilemmas.

This study points out that, contrary to some commonly held opinions, the involvement of women in paid industrial labor in developing countries does not necessarily represent the improvement of their alternatives as individuals and as members of families. Rather, their employment in maquiladoras may be a symptom of their economic vulnerability. In the absence of jobs for them and the men in their families, women opt for the only form of employment available. True, this affords survival, but it is hardly an adequate vehicle for expanding the choices of working people on whose shoulders rests the advancement of a nation. It should be clear that the argument is not against the participation of women in paid work but against the perpetuation of sexual segregation in the labor market which fosters underdevelopment and economic atrophy.

Another issue to be stressed in this concluding section refers to the heterogeneity of the maquiladora work force. Important differences were found when comparing workers by manufacturing activity. These differences are not random. Instead they are the consequence of employment policies combined with the position of women in the labor market. Thus, "older" women, many of whom are married, have a low level of schooling and/or comparatively short periods of residence in Ciudad Juárez, are more often found in the apparel manufacturing industry than in electronics. Here, plants tend to hire young, single women with comparatively more years of schooling and long periods of residence in the city. These findings underscore the need to refine our appraisal of the participation of women in socioeconomic activities. Generalizations are not warranted, and to subsume women into the even more abstract category "cheap labor" does violence to an accurate description of reality.

It has also been noted that employment policies are influenced by the requirements of industries and firms as well as by the particular levels of investment and the type of relationship of parent companies with their affiliates abroad. In this sense, electronics firms, the majority of which operate in Ciudad Juárez as direct subsidiaries of large multinational corporations are in a good position to be highly selective with respect to the personnel they employ. Such is not the case of the clothing industries, most of which are subcontracted and therefore in a more vulnerable position with respect to their principal firms.

A third argument emphasized throughout this study has been that the employment of a particular work force cannot be fully understood only by reference to the requirements of capital accumulation and expansion. Instead, the position of individuals within households and labor markets has to be considered. According to this view, the enfeebled occupational status of working-class men in Ciudad Juárez, and the economic needs of families prompt the entrance of women into the labor force. Contrary to the opinion that maquiladora workers are "supplementary" wage earners, this study demonstrates that most women working in Ciudad juárez's maquiladoras are the main source of stable income for their households.

In other words, when moving stages of their production abroad, multinational corporations can and do take advantage of previously existent high levels of unemployment and underemployment, which in turn are the legacy of economic and political dependence. By employing a majority of women, maquiladoras cause a segmentation of the labor market by gender while at the same time contributing to enlarge the pool of available unskilled and semiskilled workers of both sexes. Thus, although maquiladoras have undoubtedly created jobs during the period they have been in existence, the nature of these jobs suggests that they are not a suitable instrument to diminish the trauma of unemployment and underemployment.

In the final analysis the issue most worthy of consideration regards the understanding of maquiladoras as part of a strategy for development. To what extent is this claim accurate? Let us recapitulate some of the factors that have led to their emergence. The economic implosion of the world has made it possible for investments to cross international barriers and establish industrial operations in different parts of the globe. Corporate representatives see geographical dispersion as a path which diversifies political and economic risks. Large wage differentials maintain high profits. The absence or weakening of unions and other workers' organizations provides hospitable environments for production. Women are a docile, manipulatable, easily replaceable work force. Flexibility of this kind is good for business.

But the same factors have a different meaning when seen from the perspective of workers. For them, industry's diversification of risks may translate into precisely the opposite phenomenon: the accentuation of multiple hazards. Without the careful vigilance of responsible business representatives and public officials, the internationalization of production can entail the worsening of working conditions, the loosening of health and safety regulations, the exacerbation of urban problems and, in the long run, the increase of unemployment.

The motives that have led corporate industry to move operations to low-wage areas of the world are pristine. Yet those that guide policy development in host countries often remain vague. At times it has appeared as if public officials were merely sanctioning what had already been devised by economic interests in New York, Geneva or Tokyo, and without due regard to the needs of people at the local level. In the future, Mexican government representatives will have to consciously weigh the benefits and costs of export-processing industrialization. Careful planning, not blind servility, is needed to define the parameters of balanced development. This is a pressing need in the light of the considerations contained in this volume.

More and more women are becoming part of the international productive structure. Whether their personal and collective alternatives will be expanded or diminished is still an open question, but optimistic generalizations should be tempered by caution. One thing is certain, balanced development cannot be achieved without considering their specific needs and problems. Public indifference towards the risks of women's indiscriminate employment may be a fault for which a high price may have to be paid in the future.

Bibliography

Aguiar, N. "The Impact of Industrialization on Women's Work Roles in the Northeast of Brazil." In *Sex and Class in Latin America*, ed. J. Nash and H. I. Safa. New York: Praeger, 1976.

Alcalá Quintero, Francisco. "Desarrollo Regional Fronterizo." *Comercio Exterior* 19 (December 1969): 960–64.

Almquist, P. Y. "Women in the Work Force." *SIGNS* 3, no. 2 (Summer 1977): 843–55.

American Chamber of Commerce. *Border Industrialization Program.* Mexico D.F., 1970.

———. *Accumulation on a World Scale.* New York: Monthly Review Press, 1974*b*.

Amsden, A. "An Overview of the Economics of Women and Work." In *The Economics of Women and Work*, ed. A. Amsden. London: Penguin, 1979.

Anderson, M. *Family Structure in Nineteenth Century Lancashire.* Cambridge: Cambridge University Press, 1972.

Ariès, P. *Centuries of Childhood.* New York: Random House, 1965.

Arizpe, L. "Women in the Informal Labor Sector, the Case of Mexico City." *SIGNS* 2, no. 3: 25–37.

Armida, D. "The Organization of the Household and the Supply of Industrial Labor to Multinational Enterprise Subsidiaries: A Case Study." Mimeographed. Berkeley: University of California, 1980.

Arreola Wong, M. *El Programa Mexicano de Maquiladoras: Una Respuesta a las Necesidades de la Industria Norteamericana.* Mexico D.F.: Centro de Estudios Internacionales, El Colegio de Mexico, 1978.

Arrow, K. "Some Models of Racial Discrimination in the Labor Market." In Anthony Pascal, *The American Economy in Black and White.* Santa Monica, California: Rand Corporation, 1971.

Bach, Robert L. "Mexican Immigration and the American State." Paper presented at the Session on Mexican Immigration to the U.S. Houston: Latin American Studies Association 1976.

Bairoch, P. "Agriculture and the Industrial Revolution, 1700–1914." In *The Industrial Revolution*, ed. C. M. Cipolla. London: Collins/Fontana Books, 1973,

Baker, E. F. *Technology and Women's Work.* New York: Columbia University Press, 1974.

195

Banco Nacional De Mexico. *Review of the Economic Situation of Mexico.* Mexico, D.F.: July 1970, January 1971, January 1973, January and February 1974, January 1975, January 1976, October 1977, November 1978.

Barkin, D. "Mexico's Albatross: the U.S. Economy." *Latin American Perspectives* 2 (Summer 1975): 64–80.

Barnet, R., and Muller, R. *Las Dirigentes del Mundo.* Barcelona: Editorial Grijalvo, 1976.

Barraesen, D. W. *The Border Industrialization Program of Mexico.* Lexington, Mass.: D. C. Heath, 1971

Barrera Bassols, J. "Maquiladoras y Migración." In *Aspectos Sociales de la Migración Municipal,* ed. Margarita Nolasco. Mexico D.F.: Instituto Nacional de Antropología e Historia, 1976.

Baxandall, R.; Ewen, E.; and Gordon, L. "The Working Class Has Two Sexes." *Monthly Review* 28 (July/August 1976): 1–9.

Barthomieu, C., and Hanaut, H. "Recent Studies and Data from Western Europe on Production Sharing and the International Division of Labour." Paper presented at the Seminar on North-South Complementary Intra-Industry Trade. Mexico, D.F., (unpublished) 1979.

Baudouin, T.; Colin, M.; and Guillerm, D. "Women and Immigrants: Marginal Workers." In *The Resurgence of Class Conflict in Western Europe since 1968,* ed. C. Crouch and A. Pissorno. Ne York: Holmes and Meier Publishers, 1978.

Bayer, J. "Unidad Coordinadora Para el Empleo Capacitación y Adiestramiento, Mexican Government." Address given before the Regional Convention of Maquiladora Associations. Ciudad Juárez, Chihuahua, Mexico, February 9, 1979.

Becker, G. *Human Capital.* Washington, D.C.: National Bureau of Economic Research, 1964.

———. "A Theory of the Allocation of Time." *Economic Journal* (September 1965): 32–41.

Beechey, V. "Some Notes on Female Wage Labor in Capitalist Production." *Capital and Class* (Autumn 1977): 450–472.

———. "Reproduction, Production and the Sexual Division of Labor." *Cambridge Journal of Economics* 3 (1979): 203–25.

Beinefeld, M. "The Informal Sector and Peripheral Capitalism: The Case of Tanzania." *Institute for Development Studies Bulletin* 6, no. 3 (February 1975): 53–73.

Bender, D. R. "A Refinement of the Concept of Household: Families, Co-Residence, and Domestic Functions." *American Anthropologist* 69 (1967): 493–504.

Benería, L. "Reproduction, Production and the Sexual Division of Labor." *Cambridge Journal of Economics* 3 (September 1979).

Benería, L., and Sen, G. "Accumulation, Reproduction and Women's Role in Economic Development: Boserup Revisited." Paper prepared for Burg Wartenstein Symposium no. 85. Wenner Gren Foundation for Anthropological Research, Burg Wartenstein, Austria 1980.

Bennett, K. W. "Dawning of a New Age of Electronics?" *Iron Age* 209 (February 1972): 40–41.

Blackburn, R. M., and Stewart, A. "Women, Work and the Class Structure." *New Society* 41, no. 788 (Spring 1977): 436–47.

Blanpain, R. "Multinational Corporations' Impact on Host Countries' Industrial Relations." In *Multinational Unions and Labor Relations in Industrialized Countries,* ed. R. F. Banks and J. Steiber. Ithaca: New York State School of Industry and Labor Relations, Cornell University, 1977.

Blau, F. D. "Sex Segregation of Workers by Enterprise in Clerical Occupations." In *Labor Market Segmentation,* ed. R. D. Edwards, M. Reich, and D. M. Gordon. Lexington, Mass.: D. C. Heath, 1975.

Blau, F. D., and Jusenius, C. L. "Economists' Approaches to Sex Segregation in the Labor Market: An Appraisal." In *Women and the Marketplace: The Implications of Occupational Segregation,* ed. M. Blaxall and B. B. Reagan. Chicago: University of Chicago Press, 1976.

————. "Economists' Approaches to Sex Segregation in the Labor Market: An Appraisal." *SIGNS* 3 (Spring 1976): 181–200.

Blaxall, M., and Reagan, B., eds. *Women and the Workplace: The Implications of Occupational Segregation.* Chicago: University of Chicago Press, 1976.

Bluestone, B. "Capitalism and Poverty in America: A Discussion." *Monthly Review* 24 (1976): 65–71.

Bluestone, B. and B. Harrison, Capital and Communities: the Causes and Consequences of Private Disinvestment. Washington, D.C.: the Progressive Alliance, 1980.

Bolin, R. L. "Border Industry Facts for 1973." *Mexican American Review* 41 (September 1973): 14–23.

————. "The First Billion Dollar Year." *Mexican American Review* (June 1974): 18–19.

Bolles, L. "From Slavery to Factory: Women, Family Structures and Development in Jamaica." Paper presented at the American Anthropological Association Meetings, Cincinnati, 1979.

Boning, W. R. *Migration for Employment Project: Basic Aspects of Migration from Poor to Rich Countries.* Geneva: International Labour Office, 1976.

Boserup, E. *Women's Role in Economic Development.* London: Allen and Unwin, 1970.

Bradshow, B. "Migrant Labor Force in the Mexican Border." *International Migration Review* 10 (Summer 1976): 17–25.

Braverman, H. *Labor and Monopoly Capital.* New York: Monthly Review Press, 1974.

Bridges, W. P., and Berk, R. A. "Sex, Earnings and the Natue of Work: A Job-Level Analysis of Male-Female Income Differences." *Social Science Quarterly* 58 (March 1978): 553–65.

Briggs, V. M. "Mexican Workers in the United States Labour Market: A Contemporary Dilemma." *International Labour Review* 112 (November 1975): 351–68.

Brookfield, H. *International Dependence and Development.* London: Methuen and Co., 1975.

Brown, G. D. "How Types of Employment Affect Earnings Differences by Sex." *Monthly Labor Review* 99, no. 7 (July 1976): 25–30.

Brown, J. K. "Recruitment of a Female Labor Force." *Anthropos* 73, nos. 1, 2 (1978): 41–48.

Buckley, P. J., and Casson, M. *The Future of the Multinational Enterprise.* London: Longman, 1976.

Bukharin, N. *Imperialism and the Accumulation of Capital.* New York: Monthly Review Press, 1972.

Burawoy, M. "The Functions and Reproduction of Migrant Labor: Comparative Material from Southern Africa and the United States." *American Journal of Sociology* 81, no. 5 (March 1976): 1050–87.

———. "Toward a Marxist Theory of the Labor Process: Braverman and Beyond." *Politics and Society* 8, nos. 3, 4 (1978): 247–312.

———. "The Anthropology of Industrial Work." *Annual Review of Anthropology* 8 (1979): 231–66.

Burtt, E. J. *Influence of Labor Supply on Location of Electronics Firms.* Boston: Federal Reserve Bank of Boston, 1966.

Bustamante, J. A. *Espaldas Mojadas: Materia Prima Para la Expansión del Capital Norteamericano.* México, D.F.: Centro de Estudios Sociológicos, El Colegio de México, 1975a.

———. "El Programa Fronterizo de Maquiladoras: Observaciones Para una Evaluación." *Foro Internacional* 16 (October–December 1975b): 183–204.

———. "Maquiladoras: A New Face of International Capitalism on Mexico's Northern Frontier." Revised version of a paper presented at the 6th National Meeting of the Latin American Studies Association, Atlanta, Georgia, 1976a.

———. "Structural and Ideological Conditions of the Mexican Undocumented Immigration to the United States." *American Behavioral Scientist* 19, no. 3 (January/February 1976b): 52–65.

Buvinic, M. *Women and World Development: An Annotated Bibliography.* Washington, D.C.: Overseas Development Council, 1976.

Campero, M. P., and Guerrero, C. A. "Reflexiónes Sobre la Participación de la Obrera en la Industria Maquiladora en Mexicali, Baja California y su Impacto en la Estructura Familiar." Paper presented at the Primer Simposio Centroamericano de Investigación Sobre la Mujer, México, D.F., 1977.

Cardoso, F. H. "The Consumption of Dependency Theory in the United States." *Latin American Research Review* 12 (1977): 7–24.

Cardoso, F. H., and Faletto, E. *Dependencia y Desarrollo en América Latina.* Mexico, D.F.: Siglo Veintiuno editores, 1971.

Castells, M. "Immigrant Workers and Class Struggles in Advanced Capitalism: The Western European Experience." *Politics and Society* 5, no. 1 (1975): 33–66.

Caulfield, M. D. "Imperialism, the Family and Cultures of Resistance." *Socialist Revolution* 20 (October 1974): 67–85.

Chafe, W. H. *The American Woman: Her Changing Social, Economic and Political Role, 1920–1970.* New York: Oxford University Press, 1972.

Chaikin, S. C. "The Needed Repeal of Item 807.00 of the Tariff Schedules of the United States." Report presented before the Subcommittee on Trade. Committee on Ways and Means, U.S. House of Representatives, 1976.

Chaney, E. H., and Schmink, M. "Women and Modernization: Access to Tools." In *Sex and Class in Latin America,* ed. J. Nash and H. I. Safa. New York: Praeger, 1976.

Chang, Y. S. "The Transfer of Technology: Economics of Offshore Assembly, the Case of the Semi Conductor Industry." UNITAR Research Report no. 11, New York, 1971.

Chinchilla, N. S. "Changing Modes of Production: Industrialization, Monopoly Capitalism, and Women's Work in Guatemala." *SIGNS* 3, no. 1 (1977): 38–56.

Chomsky, N., and Herman, E. "The United States Versus Human Rights in the Third World." *Monthly Review 9*, no. 4 (July/August 1977).

Christopherson, S. M., "The Evolution of Ciudad Juárez, Mexico as an Industrial City" Geography Department, University of California, Berkeley (mimeographed), 1982.

Cohen, L. M. "The Female Factor in Resettlement." *Society* 14, no. 6 (1977): 27–30.

Cohen, Y., ed. *Man in Adaptation*. Hawthorn, New York: Aldine Publishing Co., 1974.

Comercio Exterior. "Empresas Maquiladoras Fronterizas: Facilidades Aduaneras y Debate Sobre su Futuro." (June 1970): 453.

————. "Nuevo Reglamento para las Industrias Maquiladoras de Exportación." (April 1971): 290–91.

————. "Impulso al Desarrollo de la Zona Fronteriza Norte." (May 1971): 387–89.

————. "Fomento Económico en la Frontera Norte e Industrias Maquiladoras." (July 1972): 231–234.

————. "La Industria Maquiladora: Evolución Reciente y Perspectivas." 28 (April 1978): 407–14.

————. "Las Maquiladoras en el Contexto Económico de México." 28 (August 1978): 56–68.

Comisión Económica para América Latina. *México: Notas Para el Estudio Económico de America Latina*. City, Publisher CEPAL 1976.

Comisión Nacional de los Salarios Minimos. *Salarios Minimos*. México, D.F., 1978.

Conference Board, The. *Road Maps of Industry*. New York, 1975.

Conroy, M. E. "Mexico and the U.S.: Issues in Contemporary Economic Relations and the Theory of Dependency." Paper presented at the Conference on Economic Relations between Mexico and the United States, Austin, Texas, April 1973.

Cornelius, W. A. "Impact of Government Policies on Rural Out-Migration." Program Project on Migration and Development. Center for International Studies, Massachusetts Institute of Technology, 1977*a*.

————. "Illegal Mexican Migration to the United States: Recent Research Findings, Policy Implications and Research Priorities." Paper presented at the Workshop of U.S. Immigration: Research Perspectives. Elkridge, Maryland, 1977*b*.

————. "Mexican Migration to the United States (with Comparative Reference to Caribbean-Basin Migration)." Working Paper no. 2. Center for United States-Mexican Studies. University of California, San Diego, 1979.

Darling, M. *The Role of Women in the Economy: A Summary Based on Ten National Reports*. Paris: Organization for Economic Cooperation and Development, 1975.

Deere, C. D. "Changing Social Relations of Production and Peruvian Peasant Women's Work." *Latin American Perspectives* 4, nos. 1, 2 (Winter and Spring 1977): 117–130.

————. "The Development of Capitalism in Agriculture and the Division of Labor by Sex: A Study of the Northern Peruvian Sierra." Ph.D. dissertation, University of California, Berkeley, 1978.

Deere, C. D.; Humphries, J.; and De Leal, M. "Class and Historical Analysis for the Study of Women and Economic Change." Paper prepared for the Role of Women and Demographic Change Research Program, International Labour Organization, Geneva, 1978.

————. "Class and Historical Analysis for the Study of Women and Economic Change." Paper presented for the Role of Women and Demographic Change Research Program, ILO, Geneva, March 1979.

Deere, C. D., and De Leal, M. L. "Peasant Production, Proletarianization and the Sexual Division of Labor in the Andes." Paper prepared for Symposium no. 85, Burg Wartenstein, Austria Wenner-Gren Foundation for Anthropological Research, 1980.

de Janvry, A. "The Limits of Unequal Exchange." *Review of Radical Political Economics* 11, no. 4 (Winter 1979): 3–15.

de la Rosa, M. "La Zona Libre y el Desarrollo Económico (Península de Baja California)." Tesis. UNAM Escuela Nacional de Economía, 1965.

de la Torre, J. R. *Export of Manufactured Goods from Developing Countries: Marketing Factors and the Role of Foreign Enterprise.* New York: Arno Press, 1976.

Diario Oficial de la Federacion. *Incentivos en las Zonas Fronterizas y Perímetros Libres.* Mexico D.F. 20 April, 1971.

Dillman, D. C. "Commuter Workers and Free Zone Industry along the Mexico-U.S. Border." *Proceedings of the Association of American Geographers* 2 (1970): 48–51.

————. "Mexico's Border Industrialization Program (BIP): Current Patterns and Alternative Futures." Mimeographed. Northern Illinois University, n.d.

Doeringer, P., and Piore, M. *Internal Labor Markets and Manpower Analysis.* Lexington, Mass.: Lexington Books, 1971.

Dos Santos, T. "La Crisis de la Teoría del Desarrollo y las Relaciones de Dependencia en América Latina." In *La Dependencia Político-Económica en América Latina.* México, D.F.: Siglo Veintiuno Editores, 1970.

Dos Santos, T.; Vasconi, T. A.; Kaplan, M.; and Jaguaribe, H. *La Crisis del Desarrollismo y la Nueva Dependencia.* Lima: Instituto de Estudios Peruanos, 1969.

Drucker, P. F. "The Rise of Production Sharing." *Wall Street Journal,* March 15, 1977.

————. "Production Sharing, Concepts and Definitions." *Journal of the Flagstaff Institute* 1 (January 1979): 32–45.

Duncan, C. "Economic Relations on the U.S.-Mexico Border." Thesis, Latin American Institute of the University of Texas at Austin, 1974.

Echavarria, J. J. *Assembly and Subcontracting in Colombia.* Bogotá, Colombia: FEDESARROLLO (Fundación Para la Educación Superior y el Desarrollo), 1979.

Edwards, R. C. "The Social Relations of Production in the Firm and Labor Market Structures." *Politics and Society* 5 (1975): 83–108.

————. "Worker Traits and Organizational Incentives: What Makes a 'Good' Worker?" *Journal of Human Resources* 8 (Winter 1976): 205–213.

———. *Contested Terrain: The Transformation of the Workplace in America.* New York: Basic Books, 1980.

Edwards, R. C.; Reick, M.; and Gordon, D. H. *Labor Market Segmentation.* Lexington, D.C. Heath and Co., 1975.

Een, J., and Rosenberg-Dishmen, M. B., eds. *Women and Society: An Annotated Bibliography.* Beverly Hills: Sage Publications, 1978.

Ehrenrich, B., and English, D. "The Manufacture of Housework." In *Capitalism and the Family.* San Francisco: Idea Publishing House, 1976.

Elizaga, J. C. "Participation of Women in the Labour Force of Latin America: Fertility and Other Factors." *International Labour Review* 109, nos. 5, 6 (1974): 519–38.

El Paso Economic Review. "Programa Nacional Fronterizo." Vol. 2 (January 1969).

———. "Manufacturing and Assembly in Ciudad Juárez." 9, no. 7 (July 1974): 3.

Elson, D. and R. Pearson. "Nimble Fingers Make Cheap Workers: An Analysis of Women's Employment in Third World Export Manufacturing." *Feminist Review* 4 (Spring 1981): 87–107.

Emmanuel, A. *Unequal Exchange: A Study of the Imperialism of Trade.* New York: Monthly Review Press, 1974.

Engels, F. *The Condition of the Working Class in England.* Oxford: Basil Blackwell, 1971.

———. *The Origin of the Family, Private Property and the State.* New York: International Publishers, 1972.

Engineer Agency for Resource Inventories and U.S. Department of Labor. Report of Unemployment and Underemployment in Six Border Cities of Mexico. Washington, D.C., 1970.

Ericson, A. "Mexico's Border Industrialization Program." *Monthly Labor Review* (May 1970): 33–40.

Escamilla, N., and Vigorito, M. A. "Consideraciones Sociológicas del Trabajo Femenino en las Maquiladoras Fronterizas." Paper presented at the Primer Simposio Mexicano-Centro Americano de Investigación Sobre la Mujer. México, D.F., 1977.

Evans, J. S. "Mexican Border Development and Its Impact upon the United States." *El Paso Economic Review* (June 1973): 11–20.

Farías Negrete, J. *Industrialization Program for the Mexican Northern Border.* México, D.F.: Banco Comercial Mexicano, 1969.

Fashion Institute of Technology. "Maximizing the Fashion Industry's Use of Technology." Mimeographed. New York, 1976.

Fee, T. "Domestic Labor: An Analysis of Housework and Its Relation to the Production Process." *Review of Radical Political Economics* 8, no. 1 (Spring 1976): 1–8.

Fei, J. C. H., and Ranis, G. *Development of the Labour Surplus Economy: Theory and Policy.* New Haven: Yale University Press, 1964.

Ferber, M. H., and Lowry, H. M. "Women: The New Reserve Army of the Unemployed." *SIGNS* 1, no. 3 (1976): 213–32.

Fernández, R. A. "The Border Industrialization Program on the U.S.-Mexico Border." *Review of Radical Political Economics* 5 (Spring 1975): 37–52.

Fernández, R. A. *The United States-Mexico Border, a Politico-Economic Profile.* Notre Dame: University of Notre Dame Press, 1977.

Fernández-Kelly, Patricia. "The Maquila Women." In *Anthropology for the Eighties*, ed. J. B. Cole. New York: The Free Press, 1982.

Finger, J. M. "Tariff Provisions for Offshore Assembly and the Exports of Developing Countries." *Economic Journal* 85 (June 1975): 365–71.

Firestone, S. *The Dialectic of Sex: The Case for Feminist Revolution*. New York: Bantam Books, 1970.

Flamm, K., and Grunwald, J. *Observations on North-South Complementary Intra-Industry Trade*. Washington, D.C.: The Brookings Institution, 1979.

Form, W. "International Stratification of the Working Class: System Involvements of Auto Workers in Four Countries." *American Sociological Review* 38, no. 6 (December 1973): 697–711.

Frank, A. G. *Capitalism and Underdevelopment in Latin America*. New York: Monthly Review Press, 1967.

———. *Latin America: Underdevelopment or Revolution*. New York: Monthly Review Press, 1970.

Friedman, J., and Sullivan, F. "The Absorption of Labor in the Urban Economy: The Case of Developing Countries." *Economic Development and Cultural Change* 2, no. 3 (April 1974): 385–413.

Frobel, F.; Heinrichs, J. H.; and Kreye, O. "Tendency towards a New International Division of Labour Force for World Market Oriented Manufacturing." *Economic and Political Weekly* 11 (February 1976): 71–83.

———. "The New International Division of Labour." *Social Science Information* 17, no. 1 (1978): 123–42.

———. *The New International Division of Labour*. New York: Cambridge University Press, 1979.

Furtado, C. *Development and Underdevelopment*. Berkeley: University of California Press, 1971.

———. "The Brazilian 'Model' of Development." In *Political Economy of Development and Underdevelopment*, ed. C. K. Wilber. New York: Random House, 1973.

———. *Economic Development of Latin America*. New York: Columbia University Press, 1974.

Galenson, M. *Women and Work: An International Comparison*. Ithaca: New York State School of Industrial and Labor Relations, Cornell University, 1973.

García Moreno, V. C. "La Economía Mexicana y la Economía Fronteriza del Norte." Paper delivered at the Simposio Nacional Sobre Estudios Fronterizos, Monterrey, Nuevo León, Mexico, 1979.

Garibay, L. The Border Industrialization Program of Mexico: A Case Study of the Matamoros, Tamaulipas Experience. MA thesis, University of Texas at Austin, 1977.

Garlow, D. C. "Offshore Assembly in the Caribbean Basin." *Caribbean Basin Economic Survey*. Atlanta, Ga.: Federal Reserve Bank of Atlanta, 1978.

Gendell, M., and Rossel, G. "The Trends and Patterns of the Economic Activity of Women in Latin America During the 1950's." *Estadística* 26 (1968); 561–76.

Gereffi, G. "A Critical Evaluation of Quantitative, Cross-National Studies of Dependency." Paper presented at the Panel on Dependency Theory Meetings of the International Studies Association, Toronto, 1979.

Godelier, M. *Rationality and Irrationality in Economics*. London: New Left Books, 1974.

González Salazar, G. "Participation of Women in the Mexican Labor Force." In *Sex and Class in Latin America*, ed. J. Nash and H. I. Safa. New York: Praeger, 1976.

Goode, W. *World Revolution and Family Patterns*. New York: Alfred C. Knopf, 1963.

Gordon, D. M. *Theories of Poverty and Unemployment*. Lexington, Mass.: Lexington Books, 1972.

Gough, K. "The Origin of the Family." In *Toward an Anthropology of Women*, ed. R. Rapp. New York: Monthly Review Press, 1975.

Griffin, J. *Black Like Me*. New York: Haughton and Mifflin, 1977.

Grossman, R. "Women's Place in the Integrated Circuit." *Southeast Asia Chronicle* Vol 9, nos 5, 6 (July/October 1978). p. 2-17

Hancock, R. H. *The Role of the Bracero in the Economic and Cultural Dynamics of Mexico*. Stanford, California: Stanford University Hispanic American Society, 1959.

Hareven, T. K. "The Historical Study of the Family Cycle." *The Family in Historical Perspective* 5 (1973): 12–14.

———. *Transitions: The Family and the Life Course in Historical Perspective*. New York: Academic Press, 1978.

Hareven, T., and Langenbach, R. *Amoskeag: Life and Work in an American Factory City*. New York: Pantheon Press, 1978.

Hartmann, H. "An Historical View of Women's Work in the United States." (Mimeographed. Washington, D.C., 1976.

———. "Capitalism, Patriarchy, and Job Segregation by Sex." In *Women and the Marketplace: The Implications of Occupational Segregation*, ed. M. Blaxall and B. B. Reagan. Chicago: University of Chicago Press, 1976. Reprinted in *Capitalist Patriarchy and the Case for Socialist Feminism*, ed. Z. R. Eisenstein. New York: Monthly Review Press, 1979.

Helleiner, G. K. "Manufacturing for Export, Multinational Firms and Economic Development." *World Development* 1 (July 1973a): 13–21.

———. "Manufactured Exports from Less Developed Countries and Multinational Firms." *The Economic Journal* 83 (1973b): 21–47.

Hirsh, S. *Location of Industry and International Competitiveness*. Oxford: Clarendon Press, 1967.

Hodson, R. "Labor in the Monopoly, Competitive, and State Sectors of Production." *Politics and Society* 8, nos. 3, 4 (1978): 429–80.

Humphries, J. "Class Struggle and the Persistence of the Working Class Family." *Review of Radical Political Economics* 9, no. 3 (1977): 25–49.

Hunt, L. H. "Industrial Development on the Mexican Border." Federal Reserve Bank of Dallas, *Business Review* (February 1970): 3–12.

Huntington, S. "Issues in Woman's Role in Economic Development: Critique and Alternatives." *Journal of Marriage and the Family* Vol 26 (November 1975): 1001–2.

Instituto Mexicano de Comercio Exterior. "La Industria Maquiladora en Mexico y los Efectos del Proyecto de Ley Nixon." *Informe Económico* no. 5. México, D. F., 1974.

International Labour Organisation. *The Employment and Conditions of Domestic Workers in Private Households*. Geneva, ILO D/11, 1970.

————. *Equality of Opportunity and Treatment for Women Workers.* Report 8, 60th Session, Geneva, ILO, 1975.

————. "Women in the Workforce—The General Picture." *Impact of Science on Society* 25, no. 2 (April 1975): 137–45.

————. *Employment, Growth and Basic Needs: A One-World Problem.* New York: Pareger, 1976.

Jalee, Pierre. *Imperialism in the Seventies.* New York: Third Press, 1973.

James, D., and Evans, J. "The Industrialization of the Northern Mexico Border Region: Past, Present, and Future." Paper presented to the Southwest Social Science Conference, Dallas, Texas, 1974.

Jelin, E. "The Bahiana in the Labor Force: Domestic Activity, Handicraft Production and Salaried Work in Salvador Bahia." In *Sex and Class in Latin America,* ed. J. Nash and H. I. Safa. New York: Praeger, 1976.

————. "Migration and Labor Force Participation of Latin American Women: The Domestic Servants in the Cities." *SIGNS* 3, no. 1 (Autumn 1977): 129–41.

Jenkins, J. C. "The Demand for Alien Labor: Labor Scarcity or Social Control?" Paper presented at the Annual Meeting of the American Sociological Association, New York, 1976.

Jones, M. H. *Autobiography.* Lexington, Mass.: D. C. Heath, 1962.

Juarez, A., and Villacrespo, V. "La Instalación de Plantas Maquiladoras en Mexico: Un Caso de Anexión Económica. Mimeographed. Mexico D.F., 1978.

Kanter, R. M. *Men and Women in the Corporation.* New York: Basic Books, 1977.

Kay, Geoffrey. *Development and Underdevelopment: A Marxist Analysis.* London: Macmillan Press, 1975.

Keller, J. F. "Employment Patterns of Women in California's Electronic Industry." Paper presented at the 79th Meeting of the American Anthropological Association, Cincinnati, 1979.

Kessler-Harris, A. "Stratifying by Sex: Understanding the History of Working Women." In *Labor Market Segmentation,* ed. R. D. Edwards, M. Reich, and D. M. Gordon. Lexington, Mass.: D. C. Health, 1975.

Kindleberger, C. P. *American Business Abroad: Six Lectures on Direct Investment.* New Haven: Yale University Press, 1969.

Knickerbocker, F. T. *Oligopolistic Reaction and Multinational Enterprise.* Boston: Harvard University Press, 1973.

Koslow, L., and Jones, R. R. "The Mexican-American Border Industrialization Program." *Public Affairs Bulletin* 9, no. 2 (1970): 1–27. Institute of Public Administration, Arizona State University, Tempe.

Kuhn, A., and Wolpe, A. M., eds. *Feminism and Materialism: Women and Modes of Production.* Boston: Routledge and Kegan Paul, 1978.

Kujawa, D., ed. *International Labor and the Multinational Enterprise.* New York: Praeger, 1975.

Kuznets, S. "Demographic Aspects of the Size Distribution of Income: An Exploratory Essay." *Economic Development and Cultural Change* 25 (1976): 1–94.

Ladman, J. "Economic Impact of the Mexican Border Industrialization Program: Agua Prieta, Sonora." Center for Latin American Studies, Arizona State University, Tempe, 1972.

Lall, S., and Streeten, P. *Foreign Investment, Transnationals and Developing Countries.* Boulder: Westview Press, 1977.

Lamphere, L.; Hauser, E.; and Michel, S. "The Changing Role of Female Factory Workers: A Comparison between Early and Recent French, Polish, and Portuguese Immigrants." Paper prepared for National Institute of Education, Research Conference on Educational and Occupational Needs of White Ethnic Women, Boston, Massachusetts, 1978.

Larguía, I., and Dumoulin, J. "Aspects of the Condition of Women's Labor." *NACLA's Latin America and Empire Report* 9, no. 6 (September 1975): 4–13.

Leacock, E. B. Introduction to *Origin of the Family, Private Property and the State,* by F. Engels. New York: International Publishers, 1972.

Lenin, V. I. *Imperialism: The Highest Stage of Capitalism.* New York: International Publishers, 1939.

Lewis, W. A. "Economic Development with Unlimited Supplies of Labour." In *The Economics of Underdevelopment,* ed. A. N. Agarwala and S. P. Singh. New York: Oxford University Press, 1963.

Lim, L. Y. C. "Women Workers in Multinational Corporations: The Case of the Electronics Industry in Malaysia and Singapore." Women's Studies Program Occasional Paper No. 9. University of Michigan, 1978.

Little, A. D. "Manufacture in Mexico for the U.S. Market." Mimeographed. Mexico D.F., 1966.

———. "Promoviendo Nuevas Industrias Para Ciudad Juárez." Mimeographed. Mexico D.F. Estudio para el Programa Nacional Fronterizo 1968.

Lloyd, C. B. "The Division of Labor between the Sexes: A Review." In *Sex, Discrimination and the Division of Labor,* ed. C. B. Lloyd. New York: Columbia University Press, 1975.

Loehr, W., and Bulson, M. "Mexico's Border Industry Program." *Arizona Business* 21 (October 1974): 11–16.

Lomnitz, L. A. *Networks and Marginality.* New York: Academic Press, 1978.

McEaddy, B. J. "Women Who Head Families: A Socio-Economic Analysis." *Monthly Labor Review* 99, no. 6 (June 1976): 3–9.

Mackinnon, J. B. "Investment at the Border—the Maquiladoras." *Mexican-American Review* (March 1975).

Madden, J. F. *The Economics of Sex Discrimination.* Lexington, Mass.: Lexington Books, 1973.

Mandel, E. *Late Capitalism.* London: New Left Books, 1975.

Manzoor Ahmad, Z. "The Social and Economic Implications of the Green Revolution in Asia." *International Labour Review* 105, no. 1 (1972): 9–34.

Marglin, S. A. "The Rate of Interest and the Value of Capital with Unlimited Supplies of Labor." In *Essays in the Theory of Optimal Economic Growth,* ed. K. Shell. New York: Alfred C. Knopf, 1968.

Marshall, F. R. "Economic Factors Influencing the International Migration of Workers." In *Views Across the Border: The United States and Mexico,* ed. S. Ross. Albuquerque: University of New Mexico Press, 1978.

Martin, K., and Tallock, P. *Trade and Developing Countries.* London: Croom Helm, 1977.

Martínez, O. *Border Boom Town—Ciudad Juárez since 1848.* Austin: The University of Texas Press, 1978.

Mean, M. "Women in the International World." *Journal of International Affairs* 30 (Fall/Winter 1976–77): 151–60.

Meier, R. L. "Multinationals as Agents of Social Development." *Bulletin of the Atomic Scientist* 33, no. 9 (November 1977): 30–32.

Mercado de Valores. "Actividades del Programa Nacional Fronterizo." (30 March, 1970).

———. "Plan de Ventas Fronterizas." (20 December, 1971): 1005.

———. "La Aduana y el Fomento de la Industria Maquiladora." (16 July, 1973): 983–84.

———. "Importancia de la Industria Maquiladora en Mexico." (3 February, 1975): 92, 93.

Mexican American Review. "Maquiladoras: Road Ahead." (3 November 1974): 4–7.

Milkman, R. "Redefining 'Women's Work': The Sexual Division of Labor in the Auto Industry During World War II." Mimeographed. University of California, Berkeley, 1980.

Minge-Kalman, W. "A Theory of the European Household Economy During the Peasant to Worker Transition with an Empirical Test from a Swiss Alpine Village." *Ethnology* 2, no. 4 (1978): 560–72.

———. "The Industrial Revolution and the European Family: The Institutionalization of 'Childhood' as Market for Family Labor." Mimeographed. New York, 1978.

Minge-Klevana. W. "On the Theory and Measurement of Domestic Labor Intensity." *American Ethnologist* 4 (1978): 73–84.

———. "Historical Changes in the Family Division of Labor During Industrialization in the West." Paper prepared for Symposium no. 85. Wenner-Gren Foundation for Anthropological Research, Burg Wartenstein, Austria August 1980.

Mintz, S. "Men, Women and Trade." *Comparative Studies in Society and History* 13, no. 3 (1971): 247–69.

Mitchell, J. A. "Preliminary Report on the Impact of Mexico's Twin Plant Industry Along the U.S.-Mexico Border." Mimeographed. El Paso, Texas, n.d.

Mitchell, W. L. "Economic Impact of Maquila Industry in Juárez on El Paso Texas." Mimeographed. Antonio J. Bermúdex Industrial Park, Ciudad Juárez, Chihuahua, n.d.

Molyneux, M. "Beyond the Domestic Labour Debate." *New Left Review* 116 (July/August 1979): 3–27.

Morrison, T. K. "International Subcontracting: Improved Prospects in Manufactured Exports for Small and Very Poor Less-Developed Countries." *World Development* 4, no. 4 (1976): 327–32.

Moser, C. "Women's Work in a Peripheral Economy: The Case of Poor Women in Guayaquil, Ecuador." Mimeographed. Institute of Development Studies, University of Sussex, England, 1980.

Moxon, R. "Offshore Sourcing in Less-Developed Countries: A Case Study of Multinationality in the Electronics Industry." *The Bulletin* (New York University Graduate School of Business Administration) 98, no. 99 (July 1974): 7–12.

Mujica Montoya, E. "Hacia una Política Realista de Desarrollo Fronterizo." *Comercio Exterior* 21 (April 1971): 318–21.

Murayama, G., and Muñóz, E. *La Mano de Obra Femenina en la Industria Maquiladora de Exportación.* Instituto Nacional de Estudios del Trabajo, México, D.F., 1975.

Myrdal, A., and Klein, V. *Women's Two Roles: Home and Work.* London: Routledge and Kegan Paul, 1968.

Nash, J. "Certain Aspects of the Integration of Women in the Development Process: A Point of View." Conference background paper, World Conference on the International Women's Year. New York: United Nations, 1975.

———. "A Critique of Social Science Roles in Latin America." In *Sex and Class in Latin America,* ed. J. Nash and H. I. Safa. New York: Praeger, 1976.

———. "Women, Men and the International Division of Labor." Paper presented at the 8th Meeting of the Latin American Studies Association, Pittsburgh, 1979.

Nash, J., and Safa, H. I., eds. *Sex and Class in Latin America.* New York: Praeger, 1976.

Nathan Associates, Inc. *Industrial and Employment Potential of the United States-Mexico Border.* Washington, D.C.: U.S. Department of Commerce, December, 1968.

Navarro, M. "Research on Latin American Women." *SIGNS* 5, no. 1 (Autumn 1979): 111–20.

Nayar, D. "Transnational Corporations and Manufactured Exports from Poor Countries." *Economic Journal* 88 (March 1977): 59–84.

Newton, J. R., and Balli, F. "Mexican In-Bond Industry." Paper presented at the Seminar on North-South Complementary Intra-Industry Trade. UNCTAD. United Nations Conference, México, D.F., 1979.

Nieves, I. "Household Arrangements and Multiple Jobs in San Salvador." *SIGNS* 5, no. 1 (Autumn 1979): 134–42.

Nolasco, M., ed. *La Migración Municipal en México (1960–1976).* México, D. F.: Instituto Nacional de Antropología e Historia/Secretaría de Educaión Pública, 1976.

North, D. S. *The Border Crossers: People Who Live in Mexico and Work in the United States.* Washington, D.C.: Trans Century Corp., 1970.

North American Congress for Latin America's Latin America and Empire Report. "U.S. Runaway Shops on the Mexican Border." 9, no. 7 (July 1975): 1–22. "Capital's Flight: The Apparel Industry Moves South." 11, no. 3 (March 1977 *a*): 1–25.

———. "Electronics: The Global Industry." 11, no. 4 (April 1977 *b*). p. 1–25.

Nurske, R. *Problems of Capital Formation in Underdeveloped Countries.* Oxford: Oxford University Press, 1957.

O'Brien, P. "A Critique of Latin American Theories of Dependency." In *Beyond the Sociology of Development,* ed. I. Oxaal, W. Barnett, and D. Booth. London: Routledge and Kegan Paul, 1975.

O'Connor, J. *The Fiscal Crisis of the State.* New York: St. Martin's, 1973.

Oliveira, O. *Absorción de Mano de Obra a la Estructura Ocupacional de la Ciudad de México.* México, D.F.: El Colegio de México, 1976.

Oppenheimer, V. K. "The Female Labor Force in the United States." Institute of International Studies. University of California, Berkeley, 1970.

Ortíz, F. *Cuban Counterpoint, Coffee and Sugar.* New York: Alfred A. Knopf, 1947.

Pacific Studies Center. *Silicone Valley: Paradise or Paradox, the Impact of High Technology Industry in Santa Clara County.* Mountain View, California, 1977.

Palloix, C. *Les Firmes Multinationales et le Procés d'Internationalisation.* Paris: F. Maspero, 1973.

———. "The Internationalization of Capital and the Circuit of Social Capital." In *International Firms and Modern Imperialism*, ed. H. Radice. New York: Penguin, 1975.

Panorama Económico. 27, no. 7 (November/December 1977): 6.

Parnes, H. S. "Labor Force and Labor Markets." In *Review of Industrial Relations Research*, vol. 1. Madison, Wisconsin: Industrial Relations Research Association, University of Wisconsin, 1970.

Pearson, R. "The Mexican Border Industries: A Case Study of Female Wage Employment in Labour Intensive Manufacturing Industries on the U.S.-Mexico Border." Institute of Development Studies, University of Sussex, England, 1978. Mimeographed.

Pearson, R., and Elson, D. "Internationalization of Capital and Its Implications for Women in the Third World." Paper presented at the Conference on Subordination of Women, Institute for Development Studies. University of Sussex, England, 1978.

Peña, D. G. "Female Workers and Trade Unionism in the Mexican Border Industrialization Program." Paper prepared for the 8th Annual Conference of the National Association of Chicano Studies Research, Houston, Texas, 1980.

Pescatello, A., ed. *Female and Male in Latin America.* Pittsburgh: University of Pittsburgh Press, 1973.

Petras, E. M. "Towards a Theory of International Migration: The New Division of Labor." In *The New Migration: Implications for the U.S. and the International Community.* New Brunswick: Transaction Books, 1979.

Petras, J. F., and Rhodes, R. "Comment on International Stratification of the Working Class." *American Sociological Review* 39, no. 5 (October 1974): 757–59.

Pinchbeck, I. *Women Workers and the Industrial Revolution 1750–1850.* London: Routledge and Kegan Paul, 1969.

Piore, M. J. "Manpower Policy." In *The State and the Poor*, ed. S. Beer and R. Barringer. Cambridge: Winthrop Publishing Co., 1970.

———. "The Dual Labor Market: Theory and Implications." In *Problems in Political Economy: An Urban Perspective*, ed. D. M. Gordon. Lexington, Mass.: D.C. Heath, 1974.

Pleck, E. H. "Two Worlds in One: Work and Family." *Journal of Social History* 10, no. 2 (Winter 1976): 178–95.

Portes, A. "Modernity and Development: A Critique." *Studies in Comparative International Development* 9 (Spring 1975): 247–79.

———. "Labor Functions of Illegal Aliens." *Society* 14, no. 6 (1977): 31–37.

———. "Migration and Development." *Politics and Society* 8, no. 1 (1978): 1–48.

———. "Convergences Between Conflicting Theoretical Paradigms in National Development." Paper prepared for delivery at the Thematic Session on Development Meetings of the American Sociological Association, Boston, Mass., 1979a.

———. "Dual Labor Markets and Immigration, a Test of Competing Theories of Income Inequality." Paper prepared for delivery at the Meetings of the American Association for the Advancement of Science, Houston, Texas. 1979*b.*

———. "Unequal Exchange and the Urban Informal Sector." In *Labor, Class and the International System,* ed. A. Portes and J. Walton. New York: Academic Press, 1981.

Portes, A., and Bach, R. L., "Dual Labor Markets and Immigration; a Test of Competing Theories of Income Inequality." Comparative Studies of Immigration and Ethnicity, Occasional Papers Series, Center for International Studies, Duke University, 1979.

Poulantzas, N. *Political Power and Social Classes.* London: New Left, 1973.

Rapp, R. "Family and Class in Contemporary America: Notes Toward an Understanding of Ideology." *Science and Society* 12 (1978): 278–300.

Rees, A., and Schultz, G. *Workers and Wages in an Urban Labor Market.* Chicago: University of Chicago Press, 1970.

Regional Commission of Minimum Wages. *Study of Minimum Wages, Zone No. 09.* Ciudad Juárez, Chihuahua, 1978.

Reich, M. "The Evolution of the U.S. Labor Force." In *The Capitalist Systems,* ed. R. C. Edwards, M. Reich, and T. E. Weisskopf. Englewood Cliffs, N.J.: Prentice Hall, 1972.

Reiter, R. R. *Toward an Anthropology of Women.* New York: Monthly Review Press, 1975.

Revista Económica. "Perspectivas de la Industria Maquiladora Para 1978." 1, no. 2 (July 1978): 53.

Reynolds, S. "Women on the Line." *Michigan Business Administration Journal* 9 (1975): 27–30.

Rosado Matos, M. R. *La Condición de las Obreras en las Maquiladoras de la Frontera Norte.* Mexico, D. F.: El Colegio de México, 1976.

Rosaldo, M. Z. "Women, Culture, and Society: A Theoretical Overview." In *Women, Culture and Society,* ed. M. Z. Rosaldo and L. Lamphere. Stanford: Stanford University Press. 1976.

Ross, S., ed. *Views Across the Border.* Albuquerque: University of New Mexico Press, 1978.

Rostow, W. W. "From Dependence to Interdependence: An Historian's Perspective." Paper presented at the Conference on Economic Relations Between Mexico and the United States, Austin, Texas, April 1973.

Rowbotham, S. *Women, Resistance and Revolution.* New York: Vintage Books, 1974.

———. *Hidden From History.* London: Penguin, 1976.

Sacks, K. "Engels Revisited: Women, the Organization of Production, and Private Property." In *Towards an Anthropology of Women,* ed. R. Reiter. New York: Monthly Review Press, 1975.

Safa, H. I. *The Urban Poor of Puerto Rico: A Study in Development and Inequality.* New York: Holt, Rinehart and Winston, 1974.

———. Introduction to *Migration and Development: Implications for Ethnic Identity and Political Conflict,* ed. H. I. Safa and B. Du Toit. The Hague: Mouton Publishers, 1975.

———. "Class Consciousness Among Working Class Women in Latin

America: Puerto Rico." In *Sex and Class in Latin America*, ed. J. Nash and H. I. Safa. New York: Praeger, 1976.

———. "The Changing Class Composition of the Female Labor Force in Latin America." *Latin American Perspectives* 9, no. 4 (1977a): 126–36.

———. "Women, Production and Reproduction in Industrial Capitalism: A Comparison of Brazilian and U.S. Factory Workers." Paper presented at the Institute of Development Studies, University of Sussex, England, 1978.

———. "Multinationals and the Employment of Women in Developing Areas: The Case of the Caribbean." Mimeographed. Graduate Department of Anthropology, Rutgers University, 1979.

———. "Export Processing and Female Employment: The Search for Cheap Labor." Paper prepared for Symposium no. 85. Wenner Gren Foundation for Anthropological Research, Burg Wartenstein, Austria, 1980.

———. "Work and Women's Liberation: A Case Study of Garment Workers." Paper prepared for *Urbanization and Inequality*, ed. L. Mullins. New York: Columbia University Press, forthcoming.

Saffioti, H. I. B. *A Mulher na Sociedade de Classe: Mito e Realidade.* Sao Paulo: Quatro Artes, 1969.

———. "Women, Mode of Production and Social Formations." *Latin American Perspectives* 4, nos. 1, 2 (Winter/Spring 1977): 27–37.

Santa Cruz Collective on Labor Migration. "The Global Migration of Labor and Capital." In *U.S. Capitalism in Crisis.* New York: Union for Radical Political Economics (URPE), 1980.

Sassen-Koob, S. "Recomposition and Peripheralization at the Core." *Contemporary Marxism* no. 5 (Summer 1982): 88–100.

Schlegal, A., ed. *Sexual Stratification: A Cross Cultural View.* New York: Columbia University Press, 1977.

Schmink, M. "Dependent Development and the Division of Labor by Sex: Venezuela." *Latin American Perspectives* 4, no. 1, 2 (Winter/Spring 1977): 153–79.

———. "Women, Men and the Brazilian Model of Development." Paper presented at the 8th meeting of the Latin American Studies Association, Pittsburgh, Penn., 1979.

Sciberas, E. *Multinational Electronics Companies and National Economic Policies.* Greenwood, Connecticut: Jai Press, 1977.

Scott, J. W., and Tilly, L. A. "Women's Work and the Family in Nineteenth Century Europe." *Comparative Studies in Society and History* 17 (1975): 36–64.

Secombe, W. "The Housewife and Her Labor under Capitalism." *New Left Review* 83 (January/February 1974): 3–24.

Secretaría de Industria y Comercio. *Estudio del Desarrollo Comercial de la Frontera Norte.* 1972.

———. *Industrial Possibilities Program for Assembly In-Bond Plants.* 1974b.

———. *La Frontera Norte—Diagnóstico y Perspectivas.* 1975.

———. *Zonas Fronterizas de Mexico—Perfil Socioeconomico.* 1974a.

Sepúlveda, C. *La Frontera Norte de México: Historia y Conflictos 1762–1975.* México D. F.: Editorial Porrua, 1976.

Shorter, E. *The Making of the Modern Family.* New York: Basic Books, 1975.

Shover, M. J. "Roles and Images of Women in World War I Propaganda." *Politics and Society* 5, no. 4 (1975): 469–86.

Smelser, N. *Social Change in the Industrial Revolution: An Application of Theory to the British Cotton Industry.* Chicago, Ill.: University of Chicago Press, 1959.

Snow, R. T. "The New International Division of Labor and the U.S. Workforce: An Examination of the Decrease in the Level of Production Workers and Women in the U.S. Electronics Industry." Mimeographed. Hawaii, Jan 4, 1980.

Sokoloff, N. J. "Theories of Women's Labor Force Status: A Review and Critique." Mimeographed. Sociology Department, John Jay College, City University of New York, 1979.

Solis, L. *La Realidad Económica Mexicana: Retrovisión y Perspectivas.* México. D. F.: Siglo Veintiuno Editores, 1975.

Spradley, J. P., and McCurdy, D. W. *Anthropology: The Cultural Perspective.* New York: John Wiley and Sons, 1975.

Stein, M. B. "The Meaning of Skill: The Case of the French Engine-Drivers, 1837–1917." *Politics and Society* 8, nos. 3, 4 (1978): 399–427.

Stevenson, M. "Women's Wages and Job Segregation." In *Labor Market Segmentation,* ed. R. C. Edwards, M. Reich, and D. M. Gordon. Lexington, Mass.: D.C. Heath, 1975.

Sunkel, O. *CapitalismoTransnacional y Desintegración Nacional en América Latina.* Buenos Aires: Nueva Visión, 1962.

———. "Transnational Capitalism and National Disintegration in Latin America." *Social and Economic Studies* 22, no. 1 (1973): 132–71.

Tadashi, H. "The Multinational Corporations and Japanese Industrial Relations." In *International Labor and the Multinational Enterprise,* ed. D. Kujawa. New York: Praeger, 1975.

Taira, K., and Standing, G. "Labor Market Effects of Multinational Enterprises in Latin America." *Nebraska Journal of Economics and Business* 12, no. 4 (Autumn 1973): 103–17.

Taylor, B., and Bond, M. E. Mexican Border Industrialization. Michigan State University Business Topics (Spring 1968).

Thompson, D. "Children's Work in the Period of Transition from Traditional to Mechanized Industry." Paper presented at the Anthropology and History Conference, Max-Planck Institute, Göttingen, W. Germany, June, 1978.

Thompson, E. P. *The Making of the English Working Class.* New York: Vintage Books, 1966.

Thorner, D; Kerblay, B.; and Smith, R. E. F., eds. *A. V. Chayanov on the Theory of Peasant Economy.* Homewood, New York: Richard D. Irwin, 1966.

Thurow, L. *Poverty and Discrimination.* Washington, D.C.: The Brookings Institution, 1969.

Tiffany, S. W. "Anthropology and the Study of Women." *American Anthropologist* 82, no. 2 (June 1980): 374–80.

Tilly, L. A. "Women and Family Strategies in French Proletarian Families." University of Michigan, Michigan Occasional Paper no. 4, (Fall 1978).

———. "Paths of Proletarianization, the Sex Division of Labor, and Women's Collective Action in Nineteenth Century France." Paper presented at symposium No. 85. Wenner Gren Foundation for Anthropological Research. Burg Wartenstein, Austria, 1980.

Tilly, L. A., and Moch, L. P. "Immigrant Women in the City: Comparative Perspectives." Center for Research on Social Organization, University of Michigan, 1979.

Tilly, L. A., and Scott, J. *Women, Work and Family.* New York: Holt, Rinehart and Winston, 1978.

Tinker, I. "Introduction: The Seminar on Women in Development." In *Women and World Development,* ed. I. Tinker, M. B. Bramsen, and M. Buvinic. New York: Praeger, 1975a.

———. "The Adverse Impact of Development on Women." In *Women and World Development,* ed. I. Tinker, M. B. Bramsen, and M. Buvinic. New York: Praeger, 1975b.

Todaro, M. F. "A Model of Labor Migration and Urban Unemployment in Less-Developed Countries." *American Economic Review* 7 (March 1969): 138–48.

Trajtenberg, R., and Sajhau, J. P. "Las Empresas Transnacionales y el Bajo Costo de la Fuerza de Trabajo en los Países Subdesarrollados." International Labour Organization, Geneva. World Employment Programme Research, Working Paper 15, 1976.

Tyler, W. D., ed. *Issues and Prospects for the New International Economic Order.* Lexington, Mass.: Lexington Books, 1977.

Ugalde, A. "Regional Political Processes and Mexican Politics on the Border." In *Views Across the Border,* ed. S. Ross. Albuquerque: University of New Mexico Press, 1978.

United Nations Conference on Trade and Development. *International Subcontracting Arrangements in Electronics Between Developed Market-Economy Countries and Developing Countries.* TD/B/C2/144, Supplement 1. New York, United Nations, 1975.

Uniquel, L., et al. *El Desarrollo Urbano en México.* Mexico, D. F.: El Colegio de México, 1974.

United Nations. *The Future of the World Economy, A Study of the Impact of Prospective Economic Issues and Policies on the International Development Strategy.* New York, 1977.

University of Texas. "The Ciudad Juárez Plan for Comprehensive Socio-Economic Development: A Model for Northern Mexico Border Cities." El Paso, 1974.

Urquidi, V., and Méndez Villarreal, S. "Economic Importance of Mexico's Northern Border Region." In *Views Across the Border,* ed. S. Ross. Albuquerque: University of New Mexico Press, 1978.

U.S. Department of Commerce. *Electronics Components.* Industry and Trade Administration, June 1978.

U.S. House of Representatives. *Special Duty Treatment or Repeal of Articles Assembled Abroad.* Committee on Ways and Means, Subcommittee on Trade. Hearings before the 94th Congress, 2nd Session, March 24, 25, 1976, Washington, D.C.

U.S. International Trade Commission. *Background Information and Compilation of Materials on Items 807.00 and 806.30 of the Tariff Schedules of the U.S. Subcommittee on Trade of the Committee on Ways and Means.* U.S. House of Representatives, July 12, 1976.

U.S-Mexico Commission for Border Development and Friendship. *Mexican Program of Border Industrialization.* CODAF/4. El Paso, Texas, May 1, 1968.

U.S. Tariff Commission. *Economic Factors Affecting the Use of Item 807.00 and 806.30 of the Tariff Schedules of the U.S.* Washington, D.C., 1970.

Valdés De Villalva, G. *La Problemática Social de la Mujer eu la Frontera.* Ciudad Juárez, Chihuahua: Centro de Orientación de la Mujer Obrera, n.d.

Wallace, A. "Roackdale: The Growth of an American Village." In *The Early Industrial Revolution.* ed. Eric Pawson. New York, N.Y.: Alfred A. Knopf, 1978.

Wallerstein, I. *The Modern World-System: Capitalist Agriculture and the Origins of the European World-Economy in the Sixteenth Century.* New York: Academic Press, 1974.

————. "A World-System Perspective on the Social Sciences." *British Journal of Sociology* 27 (1976): 343–52.

Weeks, J., and Dore, E. "International Exchange and the Causes of Backwardness." *Latin American Perspectives* 6, no. 2 (Spring 1979): 62–87.

Wellesley Editorial Committee. *Women and National Development: The Complexities of Change.* Chicago: University of Chicago Press, 1977.

Young, Kate. "Modes of Appropriation and the Sexual Division of Labor: A Case Study from Oaxaca, Mexico." In *Feminism and Materialism,* ed. A Kuhn and A. Wolpe. London: Routledge and Kegan Paul, 1978.

Youssef, N. H. *Women and Work in Developing Societies.* Population Monography, Series no. 15. Institute of International Studies, University of California, Berkeley, 1974.

Zaretsky, E. "Capitalism, the Family and Personal Life." *Socialist Revolution* 3 January/April 1973): 69–125.

Zysman, J. *Political Strategies for Industrial Order.* Berkeley: University of California Press, 1977.

Index